臺灣民主高峰會
二二八事件處理委員會紀念特展

Taiwan Summit for Democracy
—— The 228 Incident Settlement Committee

主辦單位｜ 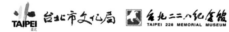 台北市文化局　台北二二八紀念館
Organized by　　　　　　　　　　　　　TAIPEI 228 MEMORIAL MUSEUM

合辦單位｜ 財團法人二二八事件紀念基金會　二二八國家紀念館
Co-organized by

執行單位｜ 純純文創
Presented by　　　Sunko Cultural & Creative Industries

協辦單位｜ 恁藝門　　　台北228協會
Co-presented by　un vœu d'art contemporain 當代藝術　TAIPEI 228 ASSOCIATION

烽火裡的民主秧苗，種入土！

　　1947年，由臺灣社會各界菁英所組成的二二八處委會，訴求依憲法保障人民權利與自由，展現了臺灣人民對民主自治的熱烈追求。在動盪的年代，二二八處委會成為戰後臺灣的第一場民主高峰會！

Planting the Seedlings of Democracy！

　　In 1947, Taiwanese social elite of various fields joined the 228 Incident Settlement Committee. They petitioned to protect people's right and freedom and eagerly expressed their pursuit of democratic self-governance. During the turbulent era, the 228 Incident Settlement Committee enbodied the first summit for democracy in postwar Taiwan！

從二二八處委會看二二八歷史

Through the Eyes of the 228 Incident Settlement Committee :
The History of the 228 Incident

2014 年下旬，臺北市政府文化局在台北二二八紀念館成功舉辦了《臺灣民主高會：二二八事件處理委員會》特展，這是對於二二八事件期間最核心的組織－「二二八處委會」第一次全面且詳實之展覽，吸引了許多市民朋友前來參觀，而在展覽結束後，也有其他縣市提出巡迴展的邀請。因此，為了讓更多民眾瞭解此一歷史事件，認識二二八處委會的重要歷史定位，臺北市政府文化局特將此一展覽內容加以編輯出書，以還原歷史事件真相。

十餘年來，臺北市政府文化局與台北二二八紀念館陸續出版了多本二二八事件歷史展覽專輯，而此書的出版也同樣引來不少期待，除了當中運用了新出土史料還原當時全臺處委會的發展與轉變，更進一步從近代臺灣人民追求民主自治的脈絡縱深，剖析了事件當時的政經背景與社會困境，並重新詮釋「二二八處委會」的角色與今日對於臺灣社會的啟示。因此，此書的出版除了一般展覽專輯的性質外，而更具有展現二二八歷史研究成果與建立具主體性史觀的目的。

在展覽論述與開幕紀實之外，本書還收錄了二二八事件處理委員會紀錄片的訪談內容，受訪者含括主要參與者的後代與受難者家屬、二二八歷史研究學者，以及紀念館營運者等，藉由第一手的訪談資料與歷史分析，使本書的內涵更為完整、豐富。此外，本書首次刊載了臺南處委會主委韓石泉後人之口述歷史，讓我們瞭解臺南以和平為原則的折衝與堅持，在表達訴求之外也讓傷亡降至最低，而藉由不同面向的史實紀錄之補充，以及倖免於難者的角度來審視，也將有助於臺灣社會對此一歷史事件更深入的探討與思索。

二二八處委會從成立到解散的時間較短，難稱得上有統一指揮與發揮全面影響，且各地方所成立之處委會在當時所面對的挑戰各有不同，例如事件爆發地點的臺北在數日後市面已暫時平靜，而在訊息傳到各地後，嘉義在水上機場爆發了武裝對抗，但在臺南的示威遊行則能和平落幕。然而，二二八處委會不僅承擔著中介、調停與穩定秩序的職責，更凝聚了當時社會的共同期待，並代表提出民主改革的整體訴求，由此觀之，此一組織所象徵的精神，實可視為戰後臺灣的第一場民主高峰會！

　　以古鑑今，在此一民主高峰會裡，由王添灯所提擬、宣讀的《三十二條處理大綱》，不僅是二二八事件的核心訴求，更蘊含了臺灣近代對於憲政民主與法治精神的不懈追求。因此，希望本書的出版能夠拋磚引玉，鼓勵相關的歷史發掘與研究工作持續進行，而對於二二八事件與二二八處委會的深入研究，不僅是臺灣近代史關鍵的一環，更是為了記取臺灣民主先賢的理想與犧牲精神，珍惜臺灣今日得來不易的民主法治社會。

臺北市政府文化局局長

THE J. F. A. K. RADIO BROADCASTING STATION, TAIHOKU.
裝新の所奏演局送放（北 臺）
スーユニろゆらあ、に醋聲、に樂音、に沉講
地源發つ分た樂歡之變歎に民市りよに

In the second half of 2014, the Department of Cultural Affairs, Taipei City Government held an exhibition, entitled "Taiwan Summit for Democracy—The 228 Incident Settlement Committee," at the Taipei 228 Memorial Museum. It was the first comprehensive exhibition of the "228 Incident Settlement Committee." The exhibition was received with enthusiasm and many counties and cities have expressed their interest in hosting a touring exhibition. Therefore, in order to raise the awareness of the importance of the 228 Incident and the committee in the Taiwanese history, the Department of Cultural Affairs came to the decision to publish this exhibition book to reveal the history of the 228 Incident from a perspective of a Taiwanese sense of self.

In the past decade, the Department of Cultural Affairs, Taipei City Government and the Taipei 228 Memorial Museum have published many books regarding the 228 Incident. As always, this book has been awaited with great expectation. The book takes into consideration the latest historical records to illustrate the development and transformation of various levels of the 228 Incident Settlement Committee throughout Taiwan. Concerning the Taiwanese people's pursuit of democracy and self-governance, this book not only analyzes the political, economic and social predicaments at that time, but also re-evaluates the position of the 228 Incident Settlement Committee and its impacts on the nowadays Taiwan's society. Thus, serving more than an exhibition record, this book seeks to build a historical view with a Taiwanese sense of self by presenting the accomplishments of the research on the history of the 228 Incident.

In addition to the exhibition statements and the documentation of the exhibition opening, this book also includes the interviews from the documentary film on the 228 Incident Settlement Committee, in which families of the 228 victims, historian of the 228 Incident and director of the museum were interviewed. With the first-hand interview materials and historical analyses, this book seeks to present a more comprehensive view of this past. Furthermore, the inclusion of the oral history of the offspring of Hahn Shyr-Chyuan, chairman of the 228 Incident Settlement Committee-Tainan Branch, would assist us in understanding how the major leaders in Tainan back then followed the principles of peace throughout their negotiation, significantly reducing the casualties in Tainan. The various aspects presented in the historical records and the survivors' viewpoints would pave the way for a deeper exploration of and contemplation upon this historical event in Taiwan's society.

The 228 Incident Settlement Committee was short-lived. Therefore, it is difficult to evaluate if the committee had a thorough impact, considering the various challenges each settlement committee encountered. For instance, after the turbulence in Taipei was under control shortly after the event erupted, armed riots took place in Chiayi Shuishang Airport, resulting in serious casualties, while the demonstration in Tainan was peacefully held. Nevertheless, the contribution of the 228 Incident Settlement Committee cannot be neglected. They took over the responsibility of an intermediary, assisting in negotiation and maintaining order, calling together a collective aspiration for a better society, as well as proposing statements of democratic reforms. Hence, the merits of the committee should certainly be considered as the first democratic summit of postwar Taiwan.

To learn from the past, the "32 Demands," proposed and declaimed by Wang Tien-Teng, not only presented the fundamental pursuit of the 228 Incident, but also embodied the consistent aspiration for a constitutional democracy and the spirit of the rule of law in Taiwan's modern history. Therefore, the publication of this book is expected to encourage continued historical researches. An extensive investigation into the 228 Incident and the Committee would not merely stand for a crucial part of Taiwan's modern history. More importantly, it would assist us in remembering the spirit and the sacrifice of those pioneers endeavoring after Taiwan's democracy, and eventually, treasuring the democracy and the rule of law that are hard to come by.

Commissioner, Department of Cultural Affairs, Taipei City Government

Ni Chung-Hwa.

目錄 • Contents

第一章/前言：為何會有二二八處委會?

Introduction: Why was there a 228 Incident Settlement Committee?

1-1 臺灣民主自治與二二八處委會

1-2 認識二二八處委會的歷史

1-1 Taiwan's Democratic Self-Government and the 228 Incident Settlement Committee

1-2 Understanding the history of the 228 Incident Settlement Committee

第一章／前言：為何會有二二八處委會？
Introduction: Why was there a 228 Incident Settlement Committee?

走進今日的臺北二二八紀念館，可以看到入口大廳裡，懸掛著代表二二八事件處理委員會（以下或簡稱「二二八處委會」）的核心訴求-《三十二條處理大綱》銅匾，以及豎立其前的二二八處委會談判代表、大綱宣讀者王添灯的銅像，此一場景，彷彿重現了二二八處委會的民主先賢們為民喉舌、犧牲奉獻的身影，同時也讓我們想追問：在68年前那個撼動人心的歷史事件裡，二二八處委會究竟扮演著什麼角色？發生了哪些事情？ 它為今日臺灣的民主社會又帶來了什麼樣的影響？

■ 1-1 臺灣民主自治與二二八處委會

美國林肯總統（President Abraham Lincoln, 1809-1865）在著名的蓋茨堡演說（Gettysburg Address）提出了「民有、民治、民享（of the people，by the people，and for the people）」的民主理念，而要實現真正的民主政府，先決條件是要有健全的地方自治制度，以賦與人民行使政權的能力、知識與經驗。正如英國著名的政治諺語：「民主政治最好的學習和民主政治成功的最佳保障，便是實施地方自治（The best school of democracy, and the best guarantee for its success, is the practice of local self government）。」

實施地方自治為民主政治之基礎，因而地方自治應受憲法所保障，「基於住民自治之理念與垂直分權之功能，地方自治團體設有地方行政機關及立法機關，其首長與民意代表均由自治區域內之人民依法選舉產生」，以處理地方之公共事務。在臺灣近代民主發展過程中，不論是1947年成立省政府，1950年代開始重劃行政區域、選舉縣市長、省議員，以及成立正式省議會，乃至1990年代國會改選、憲政改革，以及總統直接民選等，地方自治都扮演著重要的紮根角色。

回顧日本殖民時期，臺灣人民以抗爭、請願等方式追求民主自治，半世紀以來苦無所獲；到了戰後，行政長官公署採行特殊化行政管理與全面性經濟統制，如同延續了殖民時期的總督府專制統治，導致經濟凋敝與政治弊端叢生，使人民從期待到挫敗，因此，實行民主憲政、推行地方制度改革，成為當時全臺人民的迫切心聲。

因此，二二八事件爆發時，二二八事件處理委員會的成立，不僅是為了調查緝煙血案，以及協調官民對立、恢復社會秩序，更是扮演臺灣人民長久以來追求民主自治的關鍵角色。換言之，二二八事件的核心價值，其實就是爭自治、爭民權！可以說，二二八事件處理委員會的設立、立場與角色演變，不僅為探究二二八事件提供了重要線索，更是認識臺灣地方自治與民主化過程中的重要一環。

■ 1-2 認識二二八處委會的歷史

二二八事件從政治禁忌到名譽平反，從歷史缺漏到官方的建碑、紀念、道歉，許多史料也陸續挖掘出現，調查研究的成果也不斷提出。本書從二二八處委會的視角來瞭解事件發生的源頭、演變與影響，論述軸線首先從日本殖民時期臺灣人民對抗殖民威權、爭取地方自治開始，到國府接收後的失落與爭取，直至事件爆發後的折衝談判與《三十二條處理大綱》的提出，並延伸到近代臺灣民主政治的轉型努力。

在橫向分析上，本書也介紹了各層級處委會之間的聯繫關係，並將其視為一個整體架構，藉由對於處委會的角色、功能與理念分析，以及受難者的生平事蹟與理念，提供民眾深入的觀察視角，以展現二二八處委會的歷史地位。

最後，隨著社會各界對二二八事件的關注，新史料不斷挖掘整理，相關研究的成果也不斷出爐，此書也特別收錄近年新出土的史料與新研究成果展陳，包括2013年中研院臺史所研討會有關各級處委會研究最新成果，以及彰化發現的田中青年十二條要求等史料，也讓此書不同於一般展覽專輯與文獻資料的回顧，以展現與鼓勵二二八歷史的挖掘與研究工作。

中山堂-第一屆省參議會期間，因原議場空間不足，為容納更多民眾參與，曾遷移至中山堂開會

Introduction: Why was there a 228 Incident Settlement Committee ?

Entering into today's Taipei 228 Memorial Museum, you can see the core demands of the representatives of the 228 Incident Settlement Committee hanging at the entrance of the main hall. A bronze plaque of the 32 Demands, and erected in front of it is a bronze statue of Wang Tien-teng, a 228 Incident Settlement Committee negotiator, reading its main points. With this scene, it's as if the 228 Incident Settlement Committee sages of democracy had reappeared again as the mouthpiece of the people, self-sacrificing figures. At the same time it also makes us to consider: Sixty-eight years ago, what kind of role did the 228 Incident Settlement Committee play in that historical, heart-shaking incident ?

1-1 Taiwan's Democratic Self-Government and the 228 Incident Settlement Committee

The American President Abraham Lincoln's famous Gettysburg address put forth the democratic ideals of "of the people, by the people, and for the people." But to achieve a true democracy, a prerequisite is to have a sound system of local self-government, in order to give the people the ability to exercise political power, knowledge and experience. Just as the famous British political proverb says: "The best school of democracy, and the best guarantee for its success, is the practice of local self government. "

Implementing local self-government as the foundation for democracy, so that local self-government shall be protected by the constitution, is in order to handle public affairs "based on the concept of autonomy and the function of vertical decentralization, local executive bodies and legislative bodies, whose heads and representatives were elected in accordance with law by the people in the autonomous areas." During the course of Taiwan's modern democratic development, regardless if it was the provincial government founded in 1947, the redrawing of administrative areas started in 1950, the election of a county mayor, provincial parliament members, the establishment of an official Provincial Council, or even the parliamentary elections of the 1990's, constitutional reform, as well as the direct election of the President, local autonomy always played an important core role.

Looking back at the Japanese colonial period , the Taiwanese people used resistance, petitions and other methods to pursue democratic self-government. Half a century of suffering with no reward and then after the war, the Administrative Executive Office adopted a high-handed administration style and comprehensive economic control. It was as if it were a continuation of the authoritarian rule of the colonial period's Governor-General, leading to economic depression and an explosion of political abuse, frustrating the people's hopeful expectations. And so, to implement a democratic constitutional government, to pursue reform of the local system then became the whole Taiwanese people's urgent aspiration.

Therefore, when the 228 Incident erupted, the establishment of the 228 Incident Settlement Committee, wasn't only for investigating the tobacco seizure and murder case, but also to coordinate the public opposition, restore social order, and even more, to play a key role in the Taiwanese people's long time pursuit of democratic self-government. So in other words, the core values of the 228 Incident were in fact the struggle for autonomy and civil rights! It could be said that the establishment, standpoint and transitional role of the 228 Incident Settlement Committee not only provides important clues for exploring the 228 Incident, but moreover to understand it as an important part of Taiwan's process of local self-government and democratization.

1-2 Understanding the history of the 228 Incident Settlement Committee

The 228 Incident went from political taboo to being rehabilitated, from omitted history to government sanctioned monument, memorial and apology. Many historical materials are continuously uncovered, and the results of investigative research are continually being presented. This book looks at the Incident's cause, evolution and influence, from the viewpoint of the 228 Incident Settlement Committee. The treatise begins with the Japanese colonial period, when the Taiwanese people resisted the colonial authority, and started fighting for local autonomy. It continues through the struggle and loss after the retrocession to the Nationalist government, until the conciliation negotiations and then to the outbreak of the Incident, proposal of the 32 Demands and extends to the restructuring efforts of modern Taiwan's democratic politics.

On the horizontal analysis, this book also describes the relationship between the various levels of connection between the Committee, and its structure as a whole, through an analysis of the Committee's roles, functions and concepts, as well as the life stories and ideas of the victims, offering an in-depth perspective of the people, and demonstrating the 228 Incident Settlement Committee's historical status.

Finally, because of the whole community's keen interest in the 228 Incident, new historical materials are constantly being uncovered and compiled, with the results of such research continuously being published. This book also specially features newly unearthed historical materials and showcases new research results, including the latest comprehensive research results of the 2013 Academia Sinica Taiwan History Seminar on the Settlement Committee, along with the Youth Leagues 12 Demands discovered in a field in Changhua county. This and other historical documents make this book much different from an ordinary literature review, it is a very important book that shows and encourages the excavation and research of the 228 Incident's history.

（二） 中華民國三十六年三月八日 （星期六） 新生報 第五百號

處委會闡明事件眞相
向中外廣播處理大綱
除改革政治外別無他求
建議案本日可正式提出

【本報訊】臺灣省「二，二八事件處理委員會」于六日下午二時召開會議，席上除報告組織大綱及推選常務委員外，並由委員王添灯氏勸議謂本省地處孤島，致此次所發生之事件，中外人士未能透徹明瞭，諸多曲解，爰擬就二，二八事件處理大綱，內容闡明發生之遠因與近果，將以國語，客語，閩語，英語，日語，向中外宣布，俾能了解內容眞相，全體一致贊成，茲將原文誌之如次：

（一）二，二八事件的原因

這次本省發生的二，二八事件，其發端雖然是由於專賣局查緝私烟，屢次槍傷烟販，商品財產，已不歸公，又以槍桿毆打烟販，且於二，二七夜，在臺北市查緝私烟時，開槍擊斃人命而激起公憤，生出官民衝突的事態。這事件於二，二八在臺北發生即時波及全省，到處發生軍民之衝突和流血的慘狀。現在除臺北市內暫時恢復和平狀態之外其他各地還在繼續武裝混戰的地方也不少。

這樣廣汎而大規模的事件是由查緝私烟槍斃人命，這樣單純的原因所能發生的嗎？決不是！查緝私烟槍斃人命不過是導火線而已。這次的事件完全是全省人民對於一年餘來之腐敗政治的不滿同時爆發的結果。

本省光復一年餘來的政治狀況是一面陳長官在公開演講的時候說得如花似錦，說要怎樣爲人民服務要怎樣謀民生的安定。但是實際上，大小貪污互相檢舉接收之敵產者到處有之。弄文舞法或倚藉武力以欺壓人民者比比皆是。人權不能得到保障，言論出版失去自由，財政破產，物價繼續高漲，經濟倒閉農村日益貧弊，失業者成群，無法謀生者不可勝算，全省人民不堪其苦，敢怒而不敢言，因此次專賣局貪污官吏之暴行，全省民之不滿遂同時爆發。

由此可知此次事件根本是由腐敗政治之結果而來。已非單因專賣局官吏之不法行爲所致，亦非由於省界觀念而發生的事件。故對此次事件，整個臺灣政府應負全部責任。

（二）二，二八事件的經過

二，二七夜專賣局官吏擊斃人民之時，即激動市民公憤，該局人員所乘卡車及所押收香烟，立時被民衆燒燬。翌二，八日臺北市卸全體罷市十市民結隊至專賣省專賣局請願懲兇，然該局四周警備森嚴[illegible]警察，不准民衆接近。其時民衆怒氣沖天，即逕向專賣局臺北分局欲捕兇犯，但兇手已逃匿，群情激憤搗毀該局物件，並搬至路上焚燒，而民衆爲欲達到請願目的，轉向臺灣省行政長官公署，欲向長官請願，而該署亦以武裝之兵士及憲兵，如臨大敵戒備森嚴，不許民衆接近，因此於[illegible]間公署樓上之士兵竟用機槍掃射民衆，因此民衆死傷數名，民衆益憤激，其時有省一部份民衆湧到城內，將官僚資本所經營之大商店及與貪官污吏朋比爲奸之外省人所經營之店舖搗毀，並將家具物品搬出路上焚燒，[illegible]焚燒之時武裝警察及憲兵遂至開槍射殺民衆爲數不少。又翌三月一日在鐵路管理委員會前（即北門町附近）[illegible]民衆被軍隊機槍掃射以致死傷者達數十名，此消息一經傳出全省各地民情頓時激變。現臺北市內雖經二，二八事件處理委員會居間接洽，略已平靜，但中南部各地民衆則爲避免政府武裝部隊之屠殺，正繼續努力冀求解除軍隊武裝，犧牲相當慘重。

（三）二，二八事件應如何處理

這次事件已然是政治腐敗的結果，其處理者非政治上根本加以改革，以冀確保不再發生類似或更慘重之事件。故居住本省之人民不論本省人或外省人均應盡量提出處理意見，政府兩當人員應亦以公明正大之政治家態度，誠心誠意與人民共謀解決，切勿爲保持官僚威風而陷入錯誤觀念。

現在將本已獲到的對於本事件的處理意見，綜合起來，可分爲對目前的處理，根本的處理兩方面：

（一）對於目前的處理

一，政府在各地之武裝部隊，應自動下令暫時解除武裝，武器交由各地處理委員會及憲兵隊共同保管，以免繼續發生流血衝突事件。

二，政府武裝部隊武裝解除後地方之治安由憲兵與非武裝之警察及民衆組織共同負擔。

三，各地若無政府武裝部隊威脅之時，絕對不應有武裝械鬥行動，對貪官污吏不論其爲本省人或外省人亦只應檢舉轉請處理委員會協同憲警拘拿，依法嚴辦，不應加害而惹出是非。

四，對於政治改革之意見可條舉要求條件向省處理委員會提出，以候全盤解決。

五，政府切勿再移動兵力或向中央請遣兵力，企圖以武力解決事件，致發生更慘重之流血而受國際干涉。

六，在政治問題未根本解決之前，政府之一切施策，（不論軍事，政治）須先與處理委員會接洽，以免人民懷疑政府誠意，發生種種誤會。

七，對於此次事件不應向民間追究責任者，將來亦不得假藉任何口實拘捕此次事件之關係者。對於因此次事件而死傷之人民應從優撫恤。

（二）根本處理

甲，軍事方面：

一，缺乏教育和訓練之軍隊絕對不可使駐臺灣。

二，中央可派員在臺徵兵守臺。

三，在內陸之內戰未終息以前，除以守衛臺灣爲目的之外絕對反對在臺灣徵兵以免臺灣陷入內戰旋渦。

乙，政治方面：

一，制定省自治法爲本省政治最高規範，以便實現國父建國大綱之理想。

二，縣市長於本年六月以前實施民選，縣市參議會同時改選。

三，省各處長人選應經省參議會（改選後爲省議會）之同意，省參議會應於本年六月以前改選，目前其人選由長官提出交由省處理委員會審議。

四，省各處長三分之二以上須由在本省居住十年以上者擔任之（最好秘書長，民政，財政，工礦，農林，教育，警務等處長應如是）。

五，警務處長及各縣市警察局長應由本省人擔任，省警察大隊及鐵道工礦等警察即刻廢止。

六，法制委員會委員須半數以上由本省人充任，主任委員由委員互選。

七，除警察機關之外不得逮捕人犯。

八，憲兵除軍隊之犯人外不得逮捕人犯。

九，禁止帶有政治性之逮捕拘禁。

十，非武裝之集合結社絕對自由。

十一，言論出版罷工絕對自由，廢止新聞紙發行申請登記制度。

十二，即刻廢止人民團體組織條例。

十三，廢止民意機[illegible]

[illegible]關選舉辦法。

十五，實行所得統一累進稅，除奢侈品稅相續稅外不得徵收任何雜稅。

十六，一切公營事業主管人由本省人擔任。

十七，設置民選之公營事業監察委員會，日產處理應委任省政府全權處理，各接收工廠礦應置經營委員會，委員須過半數由本省人充任。

十八，撤消專賣局，生活必需品實施配給制度。

十九，撤消貿易局。

二十，撤消宣傳委員會。

二十一，各地方法院院長各地方法院首席檢察官全部以本省人充任。

二十二，各法院推事檢察官以下司法人員各半數以上省民充任。

其他改革事項候三月十日集中全省民意之後交由改組之政府辦理。

【本報訊】又昨（七）日下午二時半，處委會全會議，由臨時主席潘渠源[illegible]佈開會後，除原案共廿二項一致決議通過以外，並追加通過，一，本省陸海空軍，儘量採用本省人。二，警備司令部應撤消，以免軍權濫用。三，限至三月底，臺灣政府長官公署應改爲省政府，但未得中央核准前暫仍[illegible]二，二八事件處理委員會[illegible]

宜蘭處理分會成立
決定五項建議
蘭陽一帶秩序業已恢復

【本報宜蘭訊】爲防止二，二八事件擴大並謀蘭陽之安寧計，宜蘭市[illegible]于三日上午十時假宜蘭醫院舉行，結果于是日下午成立二，二八事件處理委員會宜蘭分會，即推舉執行委員前往市公所接洽，適市長，警務課長等均不在，至翌五日，朱市長書面表明辭職，並推舉[illegible]爲代理市長，是日處理委員會與市長等在[illegible]對爲宜蘭市之安寧起見，努力，結果決定請市內軍部解除武裝，藉免滋端，闔市內所有武裝機關均願與民間合作，唯飛機場分隊長周競宇，不願與民間合作，五日夜帶領全部隊兵離場，六日，七日市內均平靜。

【又訊】宜蘭處理分會，于六日上午十一時假消防隊樓上召開會議，列各委員暨市內各機關首長等六十餘名，首由郭主席報告該會處理情形，旋改組加強該會之組織，結果滿場一致，推舉郭章垣爲主任委員，黃再壽[illegible]議條件如下：

一，支持臺北處理委員會提出建議[illegible]。

二，即實施地方自治，省縣，市長均由民選。

三，平抑物價，救濟失業，安定民生。

四，因「二，二八」事件憤起行動之民衆均不得追究。

五，擁護蔣主席建設新中華民國。

【又訊】蘭陽地方秩序業已恢復二月二十七日以前之狀態，因此民間咸認不必再調軍隊來此，以免滋生事端云。

臺自治青年同盟
新竹市分會成立

【本報新竹訊】臺灣省自治青年同盟新竹市分會成立式，于七日上午十時假市立中學舉行，是日市內青年參加踴躍，由李世賢主持開[illegible]散。

蘇紹文捐資撫慰受傷同胞

【本報新竹訊】新竹地區防衛司令部蘇少將紹文，爲撫慰現在新竹病院治療中之受傷同胞起見，七日[illegible]捐[illegible]

忠義服務隊昨召會
討論強化治安問題
該隊電話號碼『三三六九』

【本報訊】臺灣省忠義服務隊，昨（七）日下午四時假於該隊（第二分局）會議室舉行強化治安會議，是[illegible]調後，由各隊負相繼報告三月五日該隊成立以來治安狀況，及對此後治安強化事項，熱烈討論約至五時許散會，又該會自本（八）日[illegible]

第二章/半世紀的追求—臺灣人民爭取民主自治之路
A half century's pursuit :
The road of the Taiwanese people's struggle for democratic self - government

2-1 日本殖民時期的艱辛追求（1895-1945）
2-2 國府接收後從期待到挫敗（1945-1947事件前夕）

2-1 The arduous pursuit during the Japanese colonial period (1895-1945)
2-2 The Retrocession to the Nationalist Government, from Hope to Defeat (1945-1947, the Precipice of the Incident)

第二章/半世紀的追求—臺灣人民爭取民主自治之路

A half century's pursuit :
The road of the Taiwanese people's struggle for democratic self-government

要認識二二八事件的本質,以及事件期間二二八處委會的組成與訴求,必須要先從臺灣人民在長達半世紀的殖民統治下,不斷追求民主自治的坎坷歷程,而此一前仆後繼的奮鬥過程卻不為戰後臺灣的掌權者所瞭解,使得衝突日益擴大,因而一發不可收拾。

■ 2-1日本殖民時期的艱辛追求(1895-1945)

臺灣人追求民主自治之路,始自文化啟蒙、議會設置請願與地方自治推動過程。1920年代,在當時美國總統威爾遜(Woodrow Wilson, 1856-1924)的鼓吹下,民族自決運動在全世界掀起,臺灣知識份子如蔣渭水、林獻堂、蔡培火、楊肇嘉等人,紛紛投入非武裝抗日活動,掀起了一波臺灣新文化運動風潮。

此一時期,由蔣渭水、林獻堂等人發起的「臺灣文化協會」(1921-1930)之設立,擔當起以臺灣為主體之文化啟蒙與教育工作,而《臺灣民報》的發行則為文化協會宣傳之言論機關。另外,「臺灣議會設置請願運動」(1921-34)更直接要求政治上的實踐,期望建立「臺灣議會」,改變殖民統治成為立憲政治,以打破總督專制體制,爭取臺人的自治權力。

1927年,由蔣渭水發起的「臺灣民眾黨」成立,成為臺灣人所組織的第一個政黨,其反對特權政治,主張集會結社言論出版之自由,並爭取州市街庄自治機關之人民普選及議決權。然而,在當局嚴密監控下,臺灣民眾黨於1931年被迫解散,而林獻堂等人所發起的議會設置請願

1. 1928年臺灣民眾黨於臺南市舉行第二次全島黨員代表大會,王受祿與韓石泉分任大會議長、副議長;坐在議長席的右方者為王受祿,左方者為韓石泉(韓良俊提供)
2. 『臺灣民報』為臺灣人的第一份報紙
3. 1931年王添灯所著《市街庄政之實際》一書出版,為臺灣自治重要專書

運動多年來屢遭駁回、徒勞無功，因此蔡式穀、楊肇嘉等知識份子轉而投入地方自治運動，成立「臺灣地方自治聯盟」(1930-1937)，期望增進民眾對民主政治的認識，以「確立完全地方自治制」為目標。

　　地方自治聯盟的設立，標誌著臺灣的社會運動從早期民族主義的立場，逐漸轉為對民主體制的追求，而新文化運動帶來的教育啟蒙，以及民眾對法治與民主精神的逐漸認識，使得推動政治體制改革、爭取臺灣地方自治權利，成為臺灣人民的普遍追求。許多日治時期積極參與臺灣地方自治聯盟的要角，也是日後二二八處委會的核心成員，而此一自治的主張，不但在日治時期已經萌生，更是二二八事件《三十二條處理大綱》政治改革方案之重要精神。

　　1935年底，總督府為籠絡臺人，舉辦了被譏為「假自治」的地方議會選舉，雖無民主之實，但也讓民眾的民權意識益加覺醒，並成為戰後初期民眾參政熱潮的背景因素。1937年後，日本軍國主義抬頭，在戰時體制下，臺人政治活動全面遭到打壓，「臺灣地方自治聯盟」也被迫解散。然而，臺灣民主先賢前仆後繼的抗日運動，早已在臺灣民眾的心中種下民主意識與法治精神的種籽，等待有朝一日開花結果。

1. 1915年「噍吧哖事件」被逮捕的余清芳及其同志
2. 1932年9月5日臺灣地方自治聯盟海山支部在板橋林家花園舉行成立大會，會後出席者合影紀念。左1為王添灯，左5為蔡式穀，左6為楊肇嘉，中坐者為葉榮鐘
3. 1945年10月24日陳儀抵臺擔任臺灣行政長官

■ 2-2 國府接收後從期待到挫敗
(1945-1947事件前夕)

　　在殖民者的高壓統治下，歷經半世紀的努力抗爭，臺灣人民依舊沒有政治發言權。戰後，人民在歡欣鼓舞迎接祖國的同時，並熱烈期盼民主憲政的實施，其強烈程度，甚至被稱為「政治渴望症」。1945年12月26日，臺灣省行政長官公署頒佈「臺灣省各級民意機關成立方案」，採間接選舉方式產生各級民意代表，1946年1月15日，臺灣辦理公民宣示登記，一個月後宣示登記的民眾達239萬餘人，佔全臺二十歲以上成人91.8%，可見當時盛況。

　　1946年4月15日的臺灣省參議員選舉，應選三十名，有投票權之各縣市參議員為五百二十三人，而省參議員競選人數卻多達一千一百八十三人，形成參選人數遠多於有投票權者之特殊現象。1946年5月1日，臺灣省參議會正式成立，此時臺灣人民普遍認為建設新臺灣、實現民主憲政的時刻終於來臨了，而臺灣省參議會也被視為臺灣第一次民主實踐的重要舞臺。

1945年臺灣光復節學生繞街遊行紀念

中山堂

行政長官公署－集行政、立法、司法、軍事等大權於一身的特殊體制

1. 專賣局與貿易局官員貪汙舞弊事件層出不窮（民報1946.09.20）
2. 批評官僚惡政漫畫

　　然而，臺灣省行政長官公署接收臺灣之際，為謀利用原有殖民體制以便於接管及推行新政令，因此，在政治上，由長官公署獨攬行政、立法、司法大權；在社會上，軍警違法亂紀、官員貪腐橫行；在文化上，以不擅國語、受日本奴化教育為藉口貶低臺人。種種因素，埋下不滿的集體情緒，而官員施政失去民心，更讓民眾把國府的「接收」稱為「劫收」。

　　更重要的是，長官公署不僅未致力於恢復臺灣的經濟建設，反而設立專賣局、貿易局，以專賣、獨占、轉賣公產等手段，重演殖民者對臺人的剝削，而接受自殖民政府、日產企業與部分臺人的產業，在轉換為國府資產之餘，頻頻發生官商貪腐的「戰後分贓」，釀成廣大民眾的失業，而物資短缺更引發物價暴漲、糧荒危機。

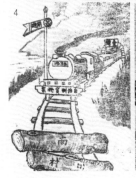

1. 從當時的漫畫可見專賣局不當的管制與緝煙問題
2. 日治時期臺灣總督府（今總統府）
3. 由蔣渭水、林獻堂（中坐者）等人所設立之臺灣文化協會召開第一次大會
4. 南村總督被諷為臺灣實施真正自治制的阻礙
5. 在專賣管制下，困苦的人民鋌而走險販售私煙

對於此一民情，行政長官公署卻毫無體察，並以省參議會為諮詢機關，只有建議權和詢問權，對於代表全臺民意之省參議會的決議與監督，並不予認真理會。甚至1947年1月1日中華民國憲法頒布後，行政長官陳儀仍以時機尚未成熟，片面宣布臺灣需先施行訓政體制，讓當時飽受惡政之苦的人民產生巨大失落感。因此，全面改革省政、實行民主憲政與地方自治，成為當時民間社會的共同期待。

弊端叢生的政治與經濟問題，以及施政不當所加重的糧食問題，使得1947年初臺灣社會的民怨已是一觸即發。可以說，1947年2月27日的緝煙血案只是壓倒駱駝的最後一根稻草，而二二八事件導致全臺的抗爭響應，證實了人民心中對於惡政的強烈不滿已無處宣洩，此時所成立的二二八事件處理委員會，也成為了戰後臺灣人民爭取民權與自治的一場民主高峰會！

1. 中山堂－第一屆省參議會期間，因原議場空間不足，為容納更多民眾參與，曾遷移至中山堂開會
2. 臺灣地方自治聯盟舉辦促進地方自治的演講會傳單，由王添灯發行。其中，1933年7月30日在臺北舉行的「全島住民北部大會」，王添灯擔任演講者之一（吳三連臺灣史料基金會提供）
3. 蔣渭水－臺灣的文化頭，推動非武裝抗日之文化啟蒙運動不遺餘力。
4. 南京國民政府派任陳儀為臺灣行政長官
5. 陳儀－光復後第一任行政長官
6. 關注民生的困苦、推行地方自治與任用臺人一直是當時臺灣社會菁英的共同期盼，也是二二八事件時的改革訴求
7. 國際媒體報導國府接收臺灣後的亂象（1946.3.21《華盛頓郵報》）

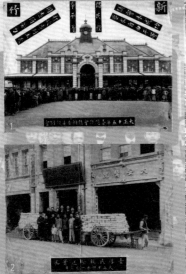

失業與救濟

王添灯

1. 臺灣議會請願團在新竹火車站歡送
2. 臺灣民報發送實況，旁邊為蔣渭水設立之大安醫院
3. 面對臺灣社會嚴重的失業與救濟問題，王添灯發表文章呼籲當局關注（台灣新生報1946.10.20）
4. 臺灣省參議會第一次大會開會現場
5. 臺灣議會設置請願書（國立中央圖書館臺灣分館提供）

臺灣議會設置請願書

請願ノ趣旨

請願ノ要旨

A half century's pursuit : The road of the Taiwanese people's struggle for democratic self-government

To understand the nature of the 228 Incident, and the formation and aspirations of the 228 Incident Settlement Committee during this event, we must first understand the Taiwanese people's half-century of being under colonial rule, their rocky road of ceaselessly striving for democratic self-government. The struggle wasn't something those in power after the war could understand and which made the conflict grow stronger day after day, soon spiraling out of control.

2-1 The arduous pursuit during the Japanese colonial period (1895-1945)

The road of the Taiwanese people's pursuit of democratic self-government began with cultural enlightenment, the process of parliament setting up petitions and the implementation of local self-government. In the 1920's, under the encouragement of the then U.S. President Woodrow Wilson (1856 - 1924), national self-determination movements took off all over the world and Taiwanese intellectuals such as Chiang Wei-shui, Lin Hsien-tang, Cai Pei Huo, Yang Chao-Chia among others, entered one after the other into the unarmed anti-Japanese movements that set off a wave of Taiwanese New Culture Movements.

During this period the establishment of the "Taiwan Cultural Association" (1921-1930) was launched by Chiang Wei-shui, Lin Hsien-tang and others, shouldering the work of cultural enlightenment and education of Taiwan, with the publication of the "Taiwan People's News" as the Cultural Association's political voice. Additionally the "Campaign for the Establishment of a Taiwanese Parliament" (1921-34), increased the demand for direct practice in politics, hoping to establish a "Taiwanese Parliament," changing colonial rule into constitutional government, in order to break the Governor-General's authoritarian regime, and to fight for the autonomy of the Taiwanese people.

In 1927, the establishment of the "Taiwanese People's Party" launched by Chiang Wei-shui became the first organized Taiwanese political party, it opposed political privilege, advocating for the freedom of speech, press, assembly, and association, and struggled for the peoples universal suffrage and the self-governing bodies of the province, city, street and village. However, under the authorities close supervision the Taiwanese People's Party was forced to disband in 1931, and Lin Hsien-tang and the others who launched the Campaign for the Establishment of a Taiwanese Parliament were repeatedly rejected over the years, and their effort was fruitless. So, Tsai Shi-Gu and Yang Chao-Chia and other intellectuals invested in the local self-government movement instead, establishing the "Taiwan Local Self-Government Coalition" (1930-1937), hoping to raise public awareness of democracy, with their goal to "establish a complete local self-government system."

The establishment of the Local Self-Government Coalition marks a gradual turning point of Taiwan's social movements from the nationalistic stance of the early days to one pursuing a democratic system. The educational enlightenment brought about by the New Culture Movement, as well as the publics gradual understanding of the spirit of the rule of law and democracy made the promotion of political reform and the fight for Taiwan's right to local self-government, the Taiwanese people's common pursuit. Many of the active participants during the Japanese occupation of Taiwan and the key players of the Taiwan Local Self-Government Coalition were also the core members of the future 228 Incident Settlement Committee. Furthermore the advocate of self-government had not only sprouted during the Japanese colonial period, but it was the central spirit of the political reform plan of the 228 Incident Settlement Committee's 32 Demands.

At the end of 1935, the Governor-General in order to win over the Taiwanese people, held what were ridiculed as "fake autonomous" local council elections. Although there was no real democracy, it still allowed the people's awareness of civil rights to increasingly awaken, and in the initial post-war stages became a background factor in the upsurge of the people's political participation. After 1937 with the rise of Japanese militarism in the wartime regime, the political activities of the Taiwanese people had been completely suppressed. The "Taiwan Local Self-Government Coalition" was also forced to disband. However, Taiwan's sages of democracy and their wave upon wave of anti-Japanese resistance movements had already planted the seeds of democratic realization and the spirit of the rule of law in the hearts of the Taiwanese people, waiting for it to one day blossom and bear fruit.

2-2 The Retrocession to the Nationalist Government, from Hope to Defeat (1945-1947, the Precipice of the Incident)

Under the colonist's oppressive rule, and after a half-century of hard struggle, the Taiwanese people still had no political voice. After the war, the people that welcomed back the motherland with great joy, also at the same time enthusiastically looked forward to the implementation of democratic constitutionalism. Their intensity was called "political yearning fanaticism." On December 26, 1945, the Provincial Administrative Executive Office issued the "Program for Establishing a People's Representative Body at All Levels of Taiwan Province", that adopted an indirect method for electing representatives of all levels. On January 15th, 1946 Taiwan processed the registration of its citizens and one month later the number of people registered had reached more than 2.39 million, accounting for 91.8% of all Taiwanese adults over the age of 20, a spectacular event of that time.

On April 15, 1946 in the Taiwanese Provincial Council elections, 30 members were to be elected, and there were 523 county and city representatives with the right to vote, but there were more than 1,183 people in the provincial senate race. This created a special phenomenon where the number of candidates was far greater than those with the power to vote. On May 1, 1946 the Taiwan Provincial Council was formally established, and this time the Taiwanese people generally agreed that the moment for building a new Taiwan and the realization of democratic constitutionalism had finally arrived, with the Taiwan Provincial Council viewed as Taiwan's first important arena for practicing democracy.

However, when the Provincial Administrative Executive Office received Taiwan, it sought to take advantage of the old colonial system in order to take over and carry out new government decrees. So, politically, all executive, legislative and judicial power was monopolized by the Executive Office; socially, the military and police behaved lawlessly, and there was rampant official corruption; culturally, they used the excuses of poor Mandarin and Taiwanese having received Japanese enslavement education to belittle the people. All these factors sowed collective feelings of discontent and the official administration lost the people's confidence, leaving the people to refer to the National Government's "receiving" of Taiwan to it's "plundering."

More importantly, the Executive Office had not only not committed to restoring the economic development of Taiwan, but instead had established a Monopoly Bureau, a Board of Trade to monopolize the selling of commodities, having exclusive ownership of and the rights to resell public goods and domains, among other ploys. They repeated the colonist's exploitation of the Taiwanese people, and received from the colonial government the Japanese enterprises and a portion of the Taiwanese industry, which they later converted into government assets. The frequent occurrence of corrupt officials and businessmen "grabbing the spoils of war," led to widespread public unemployment, material shortages, skyrocketing prices and then a food shortage crisis.

As for this public condition, the Administrative Executive Office was completely negligent, and took the Provincial Council just as an advisory body, only having the power of suggestion and the right to inquiry, but towards the resolutions and supervision of the Provincial Council, who represented the will of all Taiwan, they didn't pay any attention. Even after the enactment of the constitution of the Republic of China on January 1, 1947, Administrative Executive Officer Chen Yi still said that the opportune time had not yet come, and then he unilaterally declared that Taiwan must first undergo a system of political tutelage. This made the people so fed up with the sufferings of bad government that they felt great despair. Therefore, the comprehensive reform of the province's government, the implementation of constitutional democracy and local self-government became the common anticipation of civil society.

The numerous political abuses and economic issues, as well as poor governance all aggravated the food problems, causing Taiwan's social grievances in early 1947 to be on the verge of eruption. It could be said that the tobacco seizure and murder case on February 27, 1947 was just the last straw that broke the camel's back, and that the 228 Incident that lead to the Taiwanese responding with strong resistance, was only confirmation that the strong dissatisfaction in the hearts of the people toward bad governance had nowhere to vent. The 228 Incident Settlement Committee established at this time then became the Taiwanese people's democracy summit in the post-war struggle for civil rights and self-government !

中華日報

第 一 版

中華民國三十六年三月四日

臺北號外
發行人盧冠群
第 一 號

糧局應解決食糧問題
憲警民共同維持秩序
處理會昨已會商決定

（本報臺北專訪）二二八事件處理委員會昨今日假中山堂舉開聯席會議，到各委員及舊差觀百人，對能維持地治秩序，並表示願見舟共達下列數項事須。會議由上午十時五分開，始至十二時四十分始者結束。通過事：

一、恢復地方秩序擴定大中壓生及臺市市民出動協持秩序

二、推本委代表分赴各區勸諭市內外鄉鎮長官切莫襲武裝叛亂

三、關於此次在關鎮區金團，大家保證維持秩序

四、請求各區長官釋續治安一切平定之指揮及召集人

五、推本委員協調關治安工作者子以獎勵

六、推選委員照料傷差差人

七、一切岳加糧費支出諸由協同指揮部與金搜五萬戲量十萬及其他人 七共約三十三萬元

八、叢別武裝軍長出動搶貨城北台領讓 頑狀況及緊急解決食糧原因

九、未潰防各委員應加 速電禁華福播福等工作

推此偏融聯應速平潰食糧造成

軍民相約保太平
三日晚六時交代責任

柯參謀長廣播

（本報臺北專訪）柯參謀長頃見各界代表談稱持約安臺為目的克薪果以誠謝群眾。第三日米全市人類擾熱糧運送，誤生活隨英人類最不幸的今天，大多數代表沒復地方秩序讓圓滿。全市民生活須以決定辦法五項：

一、肅清戒嚴軍除三日晚六時，一律令營集中營

二、成立憲兵民維持治安聯合部本能維持民兵各地方與自行糧

三、交通秩序

四、自覺偶發貧糧等項之責任

五、此後市內各地如何強生純氣地方與搜辦用各界代表研討解率者遊契憲及民統推這委員會辦書司差導

六時以後貧貧糧持治安之責任

本報緊要聲明

本報總能設於臺北，仍按日出版，近因火庫停行由二日起照所有報治市內原以政人敎不限無臺北讀者 《二八事件標逃二作公正市併基之種語》頒語違述之通國

見測，至表誓歉，本報揚登羅報某之一貴上租判二．

綠，特在臺北按日出版勞外免費分途各埠，隣務服勞群眾之職責。

中華日報盧冠群謹人啓

第三章/二二八事件與二二八處委會
The 228 Incident and the 228 Incident Settlement Committee

第三章/二二八事件與二二八處委會
The 228 Incident and the 228 Incident Settlement Committee

二二八事件爆發時，官方為儘速處置事件、平息眾怒，以及民間提出處分肇事者的要求下，由官、民共組處理委員會解決此一事件，成為此時的共識，而許多社會菁英也在混亂危險的時局裡，挺身而出協調事件爭端。然而，隨著事件的影響擴大，此一事件已非地方治安與取締私菸的問題，更牽涉到省民對於官方施政不當與行政長官公署威權體制之改革訴求。由此可知，二二八事件處理委員會的設立與演變，不僅與事件發展息息相關，更是探討二二八事件歷史重要的一環。

政員林忠等四人，代表前往行政長官公署談判。行政長官陳儀允由官民共組委員會處理事件，並同意解除戒嚴、釋放被捕市民、不准軍警開槍等要求，嗣後並對民眾廣播。

■ 3-1 事件爆發與緝煙血案調查

1947年2月27日傍晚，專賣局人員因查緝私煙打傷煙販林江邁、擊斃市民陳文溪，引發臺北民眾的抗爭。28日，群眾遊行至行政長官公署前請願，竟遭機槍掃射，此一落伍野蠻的軍閥作法，讓四散逃逸的民眾群情激憤，開始尋找外省人毆打報復，臺北街頭秩序混亂。隨著消息傳遍全臺，抗爭活動蔓延開來，二二八事件衝突就此爆發。

3月1日，臺北市參議會在中山堂邀集各方召開會議，決議由國大代表、省參議員、國民參政員等各級民意代表組成「二二七緝煙血案調查委員會」，並於會上推派省參議長黃朝琴、省參議員王添灯、北市參議長周延壽、國民參

1. 2. 臺灣省專賣局向警備總部呈報查緝私煙過程
3. 1945年行政長官公署
4. 二二七緝煙血案發生後，民眾湧至新生報要求刊出此一事件（1947年2月28日《台灣新生報》）

對於行政長官公署來說，由官、民合組委員會，以恢復秩序、穩定民心，是設立「二二八事件處理委員會」的最初目的。然而，此一事件並非僅是緝菸問題，癥結在於當局專制統治導致人民窘迫的生活困境。因此，隨著事件的不斷發展，以及全臺各地紛紛響應，以臺北中山堂作為集會地點的「二二八事件處理委員會」地位益發重要，也成為事件期間最關鍵的角色。

■ 3-2 二二八處委會成立與擴編

3月2日，官、民雙方依據協議在中山堂召開了首次會議，行政長官公署派出民政處長周一鶚、工礦處長包可永、農林處長趙連芳、警務處長胡福相、交通處長任顯群等五名官員，代表官方與民間共組「二二八事件處理委員會」，協助善後事宜。

當日因旁聽群眾過多，且議論紛陳，在臺灣省政治建設協會提出擴大人民代表參與的建議下，再納入商會、工會、學生、民眾和政治建設協會等五方面代表。此外，官方代表也增加為七名，新增警備總部參謀長柯遠芬及憲兵第四團團長張慕陶，此二人正是日後進行捕殺鎮壓時的主要執行人員。

下午，二二八處委會與陳儀當局協商後，陳儀為行緩兵之計，以爭取中央派兵鎮壓的時間，因此再次廣播宣布：1.從寬處理參與事件之民眾，一律不加追究；2.被捕的民眾不需里鄰長保釋，可由父兄領回；3.死傷者不分省籍，一律撫卹，以及4.同意處委會增加其他人民代表，以容納多數意見等要求。然而，擴大改組

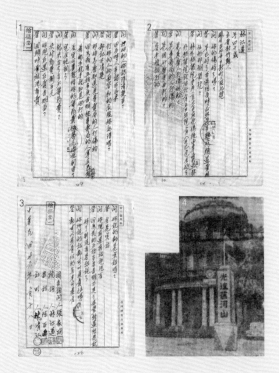

1. 2. 3. 被打傷的煙販林江邁事後所作的筆錄
4. 1945年臺灣省警備總司令部，由陳儀兼任警備總司令

後的處委會，雖可納入更多不同聲音，但參與成員也更為複雜，而此時行政長官公署代表卻不再參與處委會運作協商，反藉由情治機關派員滲透，以掌握處委會動態。

3月3日，二二八處委會決議擴大編制，設立宣傳、調查、救護、聯絡、總務等五組，並由各組召開首次會議。針對街頭仍不時傳出槍聲，以及事件爆發時警察大隊開槍濫射，處委會決議推派王添灯、林忠，以及工商、學生、青年等民眾代表二十餘人，前往長官公署與陳儀交涉，要求撤回巡邏軍隊及哨兵。協商後雙方同意軍隊需於當日撤回軍營、軍隊絕不北上、地方治安改由憲兵、警察、青年、學生共組治安服務隊維持，若再發生民眾打人毀物情事，由處委會代表負全責等事項。

為維持治安與社會秩序，二二八處委會召開了「臺北市臨時治安委員會」，由市長游彌堅擔任主席，與會者除了市參議員、青年、學生及市民代表，也混入了情治人員許德輝等人。會中決議要求由市民組織「忠義服務隊」來維持治安。此一提議旋即獲行政長官陳儀同意，原因在於提出此議的「忠義服務隊」隊長許德輝（化名高登進），為警備總部與軍統滲透至二二八處委會的情報人員。

雖然「忠義服務隊」副隊長由學生代表廖德雄擔任，負責學生隊的協助治安工作，對於維護臺北街頭治安發揮一定作用；然而，負責社會隊的隊長許德輝卻私下進行內部分化，使得「忠義服務隊」在成立之初就遭當局所掌控。同日，警總也劃定了臺北、基隆兩警戒區，以及新竹、臺中兩防衛區，由蘇紹文、黃國書任防衛司令，嘉義以南則由彭孟緝負責防範，開始進行全臺的偵防、監控。

當日會議中，處委會另決議派出林宗賢、林詩黨、呂伯雄、駱水源、李萬居等五人赴美國在臺領事館，請託將事件轉知國民政府當局與國際社會。此外，處委會也呼籲民眾不可再毆打外省同胞，並推舉王添灯擔任宣傳組長，代

1. 在官民協商後，陳儀宣布釋放二二八事件被捕民眾等處理原則
2. 二二八事件肇禍兇犯真像（台灣新生報1947.03.04）

表處委會向省民廣播，並負責發佈處委會的新聞公報。傍晚，王添灯首次代表處委會向省民廣播，說明會議經過與交涉情形，並希望民眾自發維持治安。

3月4日上午，處委會決議通告全省十七縣市，以參議會為主體組織各地之二二八處委會，以處理各地發生之事件，並推派代表參加臺北之全省性處委會，以推進工作。另外，對於上海等地方誇張扭曲此一事件，稱事件發生係臺民要求託管等言論，李萬居也在會上提出報告，強調此次事件之發生，目的為要求政治改革，並非傳言所稱有其他企圖。為此，二二八處委會決議在報上刊登《急告本市同胞書》，以說明此次事件已在交涉中，同胞應鎮靜並作為委員會後盾，勿打人燬物，以維持社會秩序。

由於臺北市區內仍有武裝軍隊巡邏，二二八處委會再度向參謀長柯遠芬交涉制止。此外，處委會還針對電力、糧食、交通、治安、宣傳等問題進行商議，協調解決，通過了包括二二八事件之新聞播送由該會統一辦理、派代表向銀行借款做為購米資金，由處委會發給採購米糧調濟證明，以及增加各工會兩名代表參與處委會等提案。最後，由王添灯代表二二八處委會向全省廣播當日議事內容，以及說明處委會決定在臺北成立本部，由各地分部派代表出席

之決議。

由於該事件並非地方治安與取締私菸的單一問題，更牽涉到省民對於行政長官公署威權體制之改革訴求。此時的二二八處委會，也從處理單一爭議事件的組織，轉為維護社會秩序，並緩和當時窘迫的米荒、交通、電力等民生問題，成為民眾所依靠的對象。

1. 柯遠芬同意軍隊撤回之報導（台灣新生報1947.03.04）
2. 抗議民眾激憤聚難平聚集於專賣局臺北分局
3. 專賣局臺北分局遭民眾抗議毀物後殘況
4. 1947年2月28日下午，《台灣新生報》以號外方式即時報導二二八事件經過及政府處置態度報導）

　　同日，蔣渭川、陳炘、青年學生與民眾代表三十餘人與陳儀及長官公署官員會面，代表們指出，事件之發生係過去政治、經濟之施政問題，此時對於政治上之改革，應開誠佈公，一舉革新臺灣政治局面，解決一切根本問題。陳儀在回覆時，表面上重申其與各處處長都願意與民眾接近，也同意由二二八處委會研擬具體辦法，提出政治改革建議，而民眾好的意見也將採納，但實際上已在佈署中央援軍登陸後的鎮壓計畫。

　　除了部分縣市在事件爆發初期已成立治安維持組織，在處委會發佈通告後的三至四天內，各縣市參議會也相繼表態支持，並陸續成立各地之處委會或相應的組織。因此，除了全省性的二二八處委會之外，可歸為第二級之全臺各縣市處委會計有十六個，截至軍隊抵臺進行鎮壓前，僅有高雄縣未及成立相對應之組織，而陸續成立中的第三級區、鄉、鎮級二二八處委會則至少有十二個。至此，二二八處委會已發展成為全省性架構。

　　當日，警總參謀長柯遠芬、調查室主任陳達元、軍統局臺灣站站長林頂立祕密開會，主張「以民眾力量對抗民眾力量」，下令以滲透、誘導、分化等手段造成內部衝突，並由「情治人員調查、監視處委會主謀人士」；此外，由林頂立(化名張秉承)出面組織的「義勇總隊

」，也乘機製造混亂局面，許多「罪證」也在此一背景下杜撰出來。

1. 3月5日，二二八處委會決議預定推派陳逸松、王添灯、吳春霖及黃朝生等4人，日後赴中央陳情事真相（1947年3月5日《台灣新生報》）
2. 1947年2月28日陳儀開始實行戒嚴，並大肆逮捕民眾
3. 遭專賣局等人員打傷之女煙販林江邁
4. 憤怒的民眾將分局內的菸、酒搬出焚毀
5. 緝煙血案發生地點天馬茶房位於日治時期的太平町（今延平北路）
6. 政治建設協會懇請政府萬勿派兵來臺

各級處委會一覽表

層　級	地　域	名　稱
第一級	全省性	二二八事件處理委員會（臺北）
第二級	省轄市、縣、縣轄市等	二二八處委會基隆分會、二二八處委會宜蘭分會、新竹市二二八處委會、新竹縣二二八處委會、臺中地區時局處理委員會、彰化市善後處理委員會、嘉義市三二事件處理委員會、臺南市二二八處委會、臺南縣二二八處委會、高雄市二二八處委會、二二八處委會屏東分會、二二八處委會澎湖分會、二二八處委會花蓮分會、二二八處委會臺東分會
第三級	區、鄉、鎮等	二二八處委會淡水分會、二二八處委會板橋支會、二二八處委會中壢分會、豐原區時局處委會、大甲時局處委會、北斗二二八處委會分會、員林二二八處委會、朴子鎮二二八處委會、臺南縣北門區二二八處委會、新營二二八處委會、羅東二二八處委會、鳳林二二八處委會

註：1945年，國民政府接收臺灣後，行政長官公署重新調整行政區制度，改為9個省轄市（臺北市、基隆市、新竹市、臺中市、彰化市、臺南市、嘉義市、屏東市、高雄市）、8個縣（臺北縣、新竹縣、臺中縣、臺南縣、高雄縣、臺東縣、花蓮縣、澎湖縣）與2個縣轄市（宜蘭市、花蓮市），另在其下設有區、鄉、鎮等行政體系。

1. 行政長官公署體制下的專賣局，與民爭利、弊端叢生。在30位省參議員中，就有27位聯名要求撤銷，由此可知臺灣社會對專賣制度的不滿情緒
2. 黃榮燦所作的「恐怖的檢查」版畫，呈現當時民眾對於查緝人員不當執勤的懼怕

■ 3-3 二二八處委會轉型 — 省政改革與民主自治

　　3月5日上午，二二八處委會在中山堂召開擴大分組會議，包括財務、糧食、宣傳、交通、治安、聯絡、救護、總組、調查等組，分別確定工作內容與提擬相關議案。其中，糧食組決議派員前往中南部採購米糧，向糧食局及工商銀行借款，交由臺北市糧食協助會作為購米資金。此外，二二八處委會也通過了宣傳組所提的《告全國同胞書》，並決議推派組長王添灯及黃朝生等四人為代表，預計赴南京向國民政府陳情，並發送電報給國民黨中央黨部、國防部長、上海同鄉會等，俾使各界瞭解事件真相。

　　下午，依據前一日陳儀同意由二二八處委會研擬具體辦法、提出政治改革建議之意見，二二八處委會召開了臨時大會，會中通過了「八項政治根本改革方案」，這也就是日後《三十二條處理大綱》的前身，這八項核心內容為：

1. 二二八事件責任應歸政府負責。
2. 公署秘書長、民政、財政、工礦、農林、教育、警務各處長及法制委員會委員，過半數以本省人充任。
3. 公營事業歸由本省人負責經營。
4. 依據建國大綱，即刻實施縣市長民選。
5. 專賣制度撤消。
6. 貿易局、宣傳委員會廢止。
7. 保障人民之言論、出版、集會之自由。
8. 保障人民生命、身體、財產之安全。

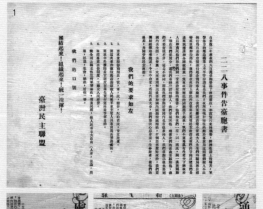

1. 228事件期間，二二八處委會與各民眾團體都紛紛提出施行憲政、推行自治的主張。圖為臺灣民主聯盟所提之二二八事件告台胞書
2. 全省各縣市組織事件處理委員會報導（台灣新生報1947.03.05）
3. 二二八處委會發出告全國同胞書（台灣新生報1947.03.07）
4. 各地方處委會成立與運作情況相關報導

此外，在臨時大會上也通過了「二二八事件處理委員會組織大綱」，開宗明義的確立處委會的宗旨為：「團結全省人民，處理二二八事件及改革省政」，首次將二二八處委會從衝突調處及維持治安之單一事件臨時組織，提升為代表臺灣人民訴求政治改革的最高民意機構。

此外，在組織架構的規劃上，二二八處委會以全體委員會為最高機構，所做出之決議由常務委員會執行，並選出七人主席團，其下設秘書室；此外，常務委員會下設立政務局和處理局，分別負責研擬政治改革建議與事件處置辦法，其下再分設交涉組、計畫組、財務組、糧食組、交通組、調查組、治安組、總務組等八組，負責執行相關任務。當晚，王添灯向全省民眾廣播，說明處委會擬提出取消專賣局與貿易局、立刻實施縣市長民選，以及行政長官公署須任用本省人等政治改革要求。

此一階段，處委會成員除最初參與緝煙血案調查委員的國大代表、國民參政員、省參議員、臺北市議員之代表外，中央及省級民意代表各再推出十至三十名代表，再加上各縣市參議員各三名、省級及縣市人民團體代表、各縣市工會代表、各縣市原住民代表、各大學中等學校以上之職員學生代表等，因此，不論從影響力或代表性來看，此時的二二八處委會都是臺

灣民眾參與政治改革最重要的管道。

1. 陳儀願與民接近改革（台灣新生報1947.03.05）
2. 要求省縣市長民選（台灣新生報1947.03.06）
3. 3月3日，二二八處委會改組後首次開會，決議維護治安，並推派王添灯等代表面見陳儀，與當局協商處理方式，並要求軍隊撤回等事項（1947年3月3日《台灣新生報》）
4. 3月10日，陳儀宣布二二八處委會為非法團體，下令解散（台灣新生報1947.03.11）

二二八處委會組織架構圖

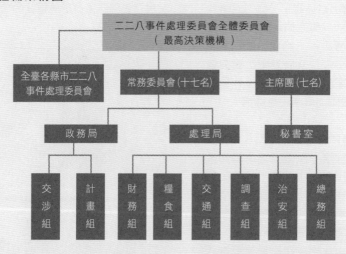

然而，陳儀當局表面上持續與二二八處委會協商，接納社會各界意見，一方面卻讓憲兵第四團密電中央，將二二八處委會羅織為「非法團體，從事叛國奪取政權叛亂」；另外，參謀長柯遠芬也召集憲兵第四團團長張慕陶、軍統局臺北站長林頂立等人，指示偵察並掌握「策動份子」動態，開始羅織一個個「黑名單」。3月5日，陳儀接到南京國民政府蔣主席手令：「已派步兵一團并派憲兵一營限本月七日由滬啟運勿念」。

3月6日，二二八處委會補開正式成立大會，完成最後一次擴大改組，成為全省性之最高民意機構，出席委員及旁聽民眾共三百餘人，會議由王添 擔任主席，並選舉出十七名常務委員。最後，主席王添灯宣讀向中央及全國廣播「二二八事件真相、全文及事件經過」內容，強調二二八處委會的目標是「肅清貪官污吏，爭取本省政治的改革，不是要排斥外省同胞參與改善本省政治」，並決議以二二八處委會名義，預計用國語、閩南語、客語、英語、日語等，向海內外進行廣播，讓中外瞭解事件真相。由此可知，二二八處委會的立場，並非陰謀叛亂或挑起省籍衝突，最終目的，就是以擴大人民參與的議會民主過程，達到政治改革的目標。

二二八處委會歷次改組比較表

時　間	名　稱／地　位	成　立／改　組　原　因	主　要　成　員
3月1日	「二二七緝煙血案調查委員會」成立	解決緝煙衝突傷亡事件	國大代表、省參議員、國民參政員、臺北市參議員等共組
3月2日	名稱改為「二二八事件處理委員會」	解決緝煙傷亡及公署開槍事件	納入行政長官公署五名官方代表
3月3日	第一次改組擴編，名稱不變，性質屬單一事件處理組織	擴大成員參與，共同解決事件爭議	擴大納入商會、工會、學生、民眾與政治建設協會等五方代表；官方代表新增兩名，共計七名，惟隨後全數退出
3月4日	第二次改組，擴大為全省性之組織	處理各地事件與協調民生需求	除全省性之二二八處委會外，由十七縣市參議會為主體設立各地之處委會
3月6日	第三次改組，性質轉為省政改革之最高民意機構	以政治改革手段根本解決省政問題	全體委員會成員含括各個階層、身分、職業代表，推選出十七人常務委員，並預計成立七人之主席團

　　同日傍晚，陳儀佯裝配合二二八處委會改革提議，再次向全省民眾廣播，內容為：1.行政長官公署將改為省政府，經中央核准後實施，改組時，省府委員、各廳長或各處長將盡量任用本省人；2.定於本年7月1日舉行縣市長民選，在尚未民選前，當地人民認為現任縣市長不稱職者，可將其免職，另由地方民意機關推選三人，由他圈選一人充任等內容。最後，陳儀呼籲：「信賴政府，切勿輕信謠言」。

　　至此，眾人以為自2月28日起風起雲湧的民主抗爭運動，將獲具體成果，然而證諸歷史，可知陳儀已獲得中央調兵支援，並主張「對於奸黨亂徒，須以武力消滅，不能容其存在」，秘密規劃軍事鎮壓計畫。

■ 3-4 王添灯宣讀《三十二條處理大綱》

　　3月7日，行政長官公署致函二二八處委會，指稱：「關於善後辦法，已組織二二八事件處理委員會，今後，各方意見希均先交處理委員會討論，訂擬綜合意見後，由該會選定代表數人，開列名單向該署建議，以便採擇實施。」當日，二二八處委會召開了全體委員大會，會中通過了《三十二條處理大綱》，並由王添灯代表宣讀，當中提出了對於事件的處理建議，以及省政改革的根本解決方針，並決議由全體常務委員向陳儀當局提出。

　　有鑒於國府接收以來，軍、警風紀不彰，肆意開槍傷人事件頻傳，而在事件期間更是變本加厲，因此，此一大綱在「對於目前的處理」方面，提出了地方治安暫由憲兵與非武裝之警察及民眾共同負擔、由憲兵隊及各地處理委員會共同保管武裝、從優撫卹死傷人員等內容。另外，在軍事的「根本處理」方面，也提出缺乏教育和訓練之軍隊絕對不可使駐臺灣等訴求，以穩定社會秩序、消弭流血衝突。

　　《三十二條處理大綱》最關鍵的內容，就是廿二條政治改革的「根本處理」內容，主要包括:制定省自治法、縣市長民選、撤銷專賣局及貿易局、廢除苛捐雜稅、保障人身安全、維護

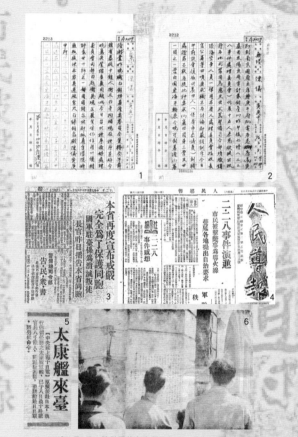

1. 2. 1947年3月8日，陳儀電蔣主席稱已使二二八處委會內部起分化作用，待軍隊抵臺即著手清除「奸匪叛徒」
3. 1947年3月10日陳儀掩蓋真相向全民廣播的歷史剪報
4. 二二八事件的發生，市民被擊斃是導火線，蔓延各地提出自治的要求（1947年3月8日《人民導報》）
5. 太康艦載運廿一師軍對來臺進行鎮壓（台灣新生報1947.03.11）
6. 軍隊鎮壓期間，陳儀為掩飾太平所發佈之安民布告

言論集會結社等人權與法治訴求,這些內容不僅是全省性處委會、各地方處委會與多數民眾的心聲,更延續了自殖民時期以來,臺灣民主先進們一直努力不懈追求的民主自治理想。

然而,在陳儀與情治機關有計畫的布置下,當天下午的會議混進許多有心人士,除了破壞會場秩序,更提出過激之軍事、政治等十項要求,例如特務份子吳國信等喧嘩要求「本省人之戰犯漢奸即時釋放」、「撤消警備司令部,以免軍權濫用」,以及「行政長官公署由二二八處委會負責改組」等涉及中央權限之虞的十項要求,也在會場混亂及特務份子叫喊聲中通過。因此,《三十二條處理大綱》與被特務份子特意另外夾帶的十項要求,被當局日後羅織為「陰謀叛亂」的「四十二條罪證」,作為軍事鎮壓的藉口。

下午,當二二八處委會全體常務委員同赴行政長官公署時,理應由雙方針對此一大綱及相關訴求續行協商,然而,陳儀因已確定軍隊抵達的時間,一改之前的協商態度,怒斥而去,也讓處委會代表對於陳儀出爾反爾的態度感到詫愕。當日,陳儀再次去電南京國民政府請兵,稱:「一團兵力,不敷戡亂之用,擬請再加開一師,至少一旅,在最短期間,予以徹底肅清」。

1. 2. 3. 4. 5. 6各地方處委會成立與運作情況相關報導
7. 處委會治安組所設之忠義服務隊已遭情治人員滲透
8. 保密局所呈臺灣事變報告書中揭露派員滲透處委會
9. 陳儀宣布處委會為非法團體予以解散(檔案局提供)

■ 二二八事件處理委員會通過王添灯所擬《三十二條處理大綱》之政治改革方案後，由王添灯代表向全臺同胞進行廣播：

《三十二條處理大綱》

二二八事件處理委員會發言人 王添灯 播講

一、對於目前的處理

1. 政府在各地之武裝部隊，應自動下令暫時解除武裝，武器交由各地處理委員會及憲兵隊共同保管，以免繼續發生流血衝突事件。
2. 政府武裝部隊武裝解除後，地方之治安由憲兵與非武裝之警察及民眾組織共同負擔。
3. 各地若無政府武裝部隊威脅之時，絕對不應有武裝械鬥行動。對貪官污吏不論其為本省人或外省人，亦只應檢舉轉請處理委員會協同憲警拘拿，依法嚴辦，不應加害而惹出是非。
4. 對於政治改革之意見，可列舉要求條件，向省處理委員會提出，以候全盤解決。
5. 政府切勿再移動兵力或向中央請遣兵力，企圖以武力解決事件，致發生更慘重之流血而受國際干涉。
6. 在政治問題未根本解決之前，政府之一切施策（不論軍事、政治），須先與處理委員會接洽，以免人民懷疑政府誠意，發生種種誤會。
7. 對於此次事件不應向民間追究責任者，將來亦不得假藉任何口實拘捕此次事件之關係者。對於因此次事件而死傷之人民應從優撫恤。

二、根本處理

甲、軍事方面

1. 缺乏教育和訓練之軍隊絕對不可使駐臺灣。
2. 中央可派員在臺徵兵守臺。
3. 在內陸之內戰未終息以前，除以守衛臺灣為目的之外，絕對反對在臺灣徵兵，以免臺灣陷入內戰漩渦。

乙、政治方面

1. 制定省自治法，為本省政治最高規範，以便實現國父建國大綱之理想。
2. 縣市長於本年六月以前實施民選，縣市參議會同時改選。
3. 省各處長人選應經省參議會（改選後為省議會）之同意，省參議會應於本年六月以前改選，目前其人選由長官提出，交由省處理委員會審議。
4. 省各處長三分之二以上須由在本省居住十年以上者擔任之（最好秘書長、民政、財政、工礦、農林、教育、警務等處長應該如是）。
5. 警務處長及各縣市警察局長應由本省人擔任，省警察大隊及鐵道工礦等警察即刻廢止。
6. 法制委員會委員須半數以上由本省人充任，主任委員由委員互選。
7. 除警察機關之外，不得逮捕人犯。
8. 憲兵除軍隊之犯人外，不得逮捕人犯。
9. 禁止帶有政治性之逮捕拘禁。
10. 非武裝之集合結社絕對自由。
11. 言論、出版、罷工絕對自由，廢止新聞紙發行申請登記制度。
12. 即刻廢止人民團體組織條例。
13. 廢止民意機關候選人檢覈辦法。
14. 改正各級民意機關選舉辦法。
15. 實行所得統一累進稅，除奢侈品稅相續稅外，不得徵收任何雜稅。
16. 一切公營事業之主管人由本省人擔任。
17. 設置民選之公營事業監察委員會，日產處理應委任省政府全權處理，各接收工廠礦應置經營委員會，委員須過半數由本省人充任之。
18. 撤銷專賣局，生活必需品實施配給制度。
19. 撤銷貿易局。
20. 撤銷宣傳委員會。
21. 各地方法院院長、各地方法院首席檢察官全部以本省人充任。
22. 各法院推事、檢察官以下司法人員各半數以上省民充任。

　　傍晚七時，王添灯再次代表二二八處委會向民眾廣播，他除了說明二二八事件真相全文、處委會的決議，以及所提要求被拒情形，同時宣讀《三十二條處理大綱》條文內容。他不改初衷的再次呼籲：「我們並無本省外省之別，我們的目標是要打倒貪官污吏，希望正義的外省同胞和我們合作，共同為民主而奮鬥」、「從今以後，這次事件已不能單由二二八處委會處理，只有全體省民的力量才能解決，同時也才能達成全體省民的合理要求，希望全體同胞繼續奮鬥！」這也成為了二二八處委會的歷史餘音。

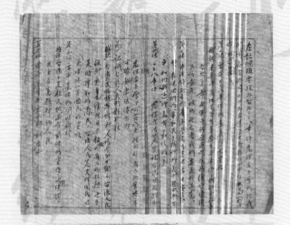

1. 陳儀宣布事件處理原則 (台灣新生報1947.03.03一版)
2. 陳儀宣布事件處理原則 (台灣新生報1947.03.03一版)
3. 蔣主席電告陳儀廿一師抵臺時間 (國史館提供)
4. 彰化田中青年同治十二條要求 (彰化縣文化局提供)
5. 彰化田中青年同治十二條要求 (彰化縣文化局提供)

■ 3-5 二二八處委會遭鎮壓、解散

　　3月8日起，軍隊陸續從基隆登陸，開始密集射擊、肅清街頭，此時陳儀仍以廣播對人民假稱：「軍隊移駐臺灣完全為保護全省人民，消滅亂黨叛徒，絕無其它用意」。是日，代表民間心聲的《人民導報》最後一次出刊，再次申明市民被擊斃是二二八事件的導火線，此一事件是「平時的積憤所致」，因而蔓延為各地提出自治的要求，最終目的，是要達成本省政治之革新。然而，陳儀當局仍儘速調集軍力，對於此一懇切的民主期盼，置若罔聞。

　　3月9日廿一師大軍開抵後，在陳儀當局的調度與部署下，開始「肅清市內奸徒」，祕密逮捕處委會成員。3月10日，陳儀再度實施戒嚴，並宣布二二八處委會為違法組織，准由各地駐軍逕行解散，並陸續解散臺灣省政治建設協會、三民主義青年團等團體，全面查封《人民導報》、《民報》等十多家言論機關，而處委會核心成員則成為首要鎮壓對象。此時的臺灣社會，不僅集會、結社、言論的自由全遭剝奪，人民的生命財產安全更毫無保障。

　　為儘速剷除異己、推諉事件責任，陳儀當局羅織了一批批的「黑名單」與「罪名」，並在逮捕後不經司法審判立即處決，避免事件真相

1. 《人民導報》刊出二二八處委會發表告全國同胞書，再次重申爭取自治非除斥外省人，目的為改進臺灣政治（1947年3月8日《人民導報》）
2. 國防部長白崇禧公告善後處理原則（秋惠文庫提供）
3. 3月7日，二二八事件處理委員會議決由王添灯所擬的「三十二條要求」，並推舉全體委員向陳儀提出（1947.3.8《人民導報》）
4. 二二八事件的發生，市民被擊斃是導火線，蔓延各地提出自治的要求（1947年3月8日《人民導報》）
5. 3月5日蔣介石主席派兵手令

為世人所知。這些名單包括了3月13日陳儀電呈蔣介石的〈辦理人犯姓名調查表〉、3月24日臺灣省警備總部軍法處呈報之《二二八事件首謀叛亂通緝要犯名冊》，以及4月18日警備總部發佈之《二二八事變首謀叛亂在逃主犯名冊》等，其中，參與二二八處委會的成員傷亡最為慘重。

在陳儀所附的報告中，甚至主張「司法手續緩慢，而臺灣情況特殊，擬請暫時適用軍法，使得嚴懲奸黨份子，以滅亂源。」因此，早在3月13日陳儀上呈〈辦理人犯姓名調查表〉之前，多位處委會的核心成員早已被捕遇害。然而，要等到臺灣解嚴後，從國家安全局公佈的1949年11月28日由王守正上呈雷萬鈞〈臺灣省『二二八』事變正法及死亡人犯名冊〉中，才證實這些被秘密逮捕的處委會成員，已遭殺害。

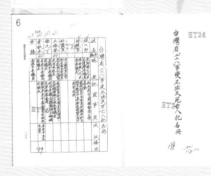

1. 3月7日陳儀再次電請加派兵力
2. 3月7日，陳儀接獲蔣介石手令，得知軍隊即將抵臺，一改之前的協商態度，悍然拒絕處委會代表所提的訴求
3. 4. 5. 3月13日陳儀呈報「辦理人犯姓名調查表」（國史館提供）
6. 1949年11月28日，國家安全局上呈《臺灣省「二二八」事變正法及死亡人犯名冊》，赫然見王添登（灯）姓名

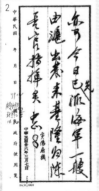

二二八處委會與行政長官公署談判大事紀

時　間	二二八事件處理委員會	行政長官公署
2月27日	發生二二七緝煙血案	專賣局等人員因查緝私菸，打傷菸販、擊斃市民
2月28日	二二八事件爆發	行政長官公署向遊行陳情緝煙血案的民眾開槍，造成數人死傷，抗爭活動蔓延開來，陳儀宣佈戒嚴
3月1日	「二二七緝煙血案調查委員會」成立，推派代表與行政長官陳儀談判	陳儀第一次向全省廣播，同意委員會代表之提議，解除戒嚴，並由官民共組委員會處理事件
3月2日	「二二八事件處理委員會」成立，並推派代表與陳儀協商，提出從寬處理抗爭民眾等意見	陳儀派出五名官員參加處委會，再次廣播宣布所謂「更寬大的措施」，卻私下調動南部軍隊，並向南京政府請兵。此時，各地街頭仍傳出槍聲與出現軍隊巡邏車
3月3日	二二八處委會擴大納入商會、工會、學生、民眾與政治建設協會等五方代表。推舉各組召集人，會後由對外廣播與發佈新聞，並呼籲民眾自發維持治安	警備總部印發《告全體市民書》，答應寬大處理，要求市民照常上課、工作，卻同時派人滲透與分化二二八處委會。另外，長官公署同意撤退街頭軍警，由「忠義服務隊」維持治安，惟該服務隊實質由警總掌控
3月4日	二二八處委會決議在臺北成立本部，由各地成立分部，並派代表出席，因而發展成為全省性組織，並宣布要求政治改革	陳儀會見陳情代表，聲稱願意多與民眾接近、握手，並同意由二二八處委會研擬辦法提出政治改革建議
3月5日	二二八處委會召開成立大會，通過「八項政治根本改革方案」及「處委會組織大綱」，並預定推派代表赴南京向中央政府陳情	警備總部參謀長柯遠芬發表談話，要求各界同胞「不可聽信謠言」。憲兵司令張鎮向蔣介石報告，「已演變為叛國奪取政權之階段」。陳儀接到蔣介石手令：「已派步兵一團并派憲兵一營限本月七日由滬啟運勿念」
3月6日	二二八處委會補開正式成立大會，成為全省性之最高民意機構，推選常務委員，並發表《告全國同胞書》，聲明肅清貪官污吏、爭取本省政治改革的目標	陳儀召集參謀長柯遠芬等幕僚，研議軍隊抵臺後之作戰計畫。陳儀向全省廣播，假稱：將改長官公署為省政府，並任用本省人士；定七月一日實施縣市長民選，目前不稱職者可予免職，由地方民意機關推選
3月7日	二二八處委會通過王添灯所擬之《三十二條處理大綱》，卻被當局滲透處委會之特務另追加十條過激要求	陳儀悍拒處委會所提要求，並再次去電向蔣介石請兵，稱：「一團兵力，不敷戡亂之用，擬請再加開一師，至少一旅，在最短期間，予以徹底肅清」
3月8日	二二八處委會及相關政治團體已被分化、人心惶惶	憲兵第四團的兩營憲兵從福建抵臺，憲兵團長張慕陶仍在處委會保證中央絕不調兵
3月9日	二二八處委會成員陸續遭捕殺	廿一師大軍登陸基隆，軍隊開始密集射擊、肅清街頭，傍晚，臺北地區槍聲大作
3月10日		3月10日陳儀宣佈戒嚴，並下令解散各地二二八處委會及一切「非法團體」

（版一第）　　　報導民人　　（六期星）　日八月三年六十三國民華中

經中華郵政登記第一類第一類新聞紙類
臺灣郵電管理局新聞紙類登記執照第三三號

二二八事件演進

市民被擊斃事為導火線

臺延各地提出自治要求

二月廿七日晚七點半鐘，太平町發生事件後民眾在憤恨之餘，擁到憲兵隊和臺北市警察局前喊口號，廿八日上午九點餘沿途打鑼通知，全市罷勤、大批民眾湧向本町專賣局，把局裡的民眾沿街打鑼通知，各盛民眾湧湧，香煙、酒、汽車、腳踏車，拋出路中、南門的專賣局亦被包圍，下午一點餘憲兵槍阻止旋而槍斃二名，傷四名，把局裡堆貨火柴、憲兵挺身向交官公者被衛兵繳槍阻止此旋而槍斃二名，傷四名，虎標永安堂，店面玻璃均被搗毀，各機關團……

事件擴大

……遠到憲兵隊和臺北市分局前進，各盛民眾湧湧，市民死傷數人，情勢愈益複雜，學生全部停課，各機關員工、生、工人、商人等都有死傷，被捕的亦不少，民眾的反抗、有加無減。二日下午三時，陳……

（轉處遊對法。）

（一）凡是參加此次事件之人民，政府念其由於衡動、缺乏理智，準予從寬，一律不加追究。

（二）因參加比次事件已被憲警拘捕之人民，准予省參議員各一人、國大代表、青年四人、三青團五人、工人二……

……件，國大代表、青年四人、三青團五人、工人二件處理委員會之二人由中山堂開會之二……由其其父兄玩家族領回，長官公署要求撤退由其其父兄玩家族領回，以免……被憲警拘捕之人民，准予釋放，均送染蓬兵團部、川、林梧村等二……不必由鄰里妥保釋，以免……

秩……

二、二八事件感想

這次二二八事件，可說是中國的不幸，但……

日來一相反比照，一般人民的行動中，如打外省人當為……合理的、可是關於邁過行憲、自治的要……事態的進展而到今……合理的要求自可……眾的同情，今後……見拋出才能夠……使政府獲得鐵制的對象……

社論

The 228 Incident and the 228 Incident Settlement Committee

When the 228 Incident erupted, the consensus at the time by the officials was to use a joint Government-civilian Settlement Committee to resolve the issue, so as to deal with the Incident as quickly as possible, to quell the public outrage, as well as to have the requirement that civilians propose punishments for the perpetrators. Furthermore, many of society's elites also bravely stepped forward into the chaos of the current situation, to assist in reconciling the disputes of the incident. However, as the impact of the event mushroomed, this incident was no longer just a problem of local law and order or cracking down on contraband cigarettes, but was concerned with the citizens' demands for reforming the official's improper administration and the Administrative Executive Office's authoritarian system. Therefore we know that the establishment and evolution of the 228 Incident Settlement Committee, is not only closely related to the development of the Incident, but is also an important part of exploring the history of the 228 Incident.

3-1 The Incident's Outbreak and the Tobacco Seizure and Murder Investigation

On the evening of February 27, 1947, because Monopoly Bureau staff member investigating and seizing contraband cigarettes, wounded tobacco trader Lin Jiang-Mai, and then fatally shot citizen Chen Wen-Xi, it triggered a public protest in Taipei. On the 28th, a mass demonstration had reached the front of the Administrative Executive Office to petition, but was unexpectedly mowed down with machine gun fire. This was the outdated practice of a brutal warlord, and it made the escaping, scattering crowd burn with rage. They started searching for mainlanders, who they beat in revenge, and then the streets of Taipei were in chaos. As the news spread throughout the island, protests spread again, and then this was the clash that erupted into the 228 Incident.

On March 1, the Taipei City Council invited all parties to convene a meeting at Chungshan Hall, sponsored by the National Assembly, Provincial Senate, National Political Assembly, as well as all other elected officials, they then formed the "227 Tobacco Seizure and Murder Case Investigation Commission," choosing Provincial Senate Chairman Huang Chao-Qin, Provincial Senator Wang Tien-Teng, Taipei Senate Chairman Zhou Yan-Shou, National Political Assemblyman Lin Zhong, to be sent as representatives to the Administrative Executive Office for negotiations. Administrative Executive Officer Chen Yi allowed the incident to be handled by the joint Government-civilian Settlement Committee, and agreed to lift martial law, release the citizens who were arrested and forbid the police and military from shooting among other requirements. This was subsequently broadcast to the public.

As far as the Administrative Executive Office was concerned, restoring public order and public confidence through a joint government-civilian committee was the original purpose for establishing the "228 Incident Settlement Committee." However, this incident was not only a tobacco seizure problem, the crux of it was that the authority's repressive rule had led to the people's plight of distress and poverty. Therefore, following the development of the Incident, as well as the overall Taiwanese response, the status of Taipei's Chungshan Hall "228 Incident Settlement Committee" became increasingly more important and then one of the key players during the Incident.

3-2 Establishment and Expansion of the 228 Incident Settlement Committee

On March 2nd, both the official and civilian parties, in accordance with the agreement, held their first meeting in Zhongshan Hall. The Administrative Executive Office sent five officials, the District Director Zhou Yi-E, the Industry and Mining Director Bao Ke-Yong, the Agriculture and Forestry Director Zhao Lian-Fang, Police Commissioner Hu Fu-Xiang, and Traffic Director Ren Xian-Qun, to represent the government in the joint 228 Incident Settlement Committee, and to help with the aftermath.

On that day, because there were too many citizens on the sidelines pushing the discussion in different directions, the Taiwanese Provincial Political Construction Association proposed expanding the people's representation to include representatives from the Political Construction Association, Chamber of Commerce, trade unions, students and citizens. In addition, the government's representatives increased to seven, newly adding Taiwan Garrison Command Chief of Staff Ke Yuan-Fen and Head of Military Police Division IV, Zhang Mu-Tao. These two officers would later be central to carrying out the future murderous crackdown.

In the afternoon, after negotiations between the 228 Incident Settlement Committee and Chen Yi's authorities, Chen Yi, as a stall tactic in order to have enough time to convince the central government to send troops for a crackdown, broadcasted: 1. The people involved with the Incident will be dealt with leniently and none will be prosecuted. 2. Those arrested will not have to post bail with the neighborhood director and can be retrieved by next-of-kin. 3. All victims would be compensated equally and 4. Agree to increase representation of the Settlement Committee, to accommodate majority opinion and similar demands. However, after the Settlement Committee expanded and reorganized to include more voices, the membership became even more complicated and it was at this time that the Administrative Executive Office representative no longer participated in the operation of the Settlement Committee negotiations, but was infiltrated by members of the intelligence agency, in order to monitor the development of the Settlement Committee.

On March 3, the 228 Incident Settlement Committee enlarge its establishment by forming five groups: the Publicity, Investigation, Ambulance, Communications, and General Services groups and each group held its first meeting. The bursts of gunfire kept occurring on the streets. The Settlement Committee resolved to send Wang Tien-teng, Lin Chung, as well as more than 20 business, student, youth and public representatives to the Executive Office to negotiate withdrawal of patrolling troops and sentries with Chen Yi. After negotiations both sides agreed that, the military needed to withdraw back to its army barracks that day, that the army in the middle and south Taiwan would not move north to Taipei, that local law and order would be maintained by a Security Service Brigade composed of gendarmes, police, youth and students and if there was any further incident of violence and destruction, then the full responsibility would be bore by these Settlement Committee representatives.

In order to maintain peace and public order, the 228 Incident Settlement Committee convened the "Taipei Interim Public Security Committee." It was chaired by Mayor You Mi-Jian, and in addition to the city council members, youth, student and citizen representatives participating, intelligence member Xu De-Hui and others were also mixed in. The meeting decided that law and order be maintained by the citizen organization, the "Loyal Service Brigade." This proposal immediately received Administrative Executive Chen Yi's approval because the one who proposed the "Loyal Service Brigade," and its captain, Xu De-Hui (alias Gao Deng-Jin) did it in order to infiltrate the 228 Incident Settlement Committee with Taiwan Garrison Command and Bureau of Investigation and Statistics secret agents.

Although the "Loyal Service Brigade's" vice captain was held by Liao De-Xiong, a student representative responsible for the role the student team played in assisting to maintain law and order in the streets of Taipei. Xu De-Hui, captain of the community team, however, secretly carried out internal reorganization to bring the "Loyal Service Brigade" under the control of the authorities from its inception. That same day, the police chief demarcated Taipei and Keelung as two alert zones, Hsinchu and Taichung as two defense zones, with Su Shao-Wen and Huang Guo-Shu as the Defense Commanders. Peng Meng-Ji was given responsibility to guard the area south of Chiayi and then they began to carry out island-wide surveillance and monitoring.

During the meeting that day, the Settlement Committee made another resolution, to send Lin Zong-Xian, Lin Shi-Dang, Lü Bo-Xiong, Luo Shui-Yuan and Li Wan-Ju, these five men to the American Consulate to request that this Incident be brought to the attention of the KMT authorities and to the international community. In addition, the Settlement Committee also called on the public to cease beating Mainlanders. Furthermore, they elected Wang Tien-Teng to serve as Publicity Chief, representing the Settlement Committee in broadcasting to citizens and to be responsible for publishing the Settlement Committee's press releases. That evening, Wang Tien-Teng made his first broadcast on behalf of the Settlement Committee to the people. He explained the experience of the meeting and the state of negotiations and that he hoped citizens would maintain law and order out of self-discipline.

On the morning of March 4, the 228 Incident Settlement Committee announced to 17 counties and cities that local councils should be the main bodies for all local 228 Incident Settlement Committees and in order to handle every localities issues, they should send a representative to participate in the Taipei's 228 Settlement Committee to promote their work. Since Shanghai and other places exaggerated and twisted this Incident, saying it was nothing more than the Taiwanese requesting to be a trustee of other country, Li Wan-Ju also gave a report in the meeting to stress that the goal of the Incident was to call for political reform and not to attempt anything like the rumors allege. For this reason the 228 Incident Settlement Committee decided to publish an "Urgent Notice to City Compatriots" in the newspaper, explaining that the Incident was already in negotiations, that compatriots should be calm and support the Settlement Committee to maintain social order, not beat people or destroy property.

Because there were still armed forces patrolling the streets of Taipei, the 228 Incident Settlement Committee once again turned to Chief of Staff Ke Yuan-Fen to stop negotiations. Furthermore the Settlement Committee, still facing electricity, food, transportation, security and communication problems entered into deliberations to coordinate and pass a solution. The Committee handled everything like this, including the news broadcasts of the 228 Incident. They sent a representative with a rice purchase order, issued by the Settlement Committee, to the bank to take out a loan for funds to buy rice. Among other measures, they also proposed to add two representatives from every trade union to participation in the Settlement Committee. Finally, Wang Tien-Teng, on behalf of the 228 Incident Settlement Committee broadcasted the proceedings of the day to the whole island and that by resolution the Committee had decided to set up headquarters in Taipei, with all branches sending a representative to attend there.

Since this Incident wasn't a singular issue of local law and order or contraband cigarettes, it moved to include demands for reform of the Administrative Executive Office's authoritarian regime. At this time, the 228 Incident Settlement Committee went from an organization handling a controversial incident into becoming the supporter of public order, easing the rice shortage, transportation, electricity and other problems. It became the object of the peoples' confidence.

That same day Chiang Wei-Chuan, Chen Xin, young students and citizen representatives, more than 30 people, met with Chen Yi and Executive Office officials. The representatives pointed out that the occurrence of the Incident was related to the problems of political and economic administration and in order to solve all fundamental problems, Taiwan's political situation should be reformed thoroughly. Chen Yi in his reply, superficially reiterated that he and every department chief were willing to work closely with the people, to agree with the concrete measures drawn up by the 228 Incident Settlement Committee, to propose suggestions of government reform, and also to adopt any useful suggestions from the people. In reality, however, they were already planning to deploy the central governments troops, after they landed, for the repression.

Except for the few cities and counties that had established peace keeping organizations early in the Incident's outbreak, within three or four days after the Settlement Committee issued the announcement, every city and county council expressed their support and in turn established their own Settlement Committees or corresponding organization. Therefore, in addition to the provincial level 228 Incident Settlement Committee, there were sixteen city and county Settlement Committees, as the second tier category, established before the military landed in Taiwan for the crackdown, and only Kaohsiung County had not yet established a corresponding organization. Moreover, there were at least twelve 228 Incident Settlement Committee's established, one after the other, in the third tier towns and districts. By this point the 228 Incident Settlement Committee had developed into a provincial framework.

On that day, the Police Chief Ke Yuan-Fen, Director of Investigations Chen Da-Yuan, and Taiwan Bureau of Labor and Statistics Director Lin Ding-Li, held a secret meeting, to propose "using the people's strength against the people," by giving the order to use methods of infiltration, deception and division to create internal conflict, and by "intelligence officers investigating and monitoring the masterminds of the Settlement Committee." In addition to this, the "Volunteer Corps" organized by Lin Ding-Li (alias Zhang Bing-Cheng), took advantage of the situation to create turmoil, and many "incriminating evidences" were fabricated in this context.

3-3 The Transformation of the 228 Incident Settlement Committee: Provincial Political Reform and Democratic Self-Government

On the morning of March 5th, the 228 Incident Settlement Committee in Chungshan Hall held an expanded group meeting that included the financial, food, publicity, transportation, police, communications, emergency services, general, investigation and others groups separated by their field of work and their correlating proposals. Among them, the Food group made a resolution to send a representative to thecentral and south part of Taiwan to procure rice. He took a loan from the ICBC and the Food Authority by handing over a Taipei City Food Assistance Certificate as funds to purchase rice. Additionally, the 228 Incident Settlement Committee passed the Publictiy Groups' proposed, "Message to the Compatriots," and resolved to send the group leader Wang Tien-teng and Huang Chao Sheng and two others as representatives, planning to send them to Nanjing to give a full account to the Nationalist government. They sent a telegram to the Nationalist government headquarters, the Ministry of Defense, the Shanghai Association and others, in order that the world would know the truth about the Incident.

That afternoon, in accordance with Chen Yi's agreement the day before, that concrete measures be developed by the 228 Incident Settlement Committee, in an interim meeting the 228 Incident Settlement Committee put forward and passed the "8 Memorandums for Fundamental Political Reform," the predecessor of the "32 Demands." The 8 core memorandums were :

1. The government shall be held responsible for the 228 Incident.
2. More than half of the Secretary-General's Office, the Director's offices of civil affairs, finance, mining, agriculture, forestry, education, police and the Legislative Committee members offices shall be held by Taiwanese people.
3. Public companies shall be operated by Taiwanese people.
4. Immediately implement county and city elections according to The Plan for National Construction.

5. Repeal the monopoly system.
6. Abolish the Board of Trade and the Propaganda Committee.
7. Protect the people's freedom of speech, press, and assembly.
8. Ensure the people's life and property.

In addition, the Interim General Assembly passed the "228 Incident Settlement Committee Memorandum," and as set forth in the opening it was aimed at the established Settlement Committee: "To unite the people to handle the 228 Incident and reform the provincial government." First, it took the 228 Incident Settlement Committee from a temporary organization of conflict resolution and protection of law and order of a singular incident and promoted it to the highest legislative body, representing the Taiwanese people's aspirations for political reform.

The organizational structure of the 228 Incident Settlement Committee took the Committee of the Whole as the supreme authority, with all of its resolutions implemented by a Standing Committee and elected a seven member Presidium including the Office of the Secretary. In addition, established under the Standing Committee were the Administrative Council and the Handling Council, responsible for developing political reform proposals and incident handling methods. Then grouped under the Negotiation group were the Project group, Financial group, Food group, Transportation group, Investigation group, Security group and General Affairs group, these eight groups were responsible for the implementation of their related tasks. That night Wang Tien-teng broadcast to the whole Taiwanese people that the Settlement Committee planned to abolish the Monopoly Bureau and the Board of Trade, to immediately implement county and city elections, as well as that the Executive Administrative Office shall employ Taiwanese people among other political demands of reform.

The 228 Incident Settlement Committee Organizational Chart

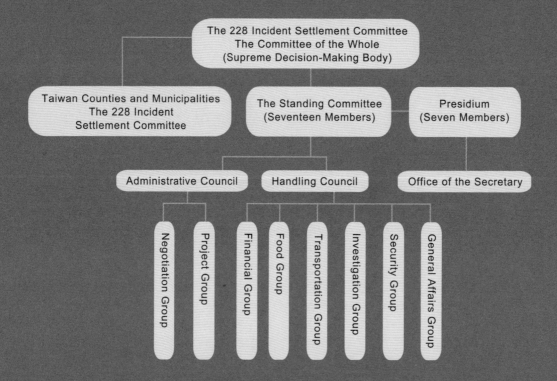

At this stage, the Settlement Committee members, in addition to the initial Tobacco Seizure and Murder Investigation Committee members, the National Assemblymen, Provincial Senators and representatives of Taipei's City Council, the Central government and all levels of provincial government each sent ten to thirty representatives, coupled with three senators of each county and municipality, provincial, county and municipal People's Organization representatives, county and municipal trade union representatives, county and municipal aboriginal representatives and faculty representatives of every university and school. Therefore, no matter if looking at it from a standpoint of influence or representation this period of the 228 Incident Settlement Committee is the Taiwanese people's most important channel for participation in political reform.

While Chen Yi's authorities continued to consult the 228 Incident Settlement Committee and accept the suggestions of the broader community on the surface, they on the other hand had the fourth regiment of the gendarme send a secret telegraph to the Central government framing the 228 Incident Settlement Committee as an "illegal organization, engaging in treason and rebellion to seize power." Additionally, the head of the gendarme chief of staff Ke Yuan-Fen assembled the gendarme's Fourth Regiment Commander, Zhang Mu-Tao, and the Taipei Bureau of Investigation and Statistics Chief Lin Ding-Li among others. He instructed them to gather intelligence and control of the "instigators" of the movement, and begin to draw up a "blacklist." On March 5, Chen Yi received the Chairman of the Nanjing National Government Chiang Kai-Shek's handwritten order: "I have already sent a regiment of infantry and a battalion of gendarme departing from Shanghai on the seventh of this month, don't worry."

On March 6th, the 228 Incident Settlement Committee resumed the official inaugural general assembly, and having completed the last of it's expansionist restructuring became the provinces highest legislative body, attending members and visiting spectators surpassed 300 people in total. The meeting was chaired by Wang Tien-Teng and elected the seventeen Standing Committee members. Finally, chairman Wang Tien-Teng read , "The Broadcast Manuscript of the Truth, Full Account and Sequence of the 228 Incident to the Central government and the Whole Nation." He stressed that the goals of the 228 Incident Settlement Committee were to "purge corrupt officials, fight for political reform of the province, and not to exclude the Mainlanders from participating in improving this province's politics." They also passed a resolution to broadcast in the name of the 228 Incident Settlement Committee, in Mandarin, Hokkien, Hakka, English, Japanese the truth about the Incident to the world. It can be seen that the position of the 228 Incident Settlement Committee was not a conspiracy of rebellion or provocation of provincial conflict, but their ultimate aim was to expand the people's participation in the process of parliamentary democracy, and to achieve the goal of political reform.

The 228 Incident Settlement Committee Restructuring Process

Time	Name/Position	Reason for Establishment/ Restructuring	Key Members
March 1st	"227 Tobacco Seizure and Murder Case Investigation Commission"	To resolve the Contraband Cigarette Death Incident	National Assembly, Provincial Senators, National Political Assemblymen, Taipei City Senator and other groups
March 2nd	Name changed to the "228 Incident Settlement Committee"	To resolve incident of contraband cigarette casualties caused by corrupt government use of firearms	Included 5 official representatives of the Executive Administrative Office
March 3rd	The first restructuring by expansion, no name change, the organization's nature is still solely for handling the incident.	To expand member participation to jointly resolve the incident's disputes	Expanded to include representatives from these five parties: the Chamber of Commerce, trade unions, student bodies, members of the public and the Political Construction Association. Official representatives were increased by two new members, for a total of seven, but soon after all withdrew.

March 4th	The second restructuring, expanding to become a provincial level organization.	To handle the incident throughout the region as well as, to coordinate the requirements of people's livelihood	In addition to the provincial 228 Incident Settlement Committee, seventeen local Settlement Committee's were established using the county and city senates as their main bodies.
March 6th	The third restructuring transformed it as the highest representative body of provincial government reform.	To use the approach of political reform to fundamentally solve the province's political issues	All members of the Settlement Committee, including every rank, position and occupation elected the Standing Committee and were planning to establish a seven-member Presidium.

In the evening of the same day, Chen Yi pretended to cooperate with the 228 Incident Settlement Committee's reform proposals and once more made a province-wide broadcast to the public: 1. The Executive Administrative Office will be changed into a provincial government after approval by the Central government for its implementation. During restructuring, the provincial government, will as much as possible, employ Taiwanese people for each Director-General or Department Head position. 2. To be scheduled on June 1st of this year are county and city elections and if the local people believe that a current county or city official is incompetent, he may be removed from his post before the elections. Then have the county and city councils suggest three other people and elect one to fill the position. Finally, Chen Yi appealed with: "Trust the government, do not believe rumors."

At this point, the people thought that since February 28th, the surging democratic resistance movement had obtained some concrete results. However, as shown from history, we know that Chen Yi had already obtained support from the Central government, they deployed troops and advocated a secret plan for a military crackdown, saying, "the riotous group of traitors must be eliminated by force, their existence cannot be tolerated."

3-4 Wang Tien-Teng reading the "32 Demands"

On March 7th, the Executive Administrative Office sent a letter to the 228 Incident Settlement Committee alleging: "We have organized the 228 Incident Settlement Committee as the approach for rehabilitation. In the future, please, first hand over and discuss the views of all parties in the Settlement Committee. After a comprehensive draft has been drawn up by a few chosen representatives of the Settlement Committee, make a list of suggestions for the office to adopt and implement. " On that day, the 228 Incident Settlement Committee convened a general meeting of all members and during the meeting they passed the "32 Demands." They were read aloud by Wang Tien-Teng and within they proposed suggestions for handling the Incident, the fundamental approach to reforming the provincial government and resolutions by the Standing Committee of the Whole proposed for Chen Yi's authorities.

In view of the military and police failures of discipline since the retrocession to the National Government, wantonly shooting people without end, and intensifying during the Incident even worse, therefore, these Demands with respect "for handling the present" propose that the burden of local law enforcement be temporarily shared equally by the gendarme, unarmed police and the general public. Weapons will be managed jointly by the gendarme and the Settlement Committee of each locale and the families of victims will be generously compensated among other things. In addition, with respect to "fundamentally handling" the military, it was proposed that military units lacking education and training must not be stationed on Taiwan for stabile social order and to avert bloodshed.

The most key content of the "32 Demands" are the contents of the 22nd article on the "fundamental handling" of political reform, mainly including: the requirements to draw up laws for provincial autonomy, to hold county and city elections, to revoke the Monopoly Bureau and the Board of Trade, to repeal exorbitant taxes, to guarantee personal safety, to safeguard the freedoms of speech, assembly, association, human rights and the rule of law. These words are not only the voice of the Provincial 228 Incident Settlement Committee, the local Settlement Committees and the majority of the people, but are a continuation of the Taiwanese democracy forerunners tireless struggle since the colonial period to pursue their democratic ideals.

However, under the planned arrangements of Chen Yi and the intelligence agencies, in the afternoon meeting that day, many scheming parties infiltrated in. In addition to the destruction of order of the meeting place, they even proposed ten additional drastic military, political and other demands. For example, the spy element Wu Guo-Xin and others tumultuously demanded the "Immediate release of all of the province's war criminals and traitors," "Repeal of the Garrison Command, in order to avoid the abuse of military power," as well as that "The 228 Incident Settlement Committee will be in charge of restructuring the Executive Administrative Office" and the other ten demands that deceptively overstepped the Central governments authority. They were passed in the confusion of the meeting and the shouts of the spy elements. Therefore, the 32 Demands were purposely sabotaged by the secret service by sneaking in ten more demands and the day after it was framed as the "42 evidences of guilt" for a "conspiracy of rebellion," as a pretext for a military crackdown.

That afternoon, when the whole Standing Committee of the 228 Incident Settlement Committee went to the Administrative Executive Office, they should have continued bi-partisan talks about the Demands, however, because Chen Yi had already confirmed the time of the army's arrival, his earlier attitude toward negotiations changed, angrily rebuking them, the Settlement Committee representatives were stunned by Chen Yi's reneging of promises. That same day, Chen Yi sent another telegram to the Nanjing Nationalist

Government requesting soldiers, saying: "One regiment of troops is inadequate for suppressing the rebellion, please plan on sending another division, at least one brigade in the shortest time possible, so they will be completely eliminated."

At seven o'clock in the evening, Wang Tien-Teng representing the 228 Incident Settlement Committee again broadcast to the people the true account of the 228 Incident, the resolution of the Settlement Committee, as well as that all of the demands had been rejected. At the same time he read aloud the provisions of the "32 Demands." His convictions unchanged, he called out: "There is no difference between us and those of other provinces, our goals are to overthrow corruption, and we hope that our righteous fellow citizens from other provinces will work together with us in this fight for democracy," "From now on this incident can no longer be handled by the 228 Incident Settlement Committee alone, but can only be resolved with the strength of the whole province, and this will simultaneously achieve all of their reasonable demands. I hope all of our compatriots continue the struggle! " This became the historical reverberation of the 228 Incident Settlement Committee.

■ The "32 Demands" the 228 Settlement Committee spokesman Wang Tien-Teng's radio broadcast :

On Handling Current Events

1. The government's armed forces everywhere should temporarily give the order to voluntarily disarm and hand over their weapons to be jointly managed by the Settlement Committee and the gendarme to avoid continued bloodshed.
2. After the disarmament of the government's armed forces, the burden of local security will be jointly bore by the gendarme, unarmed police and public organizations.
3. When there is no threat from armed government forces, do not attack them with weapons. The same for corrupt officials, no matter if they are locals or from another province, only report them to the Settlement Committee to be jointly arrested by the gendarme, and severely punished according to the law. Do not harm them yourselves and do not stir up trouble.
4. As for views on political reform, write out the conditions of your demands and present them to the Provincial Settlement Committee, afterwards there will be a comprehensive resolution.
5. The government shall not mobilize troops again, nor shall it request a deployment of troops from the Central Government to try and resolve the Incident through force, resulting in grievous bloodshed and subject to international intervention.
6. Prior to fundamental political issues being resolved, all government measures and policies (whether military or political), must first consult with the Settlement Committee, lest the people doubt the government's sincerity and various misunderstandings take place.
7. As for the Incident, there shall be no inquiries of criminal liability of the people, nor under the guise of any future excuse shall those related to the Incident be arrested. Due to this incident, the injured people should be generously compensated.

Fundamental Handling

A. The Military

1. *A military lacking in education and discipline must not be stationed in Taiwan.*
2. *The Central Government may send an official to Taiwan to conscript soldiers to defend Taiwan.*
3. *Before the end of the civil war on the mainland, and except for the purpose of defending Taiwan, Taiwan absolutely opposes military recruitment, in order that Taiwan may avoid falling into the civil war vortex.*

B. Politics

1. *Enact laws of provincial autonomy as the highest political standard of this province, in order to realize the ideals of Sun Yat-Sen's "The Plan for National Construction."*
2. *County and city mayoral elections shall be held before June of this year, as well as county and city council elections.*
3. *Each provincial director candidate must be approved by the Provincial Council. The Provincial Council should be re-elected before June of this year. The current candidates will be proposed by the Executive Office, and handed to the Provincial Settlement Committee for consideration.*
4. *More than two-thirds of all Provincial Department Directors must have resided in the province for ten years or more (preferably the Directors of the Secretary-General, Civil Affairs, Finance, Industry, Agriculture, Education, and the Police Commissioner).*
5. *The Police Commissioner and county and city police chief positions should be held by Taiwanese people. The Provincial Police Battalion and the railway, mining and other police should be abolished immediately.*
6. *More than half of the number of members of the Legislative Committees will be held by Taiwanese and the chairman will be elected from its members.*
7. *Apart from police authorities, criminal suspects may not be arrested.*
8. *Apart from military criminals, the military police may not arrest criminal suspects.*

9. Arrest and detention of a political nature is prohibited.

10. There is absolute freedom in unarmed assemblage and association.

11. There is absolute freedom of speech, of the press and strike. Abolition of the newspaper publishing registration system.

12. Immediately repeal the regulations on civic organizations.

13. The method of vetting candidates for public office is abolished.

14. Ways to improve elections of public office at all levels.

15. The implementation of a unified progressive income tax, and except for luxury and inheritance tax, miscellaneous taxes shall not be imposed.

16. All persons in charge of state-owned enterprises shall be Taiwanese.

17. Set up a democratically elected state-owned enterprise commission, and the Provincial Government shall have sole discretion on the appointment of committee members for the settlement of the former Japanese-owned enterprises. Each retroceded factory and mine shall have an Operating Committee installed and over fifty-percent of its committee members must be Taiwanese.

18. Revocation of the Monopoly Bureau and an implementation of a system of rationing basic life necessities.

19. Revocation of the Board of Trade.

20. Revocation of the Propaganda Committee.

21. Each District Court's Chief Justice, and each District Court's Chief Prosecutor positions shall all be held by Taiwanese.

22. More than half of each court's magistrate, prosecutor and judicial officer positions shall be held by Taiwanese.

3-5 The 228 Incident Settlement Committee Suffers Repression and Dissolution

On March 8th, the army began landing at Keelung and intense shooting, clearing the streets. Even at this time, Chen Yi still broadcast to people, falsely claiming, "The armies transfer to Taiwan is exclusively for the protection of the province's people, to eliminate the renegade faction and no other purpose." That day, the "People's Herald," representing the voice of the people and publishing for the last time. It reiterated that in the fuse leading up to the 228 Incident, people had been hit and killed and that the Incident was "caused by the accumulation of anger during peacetime." As a result, the demand for autonomy spread to all areas, with the ultimate aim to achieve political reform in the province. However, Chen Yi's authorities hastily mobilized the military and their sincere hope for democracy fell on deaf ears.

On March 9th, after the twenty first division of the army arrived, under the management and deployment of Chen Yi's authorities, they began to "Purge the streets of traitors," and secretly arrested members of the Settlement Committee. On March 10th, Chen Yi once again implemented martial law and declared the 228 Incident Settlement Committee an illegal organization. He had the local garrison units dismantle it and successively disband the Taiwan Political Construction Association, Three Principles of the People Youth League and other groups, completely seize the "People's Herald," "People's Daily," more than ten free speech organs and with the core members of the Settlement Committee becoming the first targets of the crackdown. At this time in Taiwanese society, not only were the freedoms of assembly, association and speech completely eroded, but also people's lives and property had absolutely no protection.

To eradicate dissidents as quickly as possible and to shift the blame for the Incident, Chen Yi's authorities blacklisted group after group with cooked up charges and upon arrest they were summarily executed without trial to prevent the world from knowing the truth about the Incident. These lists of names, included the "Investigation on the Handling of Named Criminals," that Chen Yi telegraphed to Chiang

Kai-Shek on March 13th, the Taiwanese Garrison Command Judge Advocate Department "List of the Most Wanted Lead Criminals in the 228 Incident Rebellion Conspiracy" reported on March 24th, as well as the April 18th release of the Taiwan Garrison Command's, "List of Chief Fugitive Rebellion Conspirators of the 228 Incident." Among those listed, the participating members of the 228 Incident Settlement Committee had the heaviest casualties.

In the report that Chen Yi submitted, he even advocated that "Judicial procedures are too slow and Taiwan's situation is special, please allow a temporary application of marshal law, in order to severely punish the traitorous party and to extinguish the source of chaos." As a result, early on March 13th, before Chen Yi submitted the "Investigation on the Handling of Named Criminals," many of the core members of the Settlement Committee had already been caught and killed. However, it wasn't until after the lifting of martial law in Taiwan, that from the National Security Bureau released "List of Taiwanese '228' Incident Executions and Dead Criminals" submitted by Wang Shou-Zheng to Lei Wan-Jun, on November 28th, 1949, that it was confirmed that the Settlement Committee members who had been secretly arrested had already been killed.

THE J. F. A. K. RADIO BROADCASTING STATION, TAIHOKU.
裝新の所樂演局送放（北　臺）
スーユニ ろ ゆ ち あ 、 に 都都、 に 樂督、 に 演講
。 地頭覆つ分な樂數て樂敎 に 民市 り よ に
B　行發堂高新北臺

The 228 Incident Settlement Committee and the Executive Administrative Office Negotiation Process

Time	The 228 Incident Settlement Committee	Taiwan Provincial Executive Administrative Office
February 27th	The 227 Tobacco Seizure and Murder Case	Monopoly Bureau personnel on grounds of seizing contraband cigarettes, beat a tobacco trader and killed a civilian.
February 28th	The Outbreak of the 228 Incident	The Executive Administrative Office opened fire on the crowd marching for justice on the Tobacco Seizure and Murder Case, resulting in several deaths and widespread protests. Chen Yi declared martial law.
March 1st	"The 227 Tobacco Seizure and Murder Case Investigation Commission" was established, sending representatives to negotiate with Governor Chen Yi.	In his first broadcast across the province, Chen Yi agreed to the proposal by the representatives of the Commission, lifting martial law and forming a joint Government-Civilian Committee to handle the Incident.
March 2nd	"The 228 Incident Settlement Committee" established and sent representatives to negotiate with Chen Yi, proposing leniency for the protesters and other ideas.	Chen Yi sent five officials to participate in the Settlement Committee, and again announced in a broadcast the so-called "more lenient measures," but secretly mobilized the army in the south and requested more troops from the Nanjing Government. At this time, gunshots rang out in streets everywhere and army patrol vehicles appeared.
March 3rd	The 228 Settlement Committee expanded to include representatives from five parties, the Chamber of Commerce, trade unions, students, the public and the Political Construction Association. Each Committee division elected a chairman, after the meeting a broadcast and press release were sent to the international community and an appeal to the public to use self-discipline to maintain law and order.	The Taiwan Garrison Command issued a "Notice to all Citizens," promising leniency, and asked the people to return to school and work as usual. While at the same time they sent people to infiltrate and subvert the 228 Incident Settlement Committee. Additionally, the Executive Administrative Office agreed to withdraw military and police from the streets and have the "Loyal Service Brigade" maintain law and order, but the Service Brigade was essentially controlled by the Police Chief.

March 4th	The 228 Incident Settlement Committee passed a resolution to set up headquarters in Taipei and for all other locations with established branches to send representatives there to attend. Thus it became a provincial organization, and declared demands for political reform.	Chen Yi would meet with petitioning representatives, claim a greater willingness to listen to the people, shaking hands with and agreeing to the approach of political reform proposed by the 228 Incident Settlement Committee.
March 5th	The 228 Incident Settlement Committee held their inaugural General Assembly, passing the "8 Memorandums for Fundamental Political Reform" and the "32 Demands." They planned to send a representative to the Central Government in Nanjing to give an account of the Incident.	The Taiwan Garrison Command Chief of Staff Ke Yuan-Fen issued a statement, requesting compatriots "not to listen to rumors." Provost Marshal Zhang Zhen reported to Chiang Kai-Shek, "It has already evolved to the stage of a traitorous seizure of power." Chen Yi received Chiang Kai-Shek's handwritten order: "I have already sent a regiment of infantry and a battalion of gendarme departing from Shanghai on the seventh of this month, don't worry."
March 6th	The 228 Incident Settlement Committee resumed the official inaugural General Assembly, it became the highest provincial legislative body, elected the Standing Committee and published a "Message to the Compatriots," declaring a weeding out of corrupt officials and a struggle for the province's goal of political reform.	Chen Yi assembled Chief of Staff Ke Yuan-Fen and other advisors to deliberate on the battle plan for after the army had landed in Taiwan. Chen Yi broadcast to the province, falsely stating: The Executive Administrative Office will reform into a Provincial Government and will appoint Taiwanese persons to office. County and city elections will be implemented on July 1st, and current incompetent officials may now be removed from office through a local representative body's vote.

Time	The 228 Incident Settlement Committee	Taiwan Provincial Executive Administrative Office
March 7th	The 228 Incident Settlement Committee passed all of Wang Tien-Teng's proposed "32 Demands," however an additional 10 radical demands were added by the authority's spies that had infiltrated the Settlement Committee.	Chen Yi fiercely refused the demands proposed by the Settlement Committee and once again telegraphed Chiang Kai-Shek to send troops, saying: "One regiment of troops is inadequate for suppressing the rebellion, please plan on sending another division, at least one brigade in the shortest possible time, so they will be completely eliminated."
March 8th	The 228 Incident Settlement Committee and related political groups had already been broken up and everyone was in fear.	The two battalions of the fourth regiment of the gendarme arrived at Taiwan from Fujian, while Brigadier Zhang Mu-Tao of the gendarme was still at the Settlement Committee guaranteeing that the Central Government had not mobilized any troops.
March 9th	The 228 Incident Settlement Committee members were arrested and killed one after another.	The twenty-first division of the army landed in Keelung, the military began intense shooting, clearing the streets, and by nightfall peals of gunfire rang out in Taipei.
March 10th		On March 10th Chen Yi declared martial law and ordered the dissolution of all local 228 Settlement Committees and all "illegal groups."

處理委員會分設五組
本市各界代表昨已選出

（本報紫北專訪）

北二二八事件處理委員會組織人員如次：一、會長參議會市參議員，團、省參議會全體人員，二、大代表省參政員全體人員，三、由湯市長陳局長許熱輝、生代表等組織治安維持會，

二、公務代表五人，

三、擬參議長陳炘於今晚六時召集各界代表於參議會開會，又據議昨日預定宮內分，惠民蘭一人，偏卻一人，

三、臺北市各界代表包括工商學界名單未定但如再有波漩治安秩序等情發生周治安維持命人員軍隊前六時以後軍隊再放回參送如何委選長決負賣辦亦願負全部責任。

專賣局肇事查緝員六人
確已送交地檢處法辦

【本報臺北專訪】本報記者昨訪識大代表黃國書市參議員黃朝生陳屋李仁貴民家代表等據壁據木等涌壯地監調查專賣局肇事之查緝員六人是否個子扣押，莱經邊置該局肇事者蕭得根經識夫傳懇通對趙祥錦藍渕荊子健等六名礙由東族壁替治增區有守所虹鑼鐵羅押又肇事之手犧（五五九八號及九七五四七七號）亦關存地院檢察處。

糧食調劑
調劑糧食

（一）更抑平物值，必先抑平米價！
（二）調劑糧食是民生的急政！
（三）全省同胞一致起來，全力支持糧貨調劑政！
（四）我們要堅定一致團結，信仰糧食糧斷切勿自運恐慌
（五）搞了共同生活，我們樂協助糧食調劑！
（六）糧商窟厚，希迎響管糧商團結！
（七）嚴懲糧窟頭民的奸商和糧戶！
（八）防止及嚴懲糧食定私！
（九）嚴禁糧食恶，志于石者處死刑！
（十）獎勵售糧運置及走私！
（十一）與禁征得糧食荒迎！
（十二）乃行調食運乃！

（三日本報專訪）本日下午處理委員會繼積討論決定事項：

一、通電蔣主席表示要求政治根本改革並請中央談

二、由湯市長陳局長許熱輝生代表等組織治安維持

民眾極望恢復交通

【本報臺北專訪】接有關方面消息，休復交通問題，即可實現，公已路交通業已恢復鐵路管理委員會昨日人員往復錢路交通置置前已無間題現未通車純以技術問題。然一般

無分本省人外省人
大家都是中國同胞

（本報臺北專訪）本日處理會席上，有若干委員提出讓民眾保持冷靜並不再發生殿打外省同胞，因外省人本省人同屬中華民國國民，應座委員會眾出之各並案均保證助政府性質並非反對政府云云，對此民眾對此提案一致鼓掌表示讚受。

我們的口號！
尊重民意！
信賴政府！
建設臺灣！
復興中國！

公署令與各界商決
解決緝煙事件辦法
軍隊定今日下午六時撤囘

【本報特訊】本（二八）日上午十一時在中山堂開會之二‧二八事件處理委員會，計出席代表民衆五人，工人代表三人，青年四人，婦女一人，國大代表，參政員各一人，及蔣渭川，林梧村等二十餘人到公署晉謁，要求撤囘市上巡邏軍隊，有民政處長周一鶚，省警務處長包可永，憲兵處長胡福相，交通處長任顯群，農林處長趙連芳及柯參謀長等接見，分出席報告經過，由柯參謀長宣佈處決辦法如下：

一、軍隊本（二八）日午後六時撤囘原營結集。

二、地方治安出動憲兵，警察與學生青年組織治安服務隊巡邏。

三、緝煙亦于本晚全部收囘，緝私帶應像交通警工。

四、緝煙損傷應由緝私損傷之人出頭，可與父柯參謀長接洽驗傷。

五、被毆斃囘原後，倘有十二因意氣撤斃之人因出頭，可向父柯參謀長接洽商辦。

六、軍隊撤囘後，民衆倘有持器生打人燒物之處，由二十餘名代表負責完全責任，將緝亂者法辦。

七、市民勿聽信謠言（南部軍隊北上消息不正確）。

柯民又云：此次之熱軍隊决倘不舉行，希望民衆保護交通，以便運種供應民衆。快復一月二十七日以前之秩序？深防民衆安心，恢復秩序云云。

整治安，保持東京大問題，解决小時之討論，即决讓各掌握版辛，待十二時明鑑同意，再議被决讓勸留民衆不可亂打外省同胞，至十二時許散會。

二‧二八事件的經過

二月廿七日晚七時華鐘，太平町發生緝煙，行於之校，民衆二情激一倫，緝車隊被歐拒益北市百菜局詰問嚴搗毀示，一面打經警宣佈條件的始末，廿八日上午九點鈴將，民衆投家未曾辦决，又訴得打壞違告，匝，全面商行，立即發照，相率關門閉戶心慣懷哀憤激哼，全面罷市，打政嚴傑，至太半町一丁目派出所前，該所奮起馬蹄聲，都以共事前有他的发民，送將英國打拳驚驚所內破璃兵具揆根，民衆長已達到目的，就緊翻向本町車警局繼北分局前邁，由四方八面洶湧而至，御進長稻，感體派局員二名，傷四名，把囘到燒火餐炭，香煙，酒於汽車一輛，脚踏車七，八輛……一件一件出運圍地出路中放火焚毀，一時火光沖天，達至一日尚水全想，所有門密玻璃敢亦被包圍，都存逃查的顏傷，與四的事實局亦被包圍，僅打破玻璃而已，下午一點餘鐘，都以共事前所的後官有一陣以變巧殺為藉的眾歌，約有四，五百人遍的後官不察而屠殺嘉為阻止群眾鼓動，疑散民衆，其後把一般民眾歌，市民即斃死一人，傷數人，但據報秘書長報告市警員處說：民民受傷谷一然而民衆並本囘仍而斑歡囘眾，各憲屬團關屋十，邯誘走一斧。有一部份民眾騷騷到本町正華六旅社，自家用汽車，卡，在本町，不親友，農出今忿俯俱，麥町龙磁水安堂學散欺的店面玻璃，勻避搗歧，零斑點燃股案，約有十餘部，外省人公务人員，憲氏警察於擀，幸罕戶已擊斷，仍打敷璃而已，一次市早已閉戶，大平町，美聯十方面被披，太半町，臺北公園，榮町，臺北平旗，夜市，臺北郵

台灣新生報

號外

（民國三十六年三月三日）

二‧二八處委會改組首次會

決定積極維持治安

派員指責上司命令不行

【本報訊】改組後之首屆二‧二八事件處理委員會於三日上午十時假中山堂舉行，各界代表均踴躍出席。

關於延遲議案未提交治商不在，由派副議長代表，百先報告昨日洽商情形，略稱：一，關於被捕人員釋放問題，現在進行中；二，長官已答應巡邏不予武裝，但昨晚與員後係武裝，可見命令不能徹底，本會應要設法；三，關於處理委員會同長官商洽辦法手續訂立一面，昨赴州務所在視結果，發現除會前六人外數十餘人業未扣押，據悉：本晚兒子已了扣留，同長官兄弟院命令故遲未交付；此時由民眾報告稱：據息自新竹方面卡，載士兵千幾輛花蓮，本隊必必早設法，懇切告梅；關於此事擬悉已在湖口方面阻止，使其返於新竹位治安未定，長官威令不行，開我在進行處長會議，必怕是選延之策，如不可被當局撤銷，而且本會擬組自衛隊；此時學生代表向各詢議負其責，關於此須纔長提派員向長官訊問如何；全場歡聲表示贊同，立即派選大眾代表四人，學生代表二人，工會，商會，婦女會各一人，及國代理明朝，多致員，林忠，省參議員，王添灯等國長，此時一部份的老舊死不歸，縣的時謝安問題，由的淹雄代表表示顧與起全有志歉十萬市民紛組自衛隊，以負治安之責，惟有即早可鑑，不可如無後，彼容察以先載共利用，彼被作煽流眼處理，對此點望諸位位協助。滿場歡聲，表示勢力支持。且有一帶分戎未滿諸民反示意，大場於本會，再與

號外

調委會與長官商定
緝烟事件解決方針
本案民間負責人決不追究

【本報特訊】本二日十二時十分，市參議會開全委員會，全體委員往長官公署謁見陳長官，于正午在公署四樓，討論本案之解決方針，席上有葛敬恩、交通處長任顯群，民政處長周一鶚，工礦處長包可永列席，陳長官當面答應下列數項：

一，因此案被捕之民眾，全部交交憲兵第四團無條件釋放。

二，關于本案之死者，由政府發給燃郎金，傷者由政府責成醫院治療，死傷者不分本省外省，友公務員，希望民眾調查其姓名，住址，報告，以便救濟撫卹。

三，不追究　生本案之民間負責人，（從今以後，各安其業。共謀本省之建設。）

四，即時恢復交通，（鐵路交通由國大代表館交通負責）

五，武裝警察巡邏車，逐漸減少。（槍口不向外，武器放于車內）。以維持治安。

六，從速恢復工作，各商店開門照常營業。

七，食米即運市內，供應民眾雲來。

八，路上倘有死傷者，由憲警與附近民眾設法交憲院醫療。云云。

【又訊】陳長官令（二）已下午三時向全省廣播，各委員求會分訓廣播。下午一時二十分各委員議

本訊已呈准發刊

經中華政部登記認爲第類新聞紙類

社址　臺北市重慶南路第一八七號　信箱
社長　蘇泰楷
發行人　柯台山
電話　二五八○
電報掛號　九一七○

臺灣日報

第三報

外號

中華民國卅六年三月三日下午四時

臺灣省民眾代表大會致蔣主席電原文如下

南京國民政府主席蔣鈞鑒：二月二十七日夜本省專賣局派員帶警察大隊員警十名在臺北市延平路查緝私煙塲辱死傷市民數名民眾甚爲憤慨翌日上午死難家屬暨民眾往專賣局要求究辦兇首不得要領乃轉赴長官公署請願該公署衞兵突由樓上開機鎗掃射民眾死傷數人由是激動公憤遂遷怒於公務人員致發生毆打情事警備總司令十是日下午宣布戒嚴四處開鎗斃傷市民甚衆情勢更趨擴大經國大代表參政員省市參議員暨參議員等力向長官交涉結果准於三月一日下午十二時解嚴並於上午四時開機鎗掃射死傷民衆三十餘因之更惹全省人民公憤認爲政府毫無感信舉動極野蠻且無紀律是以本省陳長官親日廣播民衆稍趨平靜分散廠家行經北門口鐵路管理委員會時樓上國軍及警察大隊竟再開機鎗掃射死傷民衆三十餘因之更惹全省人民公憤認爲政府毫無感信舉動極野蠻且無紀律是以態愈加擴大此經過真相現全體民衆要求本省政治必須根本改革蓋本省自光復以來政治惡劣軍警公務人員之不法行爲致使省民大抱不滿雖經選次要求改善仍無效果此乃造成二，二八慘案之素因爲此懇請中央速派大員蒞臺調處以平民憤並剋速實行地方自治實現真正民主政治臨電迫切不勝待命之至

臺灣省民眾代表大會　寅

第四章/二二八處委會重要成員暨受難先賢

The influential members of the 228 Incident Settlement Committee and the suffering sages

第四章／二二八處委會重要成員暨受難先賢
The influential members of the 228 Incident Settlement Committee and the suffering sages

　　二二八事件期間，許多懷抱理想的民主鬥士，為了解決流血衝突，又冀望一舉掃除政府施政的弊病，爭取臺灣民主自治的權利，因而挺身而出，最後甚至為了理念而犧牲自己。然而，二二八事件被陳儀當局定位為「奸黨叛亂」，並以此為由向中央調兵，將責任嫁禍予二二八處委會，以轉移長官公署失德失能的問題癥結，從此箝制了一個世代的臺灣人民要求民主政治之呼聲。

　　回顧事件發生過程，陳儀與情治機關首長一方面不斷向南京請兵派援，另一方面也逐步羅織「暴亂份子」名單及其「罪名」，並在軍隊抵臺後大肆捕殺；其中，以省及縣市參議會為主體的各地二二八處委會，傷亡最為慘重。

　　以省參議會為例，包括王添灯、林連宗身亡，郭國基、林日高、馬有岳等因繫獄、或遭通緝者共達十四名，約佔全體議員半數，導致第三次大會幾乎因出席人數不足而無法召開。在縣市情況，臺北市二十六名市參議員，四名死亡、七名繫獄，受難比例超過四成。影響所及，全臺各級民意代表縱使倖存，也多飽受壓力與恐懼，從此進入噤聲的年代。

　　為深入瞭解二二八處委會受難先賢的理念，以下將藉由分析部分處委會核心成員的生平事蹟、事件中扮演角色、家屬證言，以及對照當時的官方所羅列的檔案，將有助於我們更真實的貼近事件當時之情境；此外，這些受難先賢與主要成員地域涵蓋臺灣北、中、南地區，職業包括律師、醫生、教師、報人、商人等社會各階層，藉此也讓我們得以描繪出那一代臺灣民主先賢的群體輪廓。

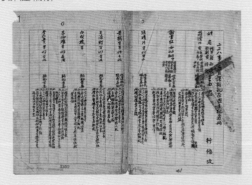

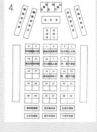

1.2.3. 警備總司令所羅織的〈二二八事變首謀判亂在逃主犯名冊〉，其中王添灯、徐春卿等人早已遭祕密捕殺，卻仍舊列在在逃名冊之中
4. 二二八事件後，臺灣省參議會召開第三次大會，除正、副議長外，參議員只剩16位；臺灣一代菁英消聲無蹤

行政長官公署羅織二二八事件參與「暴亂」民意代表「黑名單」

地　名	主動及附從者	民意代表職稱	地　名	主動及附從者	民意代表職稱
臺北市	王添灯	省參議員	新竹市	張式穀	新竹市參議長
	蔣渭川	後來遞補參議員		何乾欽	新竹市副參議長
	駱水源	臺北市參議員		李克承	新竹市參議員
	顏欽賢	省參議員		鄭作衡	新竹市參議員
	陳逸宏	國民參政員		李延年	新竹市參議員
	劉明朝	制憲國大代表		陳添登	新竹市參議員
	潘渠源	臺北市副參議長		郭福壽	新竹市參議員
	吳國信	制憲國大代表		康阿孔	新竹市參議員
	陳春金	臺北市參議員		周宜培	新竹市參議員
	黃朝琴	省參議長		李子賢	新竹市參議員
	周百鍊	臺北市參議員		郭傳芳	新竹市參議員
	吳春霖	臺北市參議員		鄭建杓	新竹市參議員
	黃純青	省參議員	新竹縣	劉闊才	省參議員
	蘇惟梁	省參議員		黃運金	新竹縣參議長
	林為恭	省參議員		朱盛淇	新竹縣副參議長
	郭國基	省參議員		劉梓勝	新竹縣參議員
	徐春卿	臺北市參議員	臺中縣	林　糊	臺中縣參議員
	陳旺成	省參議員		洪元煌	臺中縣參議員
	黃國書	制憲國大代表		黃朝清	臺中縣參議長
	林連宗	制憲國大代表		賴通堯	臺中縣參議員
	林　忠	國民參政員		張煥珪	臺中縣參議員
	李萬居	省參議會副議長		林西陸	臺中縣參議員
	周延壽	臺北市參議長		陳南山	臺中縣參議員
	林宗賢	國民參政員	彰化市	李君曜	彰化市參議長
	杜聰明	國民參政員		吳石麟	彰化市副參議長
	黃朝生	臺北市參議員	嘉義市	柯　麟	嘉義市參議員
	許振緒	臺北市參議員		潘木枝	嘉義市參議員
	李仁貴	臺北市參議員		陳澄波	嘉義市參議員
	陳　屋	臺北市參議員		林文樹	嘉義市參議員
	黃火定	臺北市參議員	臺南市	黃百祿	臺南市參議長
	陳海沙	臺北市參議員		侯全成	臺南市參議員
	林水田	臺北市參議員		陳天順	臺南市參議員
	簡檉堉	臺北市參議員		蔡丁贊	臺南市參議員
	林朝明	臺北市參議員	高雄縣	陳崑崙	高雄縣參議員
	王名貴	臺北市參議員	屏東市	葉秋木	屏東市副參議長
	林章恩	臺北市參議員		黃聯登	後來遞補參議員
	許慶豐	臺北市參議員		顏石吉	屏東市參議員
臺北縣	林日高	省參議員		邱家康	屏東市參議員
花蓮縣	馬有岳	省參議員	澎湖縣	許整景	澎湖縣參議員
				高順賢	澎湖縣參議員

註：參考整理自《臺灣戰後初期的民意代表》(李筱峰，1986)

■ 4-1 王添灯（1901－1947）

《三十二條處理大綱》宣讀者、全省性之二二八處理委員會談判代表、宣傳組長

臺北安坑人，畢業於臺北成淵學校，曾任職新店庄役場及臺北市役所社會課，對社會底層人民困苦感受深刻。日治時期，因具有強烈的民族意識與不畏強權的堅毅性格，積極推動臺灣自治運動，曾擔任臺灣地方自治聯盟理事、臺北支部主幹，代表出席地方自治聯盟第一次全島大會，並著有《臺灣市街庄政之實際》一書，提出臺灣地方自治的改革方向，為當時討論臺灣如何施行地方自治的第一本專書。然而，王添灯也曾因對抗日本殖民之政治活動，而遭日警拘留。

戰後，王添灯以「為最大多數、謀最大幸福」為己任，出任三民主義青年團臺北分團主任、臺灣省政治建設協會理事，並擔任《人民導報》社長，積極投入臺灣政治改革，為民喉舌、揭發時弊。1946年，王添灯當選臺灣省參議員，以臺灣的「政治民主化，經濟近代化」作為目標。在省參議會期間，提案範圍包括財政、民政、警務、教育、農林等議題，因問政時耿直敢言、質詢貪腐官員時不畏強權，頗受當時臺灣社會注目，被人稱為「鐵面議員」。

二二八事件爆發後，時任省參議員的王添灯等人被推派向陳儀當局談判，提出解除戒嚴、軍警不許開槍、釋放被捕市民、官民共組委員會之要求。其後，王添灯出任二二八處委會宣傳組長，代表處委會向每日省民廣播，說明處

王添灯全家福（後排左一）（純純文創提供）

王添灯家族合照於文山茶行（純純文創提供）

委會與官方交涉情形。在3月6日處委會舉行正式成立大會時，由王添灯擔任主席，並獲推舉為常務委員之一。7日，處委會表決通過王添灯所提的《三十二條處理大綱》，成為二二八事件中最重要的民主成果，然而此一訴求卻遭陳儀悍拒。當晚，王添灯在臺灣廣播電臺代表處委會最後一次向省民廣播，說明處委會立場與所追求之民主自治目標。11日凌晨，王添灯於文山茶行家中被逮捕，此後音訊全無。

依據王添灯長女王純純憶述，當時許多人勸說王添灯出逃，但他說：「我又沒有做什麼壞事情，我是為百姓在說話，為什麼要走？」。然而，3月11日清晨六點，一群穿著藍色中山裝、拿著短槍的人將茶行團團圍住，王添灯被逮捕帶上吉普車離開。八點後又有一批憲兵隊來抓捕王添灯，「一進門，就四處搜查，茶包還用槍尾刀一包包刺插，怕人藏在裡面；他們爬上二樓，翻箱倒櫃，家具都翻倒，把父親的書類文件都灑到一樓屋頂，把整套沙發椅從窗戶丟到天井去。」王純純對於尋找父親的過程仍舊記憶猶新，「只要聽說哪裡有人被打死，哪裡有屍體，我們都去看、去找，鐵路局、南港等地我都去過，但都找不到，一直到現在，還是不知道父親究竟在哪裡？」

在3月13日陳儀電呈蔣介石的〈辦理人犯姓

名調查表〉中，臚列多位二二八處委會參與人員，其中，王添灯於名冊中被列為第一位。在當局所羅織的「罪跡」中，包括「陰謀叛亂首要」、「組織偽二二八事件處理委員會自任宣傳組長」、「控制廣播電臺，發表叛國言論，

1. 王添灯手書文字
2. 王添灯與長子王政統合照 (純純文創提供)
3. 王添灯陳情省參議會秘書長的親筆信函

提出卅二條要求，鼓勵民眾附加其行動」等。而在另一份由軍統局臺灣站站長林頂立呈報南京的〈臺灣二二八事變報告書〉中，亦誣指王添灯「陰謀奪取政權」。

　　然而，在3月24日臺灣警備總部軍法處所陳列之〈二二八事變首謀叛亂在逃主犯名冊〉，王添灯卻登記為「蹤跡不明」，而4月11日陳儀還電呈南京謊稱並無捕殺無辜情事，並稱王添灯「有於混亂中被擊斃命消息」。解嚴後，由國家安全局公佈之1949年11月28日王守正上呈雷萬鈞的〈臺灣省『二二八』事變正法及死亡人犯名冊〉，才赫然看見王添灯姓名，證實其已被枉殺的事實。

　　王添灯不畏強權、執著敢言的形象，成為傳達臺灣人民心聲的最佳代表，也因此在二二八事件中，獲推舉為民眾談判代表及二二八處委會發言人。然而，從前述官方檔案與家屬證言可知，王添灯正因爭取政治改革，遭到當局忌恨，在軍隊抵臺後立即被秘密逮捕，並在官方單方面所羅織的罪名下，未經司法審判而遭到殺害。2007年，政府依據〈二二八事件處理及賠償條例〉，終於為王添灯洗刷冤屈、恢復名譽。

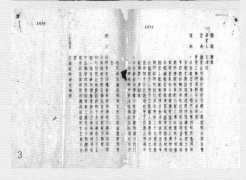

1. 任人民導報社長時的王添灯（純純文創提供）
2. 1946年5月1日臺灣第一屆省參議會第一次大會全體參議員合影後排
　立者右三為韓石泉、右七為王添灯（純純文創提供）
3. 王添灯於省參議會的提案

■ 4-2 林連宗（1905-1947）

臺中及彰化縣市參與全省性之二二八處委會代表

彰化人，畢業於日本中央大學法學部，並通過日本高等行政科及司法科試驗，取得高等文官資格。1931年返臺後，被選為臺中州律師公會會長，以及臺灣新聞社法律顧問。1945年，當選為臺灣省律師公會理事長，並陸續被選為臺灣省參議員、制憲國大代表。在擔任省參議員期間，以其法律專才提案要求撤銷統制經濟之貿易局，組織民間監督力量，並關注臺灣司法、教育、警政制度之弊端改革。

事件爆發後，臺中、彰化縣市參議會與律師公會等民間團體召開聯席會議，提出長官公署改組、實施省縣市長民選等訴求，並推派林連宗為代表前往臺北，參與全省性之二二八處委會開會運作，並在3月6日被推選為處委會常務委員之一。然而，3月10日，林連宗借住參議員李瑞漢家中，卻於當日下午與李瑞漢兄弟一併被軍憲人員帶走，從此失去音訊。

依據林連宗女兒林信貞的證言，父親林連宗在事件期間去臺北開會後，就再也沒有回音，直到3月10日經人通知，才知道林連宗當時在李瑞漢、李瑞峰兄弟家中，卻一同被憲兵抓走。當時食糧缺乏，鄰居剛好拿來兩尾魷魚，李家拿來煮魷魚粥，正在吃粥時，「這時走進來三、四位憲兵，先問李瑞漢先生是誰，繼之問我爸爸『你呢?』正直的父親便遞出名片，說明自己是制憲國大代表，來的人便說『來，出來，長官請你們去開會。』」之後卻一去不返，此後，林連宗太太林陳鳳屢次向政府機關、警備總部、憲兵隊等單位陳情，但卻始終沒有下文。

在1947年7月28日，警備總部對於林陳鳳所呈陳情書的回函中，仍稱並未派遣任何憲兵逮捕林連宗，且憲兵執行任務須出示傳票或拘票，因此「想係假冒所為，或挾仇報復」。然而，證諸日後公布的官方檔案，可知此一回函僅為託詞，林連宗早已遭密捕。

1. 林連宗結婚照（林信貞提供）
2. 3林連宗合格證書（林信貞提供）

　　依據3月12日憲兵司令部張慕陶呈蔣介石密報，載明「陳長官十日令憲兵駐臺特高組秘密逮捕國大代表林連宗、參議員李瑞峰」；另外，在〈辦理人犯姓名調查表〉中，林連宗被羅織的「罪跡」為「陰謀叛亂顛覆政府」、「強力接收臺灣高等法院第一分院並自任院長」等。在3月24日警備總部所列之〈二二八事變首謀叛亂在逃主犯名冊〉中，林連宗的「罪行」又被誣陷增加了「策動臺中地區暴動與偽臺中作戰本部謝雪紅相勾結」。

　　解嚴後，在國家安全局公佈的〈臺灣省『二二八』事變正法及死亡人犯名冊〉中，林連宗亦名列其中，其「罪名」為擔任「處理委員會委員」、「與謝雪紅勾結策動臺中暴動」等。在缺乏證據的情況下，林連宗先被秘密逮捕，且未經司法審判的程序而遭枉殺。2007年，政府依據〈二二八事件處理及賠償條例〉，為林連宗恢復名譽，進行賠償與平反。

1. 林連宗父女合照（林信貞提供）
2. 林連宗省參議員當選證書（林信貞提供）

林連宗給女兒之信函（林信貞提供）

■ 4-3 廖進平（1895－1947）

臺灣省政治建設協會參與全省性之二二八處委會代表

　　臺中縣葫蘆墩(今豐原)人，曾就讀總督府農事試驗場，以函授方式就讀早稻田大學文學科，並與詹天馬、陳清波等人設立廣福洋行，擔任專務取締役。殖民時期，廖進平曾參與臺灣文化協會，擔任《臺灣新民報》編輯，並與蔣渭水等人籌組臺灣民眾黨，積極投入對抗日本殖民統治活動。

　　戰爭結束後，廖進平曾主動接待返臺之臺灣文化協會、臺灣民眾黨同志，以及三民主義青年團成員，並至機場熱烈迎接國府前進指揮所的葛敬恩、李翼中、張邦傑等人。1946年，廖進平與蔣渭川、黃朝生等人成立臺灣民眾協會，後改名為臺灣省政治建設協會。二二八事件期間，此一組織也積極參與處委會之改組與運作。

　　1947年2月27日緝煙血案發生當晚，廖進平與政治建設協會成員張晴川、呂伯雄、黃朝生、白成枝，正在天馬茶房附近召開會議，也因此第一時間瞭解事件原委，當即於會上決議召集民眾進行遊行請願。孰料，隔日遊行隊伍竟遭長官公署開槍，使得事件全面蔓延開來。3月1日二二八處委會改組後，廖進平也加入二二八處委會，不僅積極推動會務運作，也讓其子廖德雄加入

「忠義服務隊」，擔任學生隊的隊長，協助維持臺北治安。然而，在蔣介石派遣的軍隊自上海啟程後，廖進平因遭密報而被臺北憲兵總隊逮捕，自此音訊全無。

　　依據廖進平三子廖德雄的口述，3月6日已收到電告，稱軍隊已從上海出發，3月8日將抵基隆，「父親一聽此訊，知道事態嚴重，叫我趕緊解散『忠義服務隊』，叫學生趕緊回家，否則危險。他告訴我說：『千萬要記得，這次阿兵哥一上陸，一定會大開殺戒。你眼睛要放亮一點，他們是土匪兵，你要注意喔。』」此後，在廖進平與其子廖德雄逃亡期間，軍統局人員許德輝曾派人至廖家搜人，並搶奪財物，包括當年廖進平與臺灣仕紳資助孫文革命的借款支據，也一併遺失。此時廖進平為躲避軍隊的逐戶搜查，準備坐船逃往大陸，卻遭大橋頭流氓

左-廖進平（廖德雄提供）
右-廖進平演說神情漫畫-張義雄（廖德雄提供）

李彩鑑向憲兵隊淡水分隊告密，使得廖進平於3月18日在淡水河口遭到逮捕。

　　由於政治建設協會對於行政長官公署的施政諸多不滿，在事件爆發前已與陳儀當局多有牴觸，而多位協會成員也積極參與二二八處委會之運作，因此在1947年3月7日軍統林頂立呈報南京的密件中，指控「暴動案係由臺灣政治建設協會從中主持煽動」，而廖進平作為該協會的核心成員，因而成為當局捕殺對象。

　　在陳儀電呈蔣主席的〈辦理人犯姓名調查表〉，廖進平因擔任「臺灣省政治建設協會理事兼經濟組長」而被列為「陰謀叛亂首要」，所羅織的「罪跡」包括「向美國駐臺領事館提出『將此次臺灣二二八事件真象，向國內及全世界報導，並請予主持公道』之辱國要求」、「經常利用該協會定期講演會，發表抨擊政府不滿現狀、挑撥官民之荒謬言論」等。另外，在警備總部所列之〈二二八事變首謀叛亂在逃主犯名冊〉，廖進平的「罪行」則包括擔任「政治建設協會理事兼經濟組組長暨二二八事件處委會委員」、「召集前日陸海軍人員開會號召組織武裝部隊」，以及「提議歪曲事變事實向美國新聞處發表荒謬言論」等。

　　廖進平被捕後，一直下落不明，解嚴後，從

國家安全局的〈臺灣省『二二八』事變正法及死亡人犯名冊〉，才證實廖進平被枉殺的事實。在白色恐怖時期，其子廖德雄雖然在事件後「自新」而得以保全，然而卻被列入「黑名單」，家族長期蒙受不平。2007年，政府依據〈二二八事件處理及賠償條例〉，恢復廖進平名譽，其家族後代終獲賠償與平反。

廖進平與小孩合照
（廖德雄提供）

1. 廖進平臺灣新民報社文件
　（廖德雄提供）
2. 廖進平與監禁難友的合照
　（廖德雄提供）
3. 廖進平公務人員考試及格
　證書（廖德雄提供）

■ 4-4 李仁貴（1900－1947）

全省性之二二八處委會調查組長

　　臺北縣人，畢業於蘆洲公學校，日治時期開設商行，經營日本神戶牛肉批發，以及冰果、電氣工程等事業，被選為臺北市食肉同業公會理事長、冰果店同業公會理事長，以及電氣工程同業公會理事長等，戰後經營臺北電氣工程公司等，1946年當選臺北市參議員，並擔任臺灣省政治建設協會理事長。

　　二二八事件發生後，李仁貴出任二二八處委會委員兼調查組長，協助血案事件調查。3月2日，李仁貴與其他五名代表、各報社記者赴軍法處調查緝煙兇手羈押情形。3月11日上午，遭便衣軍警強行帶走，自此下落不明。

　　依據李仁貴長子李博智憶述，3月11日早上七點，三名便衣軍警將李仁貴強行帶走，之後家屬四處尋人、打聽，卻毫無所獲，「也不知道是什麼原因被抓走？被抓到什麼地方？是不是和當時擔任二二八事件處理委員兼調查組長有關係？到現在我們都不明白原因。」

　　在陳儀當局所呈的〈辦理人犯姓名調查表〉中，李仁貴的略歷為二二八處委會委員兼調查組長、臺北市參議員、政治建設協會理事等，

其「罪跡」為「陰謀叛亂首要」、「提議將國軍武力完全解除，治安由處理委員會維持」。另外，在警備總部所呈之〈二二八事變首謀叛亂在逃主犯名冊〉中，李仁貴此時的「罪行」又被羅織為「主張撤銷政府武力禁止國軍行動」、「號召組織武裝隊伍反抗政府並主持學生接收各派出所事宜」。如同王添灯一般，名冊中也載明其「蹤跡不明」。解嚴後，國家安全局公佈的〈臺灣省『二二八』事變正法及死亡人犯名冊〉中，才證實李仁貴早已遇害。

　　然而，在1947年4月由軍統臺灣站站長林頂立呈報南京的〈臺灣二二八臺民叛亂臺北區叛逆名冊〉，李仁貴也名列其中，但未登記個人資料，也未說明「罪名」。由此可知，前述官方檔案紀錄彼此不一，各項「罪名」可以任不同機關恣意增改，毫無依據。解嚴後，政府依據〈二二八事件處理及賠償條例〉為李仁貴平反與賠償，以洗刷冤屈、恢復名譽。

李仁貴

■ 4-5 黃朝生(1904-1947)
全省性之二二八處委會治安組長

　　臺南下營人，畢業於臺灣總督府臺北醫學專門學校，在臺北圓環開設安生堂醫院。日治時期，因寄住於蔣渭水所設的大安醫院樓上，因此與蔣渭水等抗日人士相熟，並加入臺灣文化協會。曾計畫前往大陸成為軍醫參與對日抗戰，然而卻被日本特高警察監視，遭遣返回臺。戰後當選為臺北市參議員，並加入臺灣省政治建設協會，出任常務理事兼財政組長。

　　二二八事件發生後，臺北市參議會邀請各級民意代表共組「緝煙血案調查委員會」，其後於3月2日改組為「二二八事件處理委員會」時，由黃朝生出任處理委員兼治安組組長，並出席臺北市臨時治安委員會，惜於會中被軍統局策反幹員許德輝滲透，許並出任臨時治安委員會的執行機構「忠義服務隊」隊長。3月5日，黃朝生與王添灯、吳春霖等人被推派擇日前往南京陳情，說明事件真相。3月12日於家中遭憲兵逮捕後，自此失蹤。

　　依據黃朝生兒子黃瑞峰、黃瑞霖兩人的口述，黃朝生在被捕前，張晴川已來通風報信，當時黃朝生已經離家暫避風頭，然而聽到軍憲來家中抓他未遂，揚言將逮捕其子，因而返家。

　　黃瑞峰憶述當日憲兵離開後，「過了一會兒，父親回來了，母親看他回來，嚇了一跳，問他為何回來？父親說：『聽說他們還會再來，如果沒抓到我，會抓瑞霖去！』父親說他聽到有些學生被抓到臺北橋頭，就中挑了七、八個去槍斃。」最後，黃朝生為了保全家人，配合軍憲前往應訊，卻從此一去不回。

　　在陳儀當局所呈的〈辦理人犯姓名調查表〉中，黃朝生因擔任二二八處委會委員及政治建設協會理事，而被羅織「陰謀叛亂首要」、「勒令各公私醫院不得為受傷外省人醫治」、「陰謀組織『偽新華民國』政府」等「罪跡」。另外，在警備總部所列之〈二二八事變首謀叛亂在逃主犯名冊〉中，黃朝生又被羅織「脅迫

黃朝生(黃紫青提供)

政府無條件釋放人犯」、「主張解散警察大隊
」、「倡議叛亂煽惑暴動」等「罪行」。解嚴
後，從國家安全局公佈的〈臺灣省『二二八』
事變正法及死亡人犯名冊〉中，才證實黃朝生
已經死亡。

　　證諸相關史料，黃朝生作為懸壺濟世的醫
生，非但未阻止醫院救助外省受傷病患，反而
在事件期間協助維持治安，保護外省人避免無
辜遭受攻擊，包括協助李紀谷等人到陳文斌家
中避難等。2007年，政府依據〈二二八事件處
理及賠償條例〉為受難者平反及進行賠償，此
時，黃朝生終於得以洗刷冤屈、恢復名譽。

黃朝生於安生醫院（黃紫青提供）

臺灣地方自治聯盟本部合照（廖德雄提供）

■ 4-6 徐春卿（1895-1947）
全省性之二二八處委會常務委員

　　臺北錫口（松山）人，畢業於臺灣總督府國語學校後，日治時期曾擔任教職、松山庄協議會員，後從事煤炭業。1935年地方制度改革試行選舉中，獲選為庄協議會員，然日治時期也曾遭日警誣陷而入獄服刑。國府接受臺灣後，徐春卿受聘為行政長官公署諮議，後當選臺北市參議員，並加入中國國民黨。事件發生後，徐春卿參與二二八處委會運作，積極與會，3月6日獲推舉成為常務委員之一。3月11日，兩名軍警人員身著私服請其前去開會，離家後即不再復返。

　　依據徐春卿長子徐世通的憶述，3月11日「當時兩個穿便衣的來家裡說，王添灯請他去，父親便和他們出去，家人後來才知被騙了。」另外，徐世通在證言中推測徐春卿遭秘密逮捕的原因，可能與他反對陳儀拍賣日產給與其關係深厚的浙江財團有關，或者是因徐春卿擔任臺北市人權保障委員會總幹事，為保障人權與法律制度而涉入基隆要塞司令的一樁醫療糾紛，而與此糾紛事件有關係的人士，包括市參議員黃朝生、李仁貴、律師李瑞漢、醫生施江南等，都在二二八期間相繼遇害。

　　在陳儀當局所呈的〈辦理人犯姓名調查表〉中，徐春卿的略歷為二二八處委會委員、臺北市參議員，其「罪跡」被羅織為「陰謀叛亂首要」、「反對日產標售，組織日產租戶聯誼會，擴大反對政府措施」。另外，在警備總部所呈之〈二二八事變首謀叛亂在逃主犯名冊〉、軍統林頂立呈報南京的〈臺灣二二八臺民叛亂臺北區叛逆名冊〉等名冊中，都載有徐春卿的「罪行」。

　　徐春卿被抓後，妻子徐陳玉女曾向省參議會陳請代為查明，然參議會僅回覆「查照為荷」，而依據臺灣省諮議會相關檔案，省政府曾記載經電轉詢問各警備司令部，所得結果為「查徐春卿參加叛亂飭緝未獲」。解嚴後，由國家安全局公佈的〈臺灣省『二二八』事變正法及死亡人犯名冊〉，家人才得知徐春卿未經合法審判就遭逮捕殺害；2007年，政府依據〈二二八事件處理及賠償條例〉為徐春卿平反與進行賠償，以洗刷冤屈、恢復名譽。

徐春卿

■ 4-7 韓石泉（1897-1963）
二二八處理委員會臺南市分會主任委員

臺南市人，曾於其父韓子星所設私塾修讀漢文，1918年畢業於臺灣總督府醫學校，先後於赤十字社臺灣支部醫院、臺南醫院擔任內科醫生（為日治時代臺南醫院內科最早的文官「醫官補」），並於1928年開設韓內科醫院，後赴日於1940年取得熊本醫科大學醫學博士，回臺後以其醫學專業，懸壺濟世。行醫之餘，熱心參與臺灣文化協會，並擔任臺灣民眾黨臺南支部主幹，亦入股《臺灣新民報》，擔任監事，更積極投入地方自治制度的改革運動。戰後，曾受聘為自治宣導員與國民黨臺南市黨部指導員，協助穩定戰後局面與接收工作。其後當選臺南市唯一的臺灣省參議會參議員(第一屆)，所提議案相當多元，且多關注臺灣的教育、地方自治、醫藥衛生等重要問題，並參與主持防疫工作。

二二八事件發生時，由於臺南市治安一度混亂，擔任省參議員的韓石泉接受臺南市長卓高煊、議長黃百祿等懇請，與各界代表協商成立「臺南市治安協助委員會」。3月3日，韓石泉參與臺南市參議會，席間決議通過向當局提出的七項要求，包括軍憲不得任意開槍，廢止專賣局貿易局，縣市長民選、處理糧食問題、各處重要機關提拔本省人、將無能不負責之公務員解職等。

3月4日，韓石泉與市議長黃百祿、議員侯全成等，確定此一事件應採「不流血、不擴大」之處理方針。由於民眾一度群情激憤，場面幾乎無法控制，韓石泉出面安撫群眾情緒，提出且堅守與官方交涉的四項原則，包括：「不擴大、不流血、不否認現有行政機構，以及政治問題用政治方法解決」等。在各方折衝下，終於讓臺南市的局面朝向和平解決方向。

新婚的韓石泉夫婦（韓良俊提供）

1. 1929年3月11日韓內科醫院在臺南正式開業，於3月24日在《台灣民報》刊登「新設廣告」（莊永明提供）
2. 韓石泉（韓良俊提供）
3. 臺南非武裝抗日，陳、梁（加升）、黃、張四同志出獄紀念，第二排左三為韓石泉，右二為林占鰲，左二為王受祿，後排左二為蔡培火（韓良俊提供）

3月5日，臺南市參議會商議成立「二二八處理委員會臺南市分會」（簡稱臺南市分會），韓石泉被推舉為臺南市分會主任委員，並設置總務、治安、宣傳、糧食、救護、聯絡、學生等各組。3月6日，臺南市各級學校要求舉行和平示威，在韓石泉等處委會代表出面支持與維持秩序下，終讓遊行和平落幕，也讓當局瞭解當時民間心聲與處委會的立場：「確定民主政治、改革本省腐敗政治、促進地方自治實施、建設新臺灣」。

3月7日，韓石泉與地方民意代表至高雄要塞籲請市長卓高煊返回市政府辦公，以免無法推行政務；其後，在市政府召開糧食會議，決議以「二二八處理委員會臺南市分會」名義向金融機構貸款採購糧食，以解決當時嚴重的糧荒問題。當晚，韓石泉對處委會各組長進行報告，並再次重申臺南市分會之各項決議皆應符合前述四項和平處理原則，會後並推派代表北上說明情況，請當局緊急設法處置，以安民心。

3月8日，由於陳儀當局廣播，假稱行政機關將改為省政府，各處長將儘量選用本省同胞，請民意積極推薦有能力者擔任，以及辦理縣市長選舉前，現任各縣市長如有不稱職者則免職，由各參議會協商推舉候選人。因此，臺南市分會決定增設政治組，俾依據前述內容施行。3月9日，為表明為民做事、而非做官的立場，韓石泉公開表示無意競選市長。

3月10日，在軍隊陸續抵臺後，陳儀突然宣布戒嚴，並撤銷各級二二八處委會，誣指其行動「跡近叛國，國軍移防臺灣係為消滅叛徒。」3月11日，陸軍廿一師進駐臺南，並將臺南市參議會包圍，韓石泉與部份市參議員遭持槍士兵押解上車，載至臺南區指揮部，所幸韓石泉並未遭祕密處決，但後來仍被軍隊指揮官要求寫自白書，韓石泉峻拒不從，只以「處理書」了事。而侯全成則負責收繳武器、宣導政令。

1951年出版之《臺灣省首屆參議員》一書所刊載的韓石泉簡介

臺灣省參議會出版之《臺灣省首屆參議員》一書（1951年出版）所載的韓石泉照片（韓良俊提供）

1. 臺灣文化協會在臺南的鐵三角關鍵人物：蔡培火（右一）、王受祿（中間）、韓石泉（左一）（韓良俊提供）
2. 1901年韓石泉（左三）四歲時與雙親及家人合影（韓良俊提供）

二二八事件造成臺灣各地傷亡慘重，臺南也發生治安組長湯德章無辜遭當局槍決，因二二八事件而判刑入獄者亦不少；在當時一觸即發的情勢下，韓石泉不僅出面協助處理事件，安撫民眾，避免流血衝突，同時也協助救護外省傷患、保護公物，對於事件之撫平與保護臺南市市民免遭鎮壓，做出重大的貢獻。省參議會第一屆議長黃朝琴曾說，臺南市未發生不幸事件，「大部分是韓(石泉)先生的號召和熱忱，這種功勛是不可磨滅的。」因此，相較於臺北及其他縣市(尤其是鄰近的嘉義、高雄)，在韓石泉與黃百祿、侯全成、張壽齡、李國澤、林占鰲等民間人士的努力下，終能使臺南市在事件中的傷亡、犧牲降到最低。

由於少數激進分子不滿韓石泉的和平處理原則，傳出將採取對其不利的行動，面對周遭親友憂心他的安危，韓石泉曾說：「不敢明哲保身，坐視不救，是以不顧生死，置死生於度外」。在妻子莊綉鸞女士的回憶裡，說到韓石泉從日治時代就從事這些非常危險的社會、政治運動，「我從來沒有反對過，因為這些事是對臺灣人有利的。二二八當時我看見他每天早出晚歸。」對韓石泉來說，投入二二八處委會的協商折衝，是以「跪地禱告」、「背著十字架的心情去做的。」

1961年在臺南市政府所辦的雙十節大會上，韓石泉受邀發表問政的演說，直陳並批評臺灣當時的政治、教育學術、社會、國際關係等問題。此後，韓石泉與多數臺灣社會菁英一樣，對於政治深感挫折，失去參政熱情。對國民黨黨務工作也遠離而不再參與，實質上形同退黨。之後即全心投入於臺灣醫療、教育與慈善事業，曾任臺南光華女中校長及董事長、紅十字會臺南市分會長、臺南市醫師公會理事長等職，並擔任臺南市麻瘋療養院特別皮膚科診療所董事長工作。但是韓石泉晚年也曾感慨，由於民意代表缺少醫界專業人員，使得臺灣醫療水準與醫界長期缺少保障。

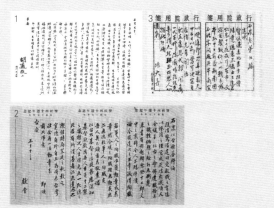

1. 胡適於1959年讀完第一版韓石泉自傳《六十回憶》後親筆來信（韓良俊提供）
2. 林獻堂寫給韓石泉的慰問信（韓良俊提供）
3. 蔡培火於1950年6月19日親筆寫給韓石泉的一封信（韓良俊提供）

The influential members of the 228 Incident Settlement Committee and the suffering sages

During the 228 Incident, many embraced the ideals of the democracy activists in order to resolve the bloody conflicts, sweep away the ills of government mal-administration and to fight for Taiwan's right of democratic self-government. Therefore, they bravely stepped forward and ultimately, even sacrificed their lives for these ideals. However, the 228 Incident was characterized as a "rebellion of a traitorous party" by Chen Yi's authorities and they used this as a pretext to get the Central Government to mobilize troops, and to shift the blame of the crux of Executive Administrative Office's problems, incompetence and misconduct, onto the 228 Incident Settlement Committee. Because of this, they strangled a generation of Taiwanese people's calls for democracy.

On reviewing the Incident's course of events, Chen Yi and heads of intelligence agencies in one hand continuously asked Nanjing to send soldier reinforcements, and in the other they gradually cooked up lists of "insurgent" names and their "charges." After the military arrived in Taiwan they wantonly hunted and killed everyone. Among those who sustained the heaviest casualties, were mainly the provincial, county and city councilmen of all the 228 Settlement Committees.

Take the provincial council as an example, Wang Tien-Teng and Lin Lien-Tsung died, Guo Guo-Ji, Lin Ri-Gao, Ma You-Yue and others who were imprisoned, as well as those who were wanted criminals totaled fourteen people, accounting for about half of their members. This resulted in their third meeting being canceled due to lack of attendance. In the counties and cities, like Taipei city's 26 city councilmen, four were killed, and seven imprisoned, with a ratio of victimization greater than 40%. The effect was far-reaching : Taiwanese elected representatives at all levels, even if they had survived, were so under duress from stress and fear that from here on, they entered into an era of silence.

王添灯

For an in-depth understanding of the ideals of the 228 Incident Settlement Committee's suffering sages, go through the following investigative section of the Settlement Committee's core member's life stories, the roles of the actors in the Incident, family member testimony and compare them with the official records of that time. It will help us get closer to the reality of the situation at that time. Additionally, these suffering sages and core members were spread across the geographic regions of the north, middle and south of Taiwan, with professions including lawyers, doctors, teachers, journalists and businessmen and were people from all levels of society. This enables us to draw a group profile for that generation of Taiwanese democratic forerunners.

4-1 Wang Tien-Teng (1901-1947)：orator of the "32 Demands," a Provincial 228 Incident Settlement Committee negotiator and the Publicity Chief

From An-Keng Taipei, he graduated from Taipei Cheng Yuan High School, and feeling deeply for those on the bottom rung of society, served in the Xindian District Office and Taipei City Government's Social Affairs Division. During the Japanese occupation, because he possessed a strong sense of national consciousness and a personality unwilling to submit to force, he actively promoted Taiwan's autonomy movement, serving as the director of Taiwan's Local Self-Government League at the main office in Taipei. As a representative, he attended the Local Self-Government League's first island-wide assembly and as author of the book, "Practical Situations of Taiwan's Local Politics," he informed the direction of Taiwan's local self-government reforms. It was the first book to discuss in detail, how to implement a local self-government in Taiwan. However, Wang Tien-Teng was ever held in custody by Japanese police because of his Anti-Japanese Colonialism political activities.

After the war, Wang Tien-Teng set out on a personal mission to "seek the greatest happiness for the most number," and served as director of the Three People's Principles Youth Corps Taipei branch, director of the Taiwanese Provincial Political Construction Association and president of the newspaper, "People's Herald." He was actively involved in Taiwan's political reforms as the mouthpiece of the people exposing the ills of the day. In 1946, Wang Tien-Teng was elected as senator of Taiwan's Provincial Council, with the "political democratization and economic modernization" of Taiwan as his goal and during his time on the Provincial Council, the scope of his proposals also included finance, civil affairs, police affairs, education, agriculture and other topics. When talking politics he was upright and outspoken, and when questioning corrupt officials he was unmoved by threats, and because of this he was popular in Taiwanese society. People called him, "The Iron Senator."

After the outbreak of the 228 Incident, as Wang Tien-Teng and others were serving as Provincial Senators, they were chosen to negotiate with Chen Yi's authorities. They demanded the lifting of martial law, the banning of the military and police from using weapons, the release of detained citizens and the formation of a joint government-civilian Settlement Committee. From then on, Wang Tien-Teng served as the 228 Incident Settlement Committee's Publicity Chief, broadcasting daily to the provincial citizens on behalf of the Settlement Committee, to describe the situation of the negotiations between the Settlement Committee and officials. On March 6, when the Settlement Committee held its official inaugural General Assembly, it was chaired by Wang Tien-Tengand he was elected as a member of the Standing Committee. On the 7th, the Settlement Committee voted on and passed Wang Tien-Teng proposed "32 Demands," becoming the most important fruit of democracy during the 228 Incident. However this appeal was met with Chen Yi's fierce refusal. That evening in Taiwan Broadcasting Station, Wang Tien-Teng, representing the Settlement Committee gave his final broadcast to the province, explaining the Settlement Committee's position and their pursuit of democratic self-government goals. Before dawn on the 11th, Wang Tien-Teng was arrested in his own home at the Wenshan Tea Company and after this he was never heard from again.

According to Wang Tien-Teng's eldest daughter, Sumiko Wang, she recalls that at that time, many people tried to persuade Wang Tien-Teng to flee, but he said, "I didn't do anything bad, I was speaking for the people, why do I need to leave?" However, on March 11th at six o'clock in the morning, a group of people wearing blue Zhongshan suits and holding pistols completely surrounded the tea company. Wang Tien-Teng was arrested, put in a jeep and then disappeared. After eight o'clock, another team of gendarme came to arrest Wang Tien-Teng, "As soon as they entered they searched everywhere, even bayoneting each sack of tea, thinking he might be hiding inside. They went upstairs rummaging through every chest and cabinet, all of the furniture was overturned. They scattered my fathers bound documents onto the first floor roof, and threw the whole set of couch and chairs out the window onto the courtyard." Sumiko Wang still vividly remembers the process of looking for her father, "As long as we heard of where someone was killed, where there was a corpse, we would all go and look. We searched the Railway Bureau, Nangang District and everywhere else, but I couldn't find him, even now. I still do not know where my father is."

On March 13th, in Chen Yi's telegraph "Investigation on the Handling of Named Criminals" to Chiang Kai-shek, it listed many 228 Incident Settlement Committee participants, and the first name among them was Wang Tien-Teng's. The "criminal evidences" formulated by the authorities, included a "Conspiracy of Rebellion against the Governor," "Self-Appointed Director of Publicity for the Illegal 228 Incident Settlement Committee," "Controlling the Broadcasting Station, Publishing Treasonous Statements, Proposing 32 Demands, and Encouraging the People to Increase their Actions." While in another report, the "Taiwan 228 Incident Report," by Lin Ding-Li, the Taiwan Stationmaster of the Bureau of Investigation and Statistics, it also falsely reported to Nanjing that Wang Tien-Teng was "Conspiring to Seize Power."

However, on March 24th, the Taiwan Garrison Command displayed their "List of the Most Wanted Lead Criminals in the 228 Incident Rebellion Conspiracy" and Wang Tien-Teng was listed as "location unknown," and on April 11th Chen Yi also telegraphed Nanjing, lying, he said that he didn't any kill innocents and that

Wang Tien-Teng "was killed in the chaos." After martial law lifted, the National Security Bureau released the November 28th, 1949, "List of Names of Taiwanese '228' Incident Executions and Dead Criminals" submitted by Wang Shou-Zheng to Lei Wan-Jun, and shockingly, Wang Tien-Teng's name was there, confirming the fact that he had already been wrongfully killed.

Wang Tien-Teng, with no fear of power, and clinging to his outspoken image, became the best representative to convey the voice of the Taiwanese people. Therefore, during the 228 Incident, he was elected as the people's negotiator and the 228 Incident Settlement Committee's spokesman. However, from the aforementioned official government records and the testimony of family members, we can know that the main reason Wang Tien-Teng was hated by the authorities was his struggle for political reform. Immediately after the military landed on Taiwan he was secretly arrested, faced official one-sided cooked charges, and was killed without judicial trial. In 2007, in accordance with the 228 Incident Disposition and Compensation Act, the government finally redressed the miscarriage of justice and rehabilitated Wang Tien-Teng's reputation.

4-2 Lin Lien-Tsung (1905-1947) : 228 Incident Settlement Committee Representative of Taichung and Changhua

A Changhua county native, he graduated from the Chuo University Law Department, Japan and passed Japan's High Administrative Branch and Judicial Branch Test, obtaining a high civil servant qualification. In 1931, after returning to Taiwan, he was elected chairman of the Taichung Bar Association, as well as counselor of the Taiwan Shinbunsha. In 1945, he was elected as director of the Taiwan Provincial Bar Association, and was subsequently elected as Provincial Senator of the Taiwan Provincial Legislature and member of the National Assembly. During his tenure as senator, Lin used his legal talent to make proposals that demanded the revocation of the Board of Trade's command economy, an organization of civilian oversight of power and corruption reforms for Taiwan's judicial, educational and police administration systems.

After the outbreak of the incident, the Taichung city and Changhua county Councils and Bar Associations and other civic groups held a joint meeting, to propose a restructuring of the Executive Office and an implementation of county and city elections among other appeals. Lin Lien-Tsung was chosen as their representative to Taipei, participating in the Provincial 228 Incident Settlement Committee operations meeting and on March 6th, he was elected as a member of the Settlement Committee's Standing Committee. However, on March 10th, Lin Lien-Tsung, staying in Senator Lee Rui-Han's home, was taken away together with Lee Rui-Han and his brother, in the afternoon by members of the gendarme and never heard from again.

According to the testimony of Lin Lien-Tsung's daughter, Lin Xin-Zhen, after her father went to the meeting in Taipei during the Incident, she didn't hear from him again until March 10th, when she was informed that Lin Lien-Tsung was staying at Lee Rui-Han and his brother, Lee Rui-Feng's home, but was arrested along with them by the gendarme. There was a food shortage at that time, and neighbors had just brought over two squid, the Lee family had made squid porridge with them and as they were eating, "In walked three or four gendarme, who first asked which one of us was Mr. Lee Rui-Han, and they continued by asking my father "Is it you?" My righteous father then handed over his name card, showing that he was a member of the National Assembly. The men who came then said, "Come, come, the governor has invited you to a meeting.'," but afterwards they were never to return. Since then, Lin Lien-Tsung's wife, Lin Chen-Feng has repeatedly petitioned the government, the Taiwan Garrison Command, the gendarme and other units but was never given any further information.

On July 28, 1947, in the letter replying to Lin Chen-Feng's petitions, the Taiwan Garrison Command said it did not send any gendarme to arrest Lin Lien-Tsung, and furthermore the gendarme is required to produce a summons or warrant when carrying out operations, and thus "believe that it was either someone impersonating the department or harboring a grudge for revenge." However, evidenced by the future released government archives, it is clear that this response was only a pretext, because Lin Lien-Tsung was secretly arrested long ago.

According to a March 12th secret report that Provost Marshal Zhang Mu-Tao sent to Chiang Kai-Shek, it specified that, "On the 10th, Governor Chen ordered an elite gendarme team stationed on Taiwan to secretly arrest National Assemblyman Lin Lien-Tsung and Senator Lee Rui-Feng." Additionaly, in the "Investigation on the Handling of Named Criminals," the "criminal evidence" framing Lin Lien-Tsung was a "Conspiracy of Rebellion to Overturn the Government," and "Usurping the First Branch of the Taiwan High Court by force and appointing himself director." On March 24th, listed in the Taiwan Garrison Command's "List of the Most Wanted Lead Criminals in the 228 Incident Rebellion Conspiracy," the "crimes" of Lin Lien-Tsung that he was again falsely accused of, adds "Instigating insurrection in the Taichung area and colluding with the Hsieh Hsueh-Hung's illegal Taichung military headquarters."

After martial law, in the National Security Bureau Office's "List of Names of the Taiwanese '228' Incident Executions and Dead Criminals," Lin Lien-Tsung ranked among them. His "crime" was for serving as a "Settlement Committee member," "and for collaborating with Hsieh Hsueh-Hung in instigating the Taichung insurrection." In the absence of evidence, Lin Lien-Tsung was first secretly arrested, and then without trial summarily executed. In 2007, the government redressed the miscarriage of justice and eventually rehabilitated Lin Lien-Tsung's reputation in accordance with the 228 Incident Disposition and Compensation Act.

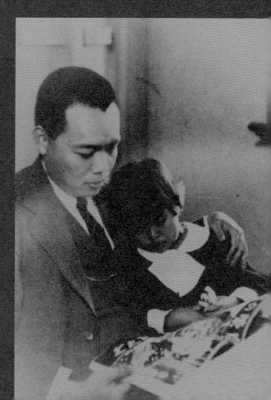

4-3 Liao Chin-Ping （1895－1947）：A Provincial 228 Incident Settlement Committee Representative from the Taiwan Provincial Political Construction Association

From Huludun (now Fengyuan) in Taichung county, he attended the Agricultural Experiment Station of the Office of the Governor General of Taiwan, studying by correspondence in Waseda University's literature department. Along with, Zhan Tien-Ma and Chen Qing-Bo and others, he established Guangfu Limited and served as senior managing director. During the colonial period, Liao Chin-Ping participated in the Taiwanese Cultural Association, serving as editor of the "New Taiwan People's News," and co-founded the Taiwanese People's Party with Chiang Wei-Shui, actively engaging in anti-Japanese colonial rule movements.

After the war, Liao Chin-Ping warmly hosted the Taiwanese Cultural Association, Taiwanese People's Party comrades, and Three People's Principles Youth Corps members returning to Taiwan. He also warmly greeted Ge Jing-En, Li Yi-Zhong and Zhang Bang-Jie of the National Government's Forward Command Post at the airport. In 1946, Liao Chin-Ping, Chiang Wei-Chuan, Huang Chao-Sheng and others co-founded the Taiwanese People's Association, that later changed its name to the Taiwanese Provincial Political Construction Association. During the 228 Incident, this organization actively participated in the restructuring and operations of the Settlement Committee.

On the night of February 27, 1947 when the tobacco seizure and murder case happened, Liao Chin-Ping and members of the Political Construction Association, Zhang Qing-Chuan, Lü Bo-Xiong, Huang Chao-Sheng, Bai Cheng-Zhi, happened to be holding a meeting in the vicinity of the Tien-Ma Tea House. Therefore, they immediately knew the whole story, and at once resolved at the meeting to assemble the people in a demonstration. Who could have guessed, that the following day the demonstrators would be fired on by the Executive Office, causing the Incident to spread all over. On March 1st, after the restructuring of the 228 Incident Settlement Committee, Liao Chin-Ping also joined it. He not only actively propelled meeting operations, but also had his son, Liao Te-Hsiung, join the "Loyal Service Corps," serving as the student leader, helping to maintain law and order in Taipei. However, after Chiang Kai-Shek ordered the troop set off from Shanghai, Liao Chin-Ping was secretly arrested by the Taipei gendarme and was never heard from again.

According to Liao Chin-Ping's third son, Liao Te-Hsiung's oral account, he had received a telegraph on March 6th saying that troops from Shanghai had already set off and would land at Keelung on March 8th. "As soon as my father heard this news, he knew the situation was serious, and told me to hurriedly disband the "Loyal Service Corps" and tell the students to quickly return home, otherwise they would be in danger. He told me: "Be sure to keep in mind that as soon as the soldiers land, they will open up a slaughter. Wise up, they are an army of bandits, you need to be careful..." Afterwards, while Liao Chin-Ping and his son, Liao Te-Hsiung were fleeing, Xu De-Hui of the Bureau of Investigation and Statistics sent men to search and plunder the Liao's house, including a fund from Liao Chin-Ping and the Taiwan gentry to loan to Sun Yat-Sen, in support of the revolution. At this time, Liao Chin-Ping, in order to escape the army's door to door searches, was preparing to flee by boat to the mainland, but he ran into a dock thug, Li Cai-Jian, who informed the head of the gendarme Tamsui branch. This led to Liao Chin-Ping's arrest on March 18th at the mouth of the Tamsui River.

Due to the Political Construction Association's many areas of discontent with the governance of the Executive Administrative Office, there had been conflict with Chen Yi's authorities before the outbreak of the Incident, and many of the Association's members were also actively participating in the 228 Incident Settlement Committee's operations. Therefore, on March 7th, 1947 in the Bureau of Investigation and Statistic's confidential report that Lin Ding-Li, sent to Nanjing, he alleged that "the series of riot cases are related to the incitement directed by the Taiwan Political Construction Association." Liao Chin-Ping was one of the Association's core members, and thus he became a hunted target for the authorities.

In Chen Yi's "Investigation on the Handling of Named Criminals," telegraphed to Chairman Chiang, Liao Chin-Ping because he was serving as the "Taiwan Political Construction Association Director and Economic Group leader," was grouped under the "Conspiracy of Rebellion against the Governor," and his cooked up "criminal evidences" included "requests that humiliated the country by proposing to the U.S. consulate stationed in Taiwan 'to report the true facts of the 228 Incident to the mainland as well as the international community, and asked them to uphold justice' " and "he often uses the Association as a public speaking platform to provoke discontent with the current government and drive a wedge between the government and people with absurd statements." In addition, the Taiwan Garrison Command listed in the "List of the Most Wanted Lead Criminals in the 228 Incident Rebellion Conspiracy," the "crimes" of Liao Chin-Ping include serving as the "Political Construction Association Director and Economic Group Leader and 228 Incident Settlement Committee member," "convening a meeting of army and navy personnel to call for the formation of an armed force," as well as "proposing absurd statements to distort the facts of the Incident to the U.S. news service," and so on.

After Liao Chin-Ping was arrested, his whereabouts had remained unclear, but after martial law, the National Security Bureau's "Taiwan Province 228 Incident Execution and Death Name List," confirmed that Liao Chin-Ping had been unjustly killed. During the era of the White Terror, and although his son Liao Te-Hsiung was "rehabilitated" after the Incident, he was however still listed on the "blacklist," and his family long suffered injustice. In 2007, the government, in accordance with the 228 Incident Disposition and Compensation Act, rehabilitated Liao Chin-Ping and his family's reputation, they were finally compensated and rehabilitated.

4-4 Lee Jen-Kuei (1900 - 1947) : Provincial 228 Incident Settlement Committee Investigation Chief

From Taipei County, he graduated from Luzhou public schools, and during the Japanese occupation he opened businesses wholesaling Japanese Kobe beef, fruit, and operating in electrical engineering among other industries. He was elected as director of Taipei's meat association, director of the fruit shop association, as well as director of the electrical engineering association. After the war, he operated a Taipei electrical engineering company in Taipei, in 1946 was elected as a Taipei City councilman, and served as Director of the Taiwan Political Construction Association.

After the outbreak of the 228 Incident, Lee Jen-Kuei served as a 228 Incident Settlement Committee member and their Investigation Chief, assisting with the Tobacco Seizure and Murder Incident investigation. On March 2nd, Lee Jen-Kuei along with five other representatives and newspaper reporters attended the Judge Advocate Department's investigation of those held in custody for the Incident. On the morning of March 11th, he was forcibly taken away by gendarme and has been missing ever since.

According to Lee Jen-Kuei's eldest son, Lee Bo-Zhi, recalled that on March 11th, at seven in the morning, three plainclothes military police forcibly took Lee Jen-Kuei away, and afterwards the family searched and inquired all over for him, but came up empty. "We didn't know for what reason he was taken away, where he was taken to, and whether or not it was related to him serving as a member of the 228 Incident Settlement Committee and the Investigation Chief. Even now we still don't know the reason."

In the "Investigation on the Handling of Named Criminals" composed by Chen Yi's authorities, Lee Jen-Kuei's profile was a 228 Incident Settlement Committee member and Investigation Chief, Taipei City councilor, Director of the Political Construction Association, and had other "criminal evidence" such as "Conspiring rebellion against the Governor," "Proposing the military be completely disarmed and that law and order be maintained by the Settlement Committee." Additionally, in the "List of the Most Wanted Lead Criminals in the 228 Incident Rebellion Conspiracy," authored by the Taiwan Garrison Command, Lee Jen-Kuei's "crimes" were again painted as "advocating the withdrawal of government force and the prohibition of military action," "calling for an armed contingent to resist the government and placing students over the affairs of the local police stations." As with Wang Tien-Teng, the list states that his "whereabouts are unknown." After the lifting of martial law, the National Security Bureau's "Taiwan Province 228 Incident Execution and Death Name List" confirmed that Lee Jen-Kuei had already been murdered.

However, in April 1947 Lee Jen-Kuei was also listed in the "List of Taipei District Rebels in Taiwan's 228 Taiwanese rebellion" sent to Nanjing by Lin Ding-Li of Taiwan's Bureau of Investigation and Statistics. Lee Jen-Kuei was listed among them, but it didn't record any personal information nor specify any "crimes." Therefore, because the aforementioned official records differ from each other, it can be seen that the "crimes" are just unfounded, arbitrary additions or changes by the different offices. After martial law, the government in accordance with the 228 Incident Disposition and Compensation Act rehabilitated and compensated Lee Jen-Kuei and his family, to clear any grievances and restore his name.

4-5 Huang Chao-Sheng (1904 - 1947) : Provincial 228 Incident Settlement Committee Security Supervisor

He was from Tainan, Xiaying District, graduated from the Taiwan Governor-General's Taipei Medical College, and in the Chien-Cheng Circle opened the An-Sheng-Tang Hospital. During the Japanese occupation, because he was lodging in the upstairs of the like Chiang Wei-Shui's Da-An Hospital, he became acquainted with anti-Japanese figures and joined the Taiwan Cultural Association. He had once planned to go to the mainland China to become a medic participating in the Second Sino-Japanese War, however he was being watched by the Japanese Tokubetsu Kōtō Keisatsu, aka Special Higher Police, and was sent back to Taiwan. After the war he was elected as a Taipei City Councilor, and joined the Taiwanese Provincial Political Construction Association, serving as the executive director and fiscal supervisor.

After the outbreak of the 228 Incident, the Taipei City Senate invited representatives from groups of all levels to form "The Tobacco Seizure and Murder Case Investigation Commission." Thereafter on March 2nd, it was restructured as the "228 Incident Settlement Committee," and Huang Chao-Sheng served as one of the committee members and concurrently as public security supervisor. He also attended the Taipei City Interim Public Security Committee, which was unfortunately infiltrated by the subversion agent of Bureau of Investigation and Statistics, Xu De-Hui. Xu also served as the director of the executive body of the Interim Public Security Committee, the "Loyal Service Corps." On March 5th, Huang Chao-Sheng and Wang Tien-Teng, Wu Chun-Lin and others were chosen to go to Nanjing to petition and send a true description of the events. On March 12th, after he was arrested by gendarme in his home, there has been no trace of him.

According to the accounts of both Huang Chao-Sheng's sons, Huang Rui-Feng and Huang Rui-Lin, before Huang Chao-Sheng's arrest, Zhang Qing-Chuan had already secretly informed them and Huang Chao-Sheng had already left home to temporarily hide out. However, he heard that when the gendarme came to his house to attempt to arrest him, they threatened to arrest his sons instead. So he returned home. Huang Rui-Feng recalled the day after the gendarme left "after a while, his father returned and when his mother saw him, she was horrified and asked him why he came back. My father said: "I heard they will still come back, and if they don't arrest me, they will take Rui-Lin!" My father said he heard some students were arrested at Taipei Bridge and they picked out seven or eight to execute." In the end, Huang Chao-Sheng, in order to protect his family, cooperated with the gendarme, going to his arraignment, but he never returned.

In the "Investigation on the Handling of Named Criminals" composed by Chen Yi's authorities, Huang Chao-Sheng served as a member of the 228 Incident Settlement Committee, director of the Political Construction Association, framed as "Conspiring rebellion against the Government," "ordering all public and private hospitals not to treat injured mainlanders," and "conspiring to create a Fake 'New Republic of China' government" among other "criminal evidences." Additionally, in the "List of the Most Wanted Lead Criminals in the 228 Incident Rebellion Conspiracy" of the Taiwan Garrison Command, Huang Chao-Sheng was again framed as "coercing the government to unconditionally release prisoners," "advocating the dissolution of the police," and "initiating rebellion to incite insurrection" among other "crimes." After the lifting of martial law, the National Security Bureau published the "List of Names of Taiwanese '228' Incident Executions and Dead Criminals" and it could be confirmed that Huang Chao-Sheng had already died.

Evidenced from relevant historical data, Huang Chao-Sheng was a doctor of the people, for not only did he not prevent hospitals from saving patients from other provinces, but during the event he helped maintain law and order, and protected innocent mainlanders from attack. Including, assisting Li Ji-Gu and others to take refuge in Chen Wen-Bing's house. In 2007, the government, in accordance with the 228 Incident Disposition and Compensation Act, rehabilitated the victims and compensated them. At this time, Huang Chao-Sheng was finally able to have any grievances cleared and his good name restored.

4-6 Hsu Chuen-Ching (1895－1947) : Provincial 228 Incident Settlement Committee Executive Member

Hsu Chuen-Ching was a teacher and also served as Songsang Village councilor during the Japanese Occupation. During that time, Hsu was framed by the Japanese police and subsequently sentenced to imprisonment. After the restoration, Hsu was employed as counselor of the Taiwan Provincial Administrative Executive Office and later elected as Taipei City councilor. After the 228 Incident, Hsu had been actively engaged in the operation of the 228 Settlement Committee and was accordingly elected as one of the executive members. On March 11, Hsu was arrested by the military police and disappeared. His son, Hsu Hsi-Tong, recalled that Hsu Chuen-Ching might have been arrested due to his opposition to Chen Yi's policy of confiscating and auctioning the Japanese-owned properties and encouraging business-government collusion, or, Hsu's advocacy of human rights. After the lifting of Martial Law, the government redressed the miscarriage of justice and eventually rehabilitated Hsu Chuen-Ching's reputation in accordance with the 228 Incident Disposition and Compensation Act.

徐
春
卿

4-7　Hahn Shyr-Chyuan (1897-1963) : Chairman of the 228 Incident Settlement Committee-Tainan Branch

Born in Tainan, Hahn Shyr-Chyuan once studied Chinese at the private institute founded by his father, Hahn Zi-Xin. Graduated from the Medical School of the Taiwan Governor-General Office in 1918, Hahn Shyr-Chyuan successively worked as an internist at the Red Cross-Taiwan Branch Hospital and Tainan Hospital. Hahn was the first "medical officer" in Tainan Hospital during the Japanese colonial era. Afterwards, he founded the Hahn Clinic (Internal Medicine) in 1928, and later obtained his M.D. from Kumamoto University in Japan in 1940. After returning to Taiwan, Hahn continued to help the public with professional medical practices. Aside from his medical practices, he also devoted himeself to the Taiwanese Cultural Association, and became the chairman of the Taiwanese People's Party - Tainan Branch. Meanwhile, he invested in and served as the supervisor of the "New Taiwan People News," and enthusiasticlly participated in the reformation of the local self-governing system. After the Chinese Civil War, Hahn was recruited as a local self-governance advocator and the director of the KMT Tainan division to assist with maintaining and handling the postwar circustance and transition. Hahn was then elected as a provincial senator, the first and only in Tainan City. During his term as a provincal senator, he put forward numerous proposals, concerning issues of education, local self-governing system, medicine and health care, and also conducted the epidemic control.

The 228 Incident severely damaged the public order in Tainan City. Responding to this unforeseen event, Hahn Shyr-Chyuan, provincial senator at that time, as requested by Tainan City Mayor Cho Gao-Xuan and Prolocutor Huang Bai-Lu, consulted with the local representatives and established the "Tainan City Public Security Committee." On March 3rd, Hahn attended the Tainan City Council meeting, during which the seven principles he proposed to the authorities were passed. These seven principles included implementing open-fire restriction on military police, abolishing the monopoly bureau, implementing magistrate and mayoral elections, solving the provisions-shortage problem, cultivating local Taiwanese for governmental administrative agencies, and dismissing irresponsible, incompetent public officials.

On March 4th, Hahn Shyr-Chyuan, City Prolocutor Huang Bai-Lu and Senator Hou Quan-Cheng reached a consensus on the principle of "no bloodshed, no escalation." Responding to the public rage that almost crashed the meeting, Hahn addressed the four principles of peace, including "Do Not Escalate," "Without Bloodshed," "Do Not Deny Existing Authorities" and "Solve Political Issues with Political Methods." These four principles of peace, together with the consensus among various parties, eventually directed Tainan City to a more peaceful resolution.

On March 5th, Tainan City Council established the 228 Incident Settlement Committee-Tainan Branch (hereinafter referred to as Tainan Branch). Hahn Shyr-Chyuan was elected to act as committee chairman. Various departments, including general affair, public security, publicity, provisions, medical care, communication and student affairs, were also established. On March 6th, students at all levels of school in Tainan City came together and requested to march on the street. Under the supervision of Hahn Shyr-Chyuan and his fellow committee members, the demonstration completed its entire route and had a peaceful ending. The demonstration delivered to the authorities the aspiration of the public and the position of the committee. That is, "establishing democracy, reforming Taiwan Province's corrupted politics, advancing the implementation of a local self-government, and also building a new Taiwan."

On March 7th, Hahn Shyr-Chyuan and the local representatives left for Kaohsiung, appealing for Mayor Cho Gao-Xuan's return to the office to ensure the operation of government affairs. Afterwards, during the provision's meeting, the city government made the decision to borrow money from financial institutions in the name of the 228 Incident Settlement Committee-Tainan Branch to purchase enough provisions to solve the severe food-shortage problem. That evening, Hahn reported to all the department leaders in the committee, and reiterated that all the resolutions made by the 228 Incident Settlement Committee-Tainan Branch should conform to the four principles of peace. After the meeting, representatives of the Tainan Branch were sent to explain the situation and appeal for the authorities' immediate response to the event in order to soothe the anxious citizens.

On March 8th, Chen Yi, Chief Executive and Garrison Commander of Taiwan, broadcasted a fraud message, claiming that the administrative authorities would become the provincial government, in which each bureau would employ as many local Taiwanese as possible and would encourage the public to recommend competent candidates for the positions. Moreover, any mayor or magistrate incompete at his job during his term should be unseated and replaced by the candidate elected by the city council. Correspondingly, the 228 Incident Settlement Committee-Tainan Branch made a decision to add a department in charge of political affairs, which would opperate according to policy announced by Chen. On March 9th, in order to show his aspiration to serve the public, rather than to become an official, Hahn announced that he had no interest in joining the mayoral election.

On March 10th, at the arrival of the KMT troops, Chen Yi immediately initiated the Martial Law and revoked all levels of 228 Incident Settlement Committee, incriminating the committee for treason and claiming that "the KMT troops were relocated to Taiwan for the elimination of the traitors." On March 11th, Tainan City Council was surrounded by the KMT troops. Hahn and several city senators were forced onto a military vehicle by armed soldiers, and were escorted to the military's southern district headquarters for interrogation. Fortunately, Hahn was not executed. While he was asked to write a confession, Hahn sternly refused and eventually wrote only an official report. Hou Quan-Cheng, on the other hand, was assigned to collect weapons and promote the government decree.

The 228 Incident caused severe casualties all over Taiwan. In Tainan, Tang De-Zhang, leader of the public security department, was executed by the firing squad. A considerable amount of people was sentenced to imprisonment. Under the harsh circumstance, Hahn Shyr-Chyuan not only helped handle the incident, pacifying the Taiwanese people to avoid further conflicts and bloodshed, but also helped rescue wounded Mainlanders and protect public property. Hahn had a significant contribution towards handling this unforeseen incident and keeping Tainan citizens from being brutally suppressed. Huang Chao-Chin, the first prolocutor of the provincial council attributed the peaceful result to Hahn's charisma and enthusiasm, and considered the accomplishment of Mr. Hahn Shyr-Chyuan "remarkable and unforgettable." Compared to Taipei and other cities such as the neighboring Kaohsiung and Chiayi, the casualties and sacrifice in Tainan City caused by the 228 Incident were considerably minimized through the endeavor of local elite such as Hahn Shyr-Chyuan, Huang Bai-Lu, Hou Quan-Cheng, Zhang Shou-Ling, Lee Guo-Ze and Lin Zhan-Ao.

Some activists could not adhere to Hahn Shyr-Chyuan's principles of peace and threatened to take adverse action against him, making Hahn's relatives and friends concern for his safety. Hahn once responded, "I could not bear to see others suffer. I would rather die for the cause of putting others' needs before mine and promoting the principles of peace." It was in Hahn's wife, Juang Shiow-Luan's recollection that ever since the Japanese colonial era, Hahn had been participating in extremely dangerous social and political movements. She mentioned, "I was never against my husband's involvement in those movements because they are beneficial to the Taiwanese people. During the 228 Incident, I watched him working diligently and conscientiously without much rest." To Hahn, his commitment to the 228 Incident Settlement Committee was coupled with his faith and prayers and the calling to "bear the weight of the cross."

In 1961, at the National Day (Double Tenth Day) celebration, Hahn Shyr-Chyuan was invited to give a speech about his participation in politics. Hahn criticized the politics, education, social and international relations of Taiwan at that time. Like the other elite, Hahn also felt frustrated and lost the enthusiasm for further involvement in politics. Gradually withdrawing from the KMT affairs, Hahn devoted himself to health care, education, and humanistic events. Hahn had served as the principal and chairman of Kuang-Hua Senior High School in Tainan, the director of Red Cross-Tainan, the president of Tainan City Medical Association, and the chairman of the dermatology clinic at the Leprosarium in Tainan City. However, feeling lamentable in his later years, Hahn Shyr-Chyuan expressed his disappointment that the medical level and medical profession have long been overlooked due to the lack of medical professionals among the elected representatives.

爭取本省政治改革
並非排斥外省同胞

【本報訊】二·二八事件處理委員會于昨發表聲明如下：

親愛的各省同胞，這次二·二八事件的發生，我們的目標，在肅清貪官污吏，爭取本省政治的明朗，早日達到目的，藉以改革本省政治的工作，不是要排斥你們外省同胞，頭腦冷靜和我們握手，爭取這次鬥爭的勝利，親愛的同胞們，我望關心國家的各省同胞，踴躍參加我們的好漢，漢皇族，國家政治的好壞，每個國民都有責，大家拿出愛國的熱誠，和我們共同推進，我們同是黃帝的子孫，至于二·二八那天有一部份外省同胞被毆打，這是出于一時的誤會，我們實深很痛心，各省同胞的犧牲，協助，今後絕對不再發生這種事件，希望大家放心出來共同，我們很誠意深深歉疚，但也是一個我們同胞的災難，這目標邁進，我們的口號是改進臺灣政治。

中華民國萬歲。
國民政府萬歲。
蔣主席萬歲。

各組長會議

【本報訊】事件處理委員會昨（六）日上午十一時，在中山堂召開正副組長會議，決議一，每日上午九時半，各組正副組長集合於貴賓室，報告各組情形。二，各委員每日上午十時，集合於各組集合室。三，各種民意及報告，由總務組接受，分配辦理。四，各組向各報或廣播發表事項，每日下午二時以前，提交宣傳組。五，對各報社發表消息，規定每日下午三時，由宣傳組負責發表云。

郭國基遄返省垣
談稱臺東蘇宜等地安靜

【本報訊】據省參議員郭國基談稱，余在恒春考察漁林情形時，聞悉臺北之二，二八事件，即縮短行程，二日至墨東縣，三日上午，本省青年及高山青年，召開縣民大會，全付武裝，在縣政府前廣場開青年大會。要求肅清貪官污吏，改進政治，因縣府等所有幾個外省人員逃容，縣府人員皆已逃走一空，秩序頗為安靜，後經要求，決議要求改進政治，維持治安，蘇澳軍站／憲兵，已不見攜四日抵花蓮縣，下午二時舉行縣民大會，參加者有民眾五千餘名，五日下午二時左右到蘇澳，本省同胞均已武裝，軍繫不准攜帶武器，後至羅東，宜蘭，瑞芳等，地方之治安，均由本省同胞維持秩序頗佳，平靜如常。

臺南市處理會成立
席上各界代表熱烈提供意見

【本報臺南六日下午四時特訊】委員會臺南市分會，於五日晚八時在市參議會議廳開，席上由各界代表盡量貢獻意見，熱烈討論，結果即成立，並推舉省參議員韓石泉為主任委員，市參議員黃百祿，青年團主任莊益〔□〕侯為副主任委員，洪榮勳為總務組長，湯德章為治安組長，侯全成為宣傳組長，陳天順為糧食組長，翁金護為救護組長，李顧能為連絡組長，學生組長（未定）半許始散會。

【文訊】本市分會，於

新生報　（星期五）　中華民國三十六年三月七日

台灣新生報

中華民國卅四年十月廿五日創刊

內政部登記證京警臺字第零零零四號

經中華郵政登記認爲第二類新聞紙類

發行人　李萬居

處理委員會發出
告全國同胞書

爭取本省政治改革
並非排斥外省同胞

【本報訊】二二八事件處理委員會於昨發表聲明如下：

親愛的各省同胞，這次二二八事件的發生，我們的目標正在肅清貪官污吏，爭取本省政治的改革，不是要排斥外省同胞，我們歡迎你們來參加這次改革本省政治的工作，以便養清政治的明朗，早且達到目的，希望關心國家的各省同胞，頭腦清楚的各省同胞，興省同胞攜手，爭取這次鬥爭的勝利，親愛的同胞們，我們同是黃帝的子孫，漢呈族，國家政治的好壞，綠個國民都有責任，大家拿出愛國的熱藏，和我們共同推進，我們很誠意地歡迎，各省同胞的幫忙，協助，至于二二八那天害一部份外省同胞被毆打，還是出于一時誤會，我們覺得很痛心，但也是一個我們同胞的災難，今後絕對不再發生這種事件，希望大家放心出來向倘

遠目標邁進，我們的口號是改進臺灣政治。

中華民國萬歲。

國民政府萬歲。

（下略）

監院電，【中央……】

監察使署亮……

六日上午十一時議閉，召開此會……討論此案……，先強化各組織……，任務及問題，並開明全……政治，切實的……本省腐敗的政治……，提出關……員，下午一時許……

有死傷情勢……

自

第五章／解讀二二八處委會：立場、角色與歷史定位

The Analysis of the 228 Incident Settlement Committee：Standpoints, Roles and the Demonstration of its Historical Status

第五章／解讀二二八處委會： 立場、角色與歷史定位

The Analysis of the 228 Incident Settlement Committee：
Standpoints, Roles and the Demonstration of its Historical Status

■ 5-1 處委會的核心立場與洗刷汙名

隨著事件逐漸發展，以及二二八處委會不斷擴編，參與者也日益複雜，並引發了派系間的爭鬥。中山堂的派系鬥爭，依警備總部的歸納，將處委會派別分為：1.省縣市參議員、參政員、國大代表之一部份，代表者為王添灯；2.政治建設協會：代表者為蔣渭川；3.學生自治同盟；4.律師公會，以及5.工會等。此外，政府情治機關，如軍統(保密局)、中統(CC派)及政學系之間的鬥爭、滲透與煽動，再加上三青團等政治外圍團體的參與，使得二二八事件的情勢發展錯綜糾葛。

雖然派系間各有不同的利害考量，例如蔣渭川就自承遭當局設計，出面成立了抗衡性的組織，加深派系間之衝突，但是在二二八處委會中，不論是被稱為天真懷抱改革目標的青年學生、保守觀望的右派仕紳階級、基進的左傾思想者，以及對於政治渴望而爭取獲得政治舞臺者等等，卻都懷抱著相同的政治改革目標，使得處委會能夠高度展現臺灣社會的集體訴求，並凝聚在《三十二條處理大綱》的條文中。

這不僅是二二八處委會的共同立場，當時臺灣各地的有識之士與各個外圍團體，包括彰化縣田中地區的青年連署運動，或是「臺灣省自治青年同盟」、「臺灣民主同盟支部」、「臺灣省警政改革同盟」、「青年復興同志會」、「臺灣省政治改革委員會」等，也都提出相近的自治主張。例如，由蔣渭川成立的最具規模之外圍團體「臺灣省自治青年同盟」，就提出了建設高度自治、省縣市長民選等訴求，同時也表達了「絕對擁護中央，打倒臺灣省貪官汙吏」的立場。此外，就連在處委會與官方談判期間，於臺中地區進行武裝鬥爭的臺共謝雪紅，也聲明對抗目的在於「爭取臺灣真正的自治，掃清貪污、改革政治」。

另一方面，事件初期雖然爆發了群眾毆人燬物的情形，然而，二二八處委會從未出面組織作戰之武裝力量，甚至由臺中仕紳所組成的「臺中地區時局處理委員會」與「治安本部」，就是為了牽制謝雪紅所掌握的「作戰本部」，避免事件衝突擴大。由此可知，二二八處委會自始至終堅持團結群眾力量，期望以和平協商方式解決此一事件，並促成改革的實現。

左-二二八處委會出面協調解決民生困境，尤其是當時嚴重的米荒問題
右-3 月 6 日下午，二二八處委會於中山堂補開成立大會，由王添灯擔任主席，並推選王添灯等17位常務委員；當日並決議調度煤炭廉價配售供應民生所需。(1947.3.7《新生報》)

在此一背景下，回頭檢視陳儀當局對二二八處委會所羅織的「罪名」，歷史的真相也就清晰了。首先，處委會最初係依據陳儀的指示由官民合組之團體，而不論是事件期間官方多次與處委會談判後的廣播，或是3月7日長官公署致函處委會的公文內容，都證實了處委會係代表臺灣最高民意、提出政治改革建議的合法組織，因此並非「非法組織」。

其次，全省性之處委會成立期間不到十日，而部分縣市處委會甚至僅成立一至二日，如此短的時日，難以發展為陳儀當局毫無實證之下所稱的有計畫之「陰謀叛亂」。此外，在國府軍隊抵臺時，處委會多位成員因為民請命、胸懷坦蕩，對於軍隊鎮壓毫無防備，因而紛紛遭捕殺，亦可證實官方的指控缺乏依據。

最重要的是，由處委會所提的《三十二條處理大綱》，事後證實遭到當局特務人員煽動、附加了十項過激政治要求，被當局羅織為四十二條「叛國罪證」。因此，此一大綱理應作為官民續行協商的民意依據，陳儀卻以此遂行鎮壓，暴露了當局對於民眾期盼改革之訴求毫無體察，而此一混淆視聽、剷除異己之手段，導致了一代社會菁英慘烈犧牲，也讓後世關心此一事件者，陷入了三十二條抑或四十二條的爭論迷霧中。

從官方事後的宣慰與處置態度來看，3月17日國防部長白崇禧來臺宣慰，期間遍訪及聽取了林獻堂等臺民領袖心聲，因此，白崇禧在報告中就直接要求撤換陳儀，廢除行政長官公署，並儘速推行省政改革。此外，在他向全臺民眾發表的第一號佈告中，也提出了四項基本處理原則，包括：1.由省政府制度取代行政長官公署，各縣市長提前民選；2.省府廳處主管大量任用本省人；3.公營事業範圍縮小，獎助民營企業以發展國民經濟，以及4.與事變有關的人民從寬免究。

因此，在4月20日的行政院會議中，就決議改組行政長官公署，成立省政府，由魏道明出任第一任省主席。此外，行政院也決議設置省府委員15人，其中臺籍人士占7位，而在改制完成的省政府方面，臺籍人士占了四分之一，在16位行政首長中有4位臺籍人士，分掌警務、糧食、農林及衛生，相較於長官公署時期無臺人擔任首長的情形，有明顯的成長。

這些宣慰處理原則與改制政策雖然屬於善後措施，但是改革的方向與《三十二條處理大綱》精神卻是一致的，這證實了《三十二條處理大綱》作為二二八處委會的核心立場，是此一歷史事件中的重要民主成果，也為二二八處委會間接洗刷了污名。

■ 各地方處委會與青年團體代表之改革訴求

提案單位	提案日期	改革訴求
臺南市參議會	3月3日	一、要求警憲軍不得任意開槍並有挑撥民情之行動 二、要求專賣局貿易局即時廢止 三、要求即時解職無能不負責公務人員 四、負責辦理糧食問題 五、縣市長民選即時實施 六、省各處長及重要機關主管人員須要提拔省人 七、臺灣省接收公司、工廠移交省人主管辦理
臺中地區時局處理委員會	3月5日	一、刻日準備施行憲政，即時選舉省縣市鄉鎮長，實行完全省自治 二、即刻改組各級幹部，起用本省人才，協力建設臺灣 三、即刻開放官軍民糧倉，配給省民，以安定民食 四、廢止專賣制度，各種工廠交人民管理 五、確保司法獨立，肅清軍警暴行，尊重民權，保障人民七大自由（人身、言論、出版、思想、集會、結社、居住） 六、因二二八事件憤起之民眾行動，一切不得追及 七、平抑物價，救濟失業，安定民生
二二八處委會 新竹分會	3月5日	一、關於本事件公署要負全責 二、市縣長民選即時實施 三、公署秘書長由本省人選出，各處長及各重要幹部、法制委員會委員，半數以上應以本省人充之 四、一切公營事業改為民營 五、專賣事業、貿易局、宣傳委員會即時廢止 六、人民、言論、出版、結社、集會之自由 七、人生命財產之確保 八、緊急成立臺灣省經濟委員會，管理金融、物價、糧食問題 九、關於失業青年，緊急措施 十、學校師資改革
彰化縣田中地區青年同志	3月6日	一、要求二二八事件的意義作文宣明 二、本事件死亡的青年學徒及其他勇士要嘉獎，表現他們的（爭取民主精神的義士、自由平等平和的戰士）行為有最後的美 三、二二八事件之處理方法是實現臺灣自治政府，處委會不可落入老獪的外省人的策略，不可解散，要繼續努力 四、認識臺灣人民的特殊性 五、要求憲法的同時實施 六、要求行政長官制度的即刻廢止

提 案 單 位	提案日期	改 革 訴 求
彰化縣田中地區青年同志	3月6日	七、要求行政長官的即辭職 八、民主政治在憲法實施以前也要各自治團體的徹底改革 九、日常想昇官發財、榨油、無技術專門的外省公務員的排斥，官僚資本之絕滅，拒絕惡德商人之來臺 十、假借民生主義的美名，凡國營之事業獨占，反而釀成貪官汙吏，要求這制度廢止 十一、要求處理委員會之處理狀況，以廣播電台或各報紙以統一的正確明瞭公開報告 十二、要求某某機關的地下工作之名義之下，施暗黑政治與危險政治即刻廢止
二二八處委會宜蘭分會	3月6日	一、支持臺北處理委員會提出之建議事項 二、即時實施地方自治，省、縣、市長均由民選 三、平抑物價，救濟失業，安定民生 四、因二二八事件憤起行動之民眾均不得追究 五、擁護蔣主席建設新中華民國
二二八處委會臺南市分會	3月6日	一、軍警不得任意開槍及不可有挑釁行動 二、省縣市長即時民選 三、省公署各處長及重要機關起用省民 四、負責辦理糧食問題 五、即時廢止貿易局、專賣局，各公司、工廠重要位置起用省民 六、無能及不負責公務員即時解職 七、確實履行民意機關之決議 八、儘速分配公有土地，以救濟失業 九、各地方之治安，由各鄉鎮長、各村里長為中心而組織，挺身實行自警自衛
二二八處委會臺中市分會	3月7日	一、慰問此次事件死傷者 二、對治安隊表示敬意 三、促進回復治安及各機關照常辦公 四、成立臺中市政臨時委員會，以檢討過去之市府及檢舉貪官污吏，並協助目下工作中之本省人，選出各科課負責人，趕速開始市政 五、即刻實施市長民選，將速準備工作 六、希望市民有識階級，踴躍幫助市政

■ 各地方處委會派員參與全省性處委會情形

單位名稱	時　間	內　容
二二八處委會新竹分會	3月3日	推派代表參加全省性之處委會開會
彰化市善後處理委員會	3月5日	決議派代表呂世明等赴臺北出席會議
新竹二二八處委會	3月6日	派七名代表赴臺北參加會議，提出：縣市長民選、任用本省人士、廢除專賣事業及貿易局等要求
二二八處委會板橋分會	3月6日	決議派代表參與全省性之處委會，以促成重要要求儘速施行
二二八處委會臺中市分會	3月7日	派代表童炳輝赴臺北聯絡
二二八處委會宜蘭分會	3月7日	派游如川等代表赴臺北請願

■ 5-2 穩定社會秩序與解決民困

1. 維護社會治安與制止衝突

　　二二八事件爆發後，由於不滿行政長官公署開槍，各地紛傳毆人燬物的暴力事件，警察機關人員逃跑一空，為了維持治安、恢復秩序，二二八處委會一方面安撫民眾情緒，每日透過報刊及對民眾廣播等方式說明與官方談判進程，另一方面也通過決議，呼籲民眾不可毆打外省人而滋生事端。

　　在二二八處委會的內部組織中，維持治安是首要工作之一，而且處委會最初成立目的之一就是解決衝突、維持社會秩序。因此，除了臺北設有「忠義服務隊」之外，各縣市之處委會組織內均設有類似的保安隊、消防組、治安組等，此外，區、鄉、鎮層級的處委會事務相對單純，因此主要工作多集中於治安維護方面，例如板橋支會的治安組設有青年、學生兩隊，各里亦設有警衛隊等，而臺中、豐原、北斗、北門區、新營等處委會均設有保安組。

　　這些全省性及各縣市處委會所成立之治安維持組織，主要借重青年與學生之力，協助治安維護工作。例如，當時參與忠義服務隊的學生來自於臺灣商工（今開南商工）、臺北工業學校（今臺北科技大學）、法商學院（今臺大法商學院）、成功中學、延平大學、泰北中學、建國中學等學校學生，共計一千多人，共同協助治安維持，以及看守派出所避免遭人掠奪武裝等。

　　整體而言，除了嘉義、臺中等地區組織了武裝對抗團體，以及臺北之「忠義服務隊」遭情治單位滲透與利用，部分成員還被當作引發事端的暴徒而遭鎮壓外，各地之二二八處委會與其所設立之地方治安維護團體，不論是安撫民眾情緒、集中保護外省人、緩減對立、看管軍警槍械避免濫用、與地方軍政機關談判等，都有助於遏止暴亂蔓延，協助維護治安。

2. 調濟米荒與協調民生需求

　　1947年初，由於戰爭甫結束，民生凋敝，且戰爭末期的殖民政府物資轉移，以及國民政府接收官員貪汙腐敗、施政不當，甚至有官員盜賣物資案件層出不窮，此時的臺灣已成風雨飄搖之勢，許多縣市都陷入了民生物資困乏的問題，甚至爆發糧荒危機。而在事件發生後，社會局勢紊亂，多處交通受阻，更加重了糧食調濟運輸的困難。

　　為此，二二八處委會特地設置了糧食組，並委由簡檉堉、劉明朝等人任糧食委員，並要求糧食局長李連春到會報告米糧供應實際情形。此時，由於臺北需糧孔急，在工商銀行董事長黃朝琴提議下，處委會決議向工商銀支借購米資金二千萬元，另外，向糧食局領出二千萬元，以及臺北糧食協助會糧商自籌之一千萬元，共計五千萬元，由處委會派人前往南部採購米糧。

3月6日，臺北處委會派糧食組代表至彰化處委會接洽米糧及番薯籤等糧食調濟事宜，並向臺南新化米商購買米二十噸，以及向二水等處洽運糧食，總計共得米五十二噸，每日可供應米一至兩千包。此外，處委會也向農產公司領出糧食八百包，由松山酒廠撥出造酒米三千包，於士林購買糧食五百包，以及由糧食局撥出黃豆一萬包，以解燃眉之急，成為當時穩定民情的重要舉措。

各縣市地方處委會也多設有糧食組，除赴南部採購糧食，並平抑配售價格，將調濟、購買米糧作為重要協調工作。例如臺中處委會主張應開放官軍民糧倉進行配給，以安定民食；彰化處委會委由吳蘅秋、陳煥章等協議糧食對策；新竹處委會也派代表南下採購米糧，以應市民急需。另外，由於花蓮地區糧食問題嚴重，因此在當地處委會遭勒命解散後，仍舊組織糧食調濟委員會，並設有運輸、救濟、採購、募捐、配銷、總務等組。由此可見當時糧食問題之嚴重，以及處委會所肩負的重責大任。

在其他各項民生問題方面，處委會也協調了煤炭運市配售，臺灣省煤炭公會決議拋售煤炭一萬噸，以解決煤炭不足，協助民眾度過1947年初的寒冷氣候。此外，處委會也決議要求電力公司應持續穩定供電，向全省郵政機關發出通知，恢復郵訊工作，並請市民協助電信局員工修復故障電話等。另外，事件發生時，火車全線停駛，處委會委由運輸背景出身的國大代表簡文發負責協調鐵路交通，因而火車全線得於4日恢復通行。

從前述種種緊急措施可知，在事件期間，不論是物資調配、平抑物價，以及民生解困等方面，二二八處委會都扮演著關鍵性的角色。

臺灣廣播電台(今日之台北二二八紀念館)－二二八事件期間，不論是官方宣達政令，或是王添灯代表二二八處委會向全民廣播，這裡都是最關鍵的訊息傳播站

■ 5-3 臺灣民主自治的時代之聲

處委會與官方的初期談判係為訴求解決事件，主要內容為懲兇、撫卹、禁止軍警開槍、解除戒嚴等。此外，處委會也在安撫群眾情緒，調濟米糧，以及協助恢復交通、電力、郵政等方面進行努力，使得事端得以避免擴大，並化解衝突，各地秩序已逐漸恢復，僅剩等地區的武裝對抗衝突。

然而，緝煙血案僅是冰山一角，官方的態度並無法根本解決問題，在陳儀當局的統治下，臺灣的省政建設可謂千瘡百孔。因此，在社會各界的期待下，處委會通過了組織大綱，擴大改組為全省性的組織，在全省性之處委會外，其他十多個縣市也成立了以參議會為主體之地方處委會，這也讓處委會從解決衝突事件的救火隊，成為呼籲政治改革的民意機構。

由於歷經殖民地不平等待遇，使得臺人極為渴望自由平等與憲政民主，面對威權的公署體制，以及省參議會地位不清，淪為問詢機構，質詢提案的議決皆無法施行，此時全省性及各縣市之二二八處委會的成立，提供了彙整與傳達民眾訴求的重要管道，雖然各地處委會成立時間不長，但透過北上請願、提案、參與開會討論等方式，彼此得以迅速凝聚並達成一定共識，成為當時政治改革的發動機與民意傳聲筒。

二二八事件政治改革訴求（處委會所提三十二條處理大綱）

壹、對於目前的處理

1. 政府在各地之武裝部隊，應自動下令暫時解除武裝，武器交由各地處理委員會及憲兵隊共同保管，以免繼續發生流血衝突事件。
2. 政府武裝解除後，地方之治安由憲兵與非武裝之警察及民眾組織共同負責保護。
3. 各地若無政府武裝部隊威脅之時，絕對不應有武裝衝突，對於政府武裝部隊之行動，絕對不應加害而檢舉。

貳、根本處理

甲、軍事方面

1. 缺乏教育和訓練之軍隊絕對不可使駐台灣。
2. 中央可派員在台徵兵守台。

乙、政治方面

1. 制定省自治法，為本省政治最高規範，以便實現國父建國之遺教。
2. 縣市長於本年六月以前實施民選，縣市參議會同時改選。
3. 省各處長人選應經省參議會（改選後的省參議會）之同意，省參議會未成立前，由省府委員暫充。
4. 省各處長三分之二以上須由在本省居住十年以上者擔任之（最好由本省人擔任）。
5. 警務處長及各縣市警察局長應由本省人擔任，省警察大隊及鐵道工礦等警察即刻廢止。
6. 法制委員會委員數半數以上由本省人充任，主任委員由委員互選。
7. 除警察機關之外，不得逮捕人犯。
8. 憲兵除軍隊之犯人外，不得逮捕人犯。
9. 非武裝之集合結社絕對自由。
10. 言論、出版、罷工絕對自由，廢止新聞紙發行申請登記制度。
11. 即刻廢止人民團體組織條例。
12. 廢止民意機關選舉辦法。
13. 改進各級司法機關之人員，各級司法人員應儘量任用本省人。
14. 廢止專賣制度。
15. 一切公營事業之主管人由本省人擔任。
16. 設置民選之公營事業監察委員會，日產處理應委任省政府，並應儘量接收。生活必需品實施配給制度。
17. 撤銷專賣局，各接收工廠應委託省政府經營。
18. 撤銷貿易局。
19. 撤銷宣傳委員會。
20. 各地方法院院長、各地方法院首席檢察官全部以本省人充任。
21. 各法院推事、檢察官以下司法人員，各半數以上省民充任。

　　檢視前述各級處委會與相關組織所提出的改革訴求，可以發現無論在政治革新與經濟整頓層面，所提出來的理念都十分相近，除了對於當時事件的解決措施外，最主要的政治改革訴求包括：臺灣不是殖民地、廢除殖民體制長官公署、廢除經濟統制之專賣制度、立即實施憲政、制定省自治法、縣市長民選、廢除苛捐雜稅、保障人權自由、啟用臺人等。

　　彙整自前述各項政治訴求，最終由王添灯代表宣讀之《三十二條處理大綱》，不僅是由臺灣當時的各界菁英，以及多位瞭解省政弊端甚深的國大代表、參政員、省縣市參議員等共同決議通過，也高度整合了臺灣社會各界的心聲。因此，此一大綱的重要性不能從個別條文內容來臧否其意涵，必須將之視為一個整體，並回歸事件的歷史脈絡來理解。

　　惟有如此，方能瞭解《三十二條處理大綱》不僅是對當時省政弊端的具體改革訴求，更展現了半世紀以來臺灣人民一直努力不懈追求的民主自治理想，也是今日瞭解臺灣在民主憲政與地方自治荊棘道路上的歷史縮影。

■ 各級「二二八事件處理委員會」的組織運作及主要訴求

名　稱	主事者	內部組織	主要訴求／事件活動
二二八處委會全省總會（臺北）	王添灯、徐春卿等	以全體委員為最高機構，設有常務委員會，並選出七人主席團，下設秘書室；另設有政務局和處理局，其下分設交涉組、計畫組、財務組、糧食組、交通組、調查組、治安組、總務組等八組	3月1日「緝煙血案調查委員會」成立，並推派代表向長官公署提出五點要求，陳儀同意由官民共組委員會處理事件；3月2日改組為「二二八事件處理委員會」，長官公署派出五名官員代表參加；3月3日擴大納入商會、工會、學生、民眾與政治建設協會等五方代表；3月4日發展為全省性之組織；3月5日通過「政治改革八項綱領」及「處委會組織大綱」；3月6日發表「告全國同胞書」，選出十七名常務委員；3月7日通過《三十二條處理大綱》及十項要求，但為陳儀所拒；3月8日軍隊抵臺後，遭到鎮壓

名　　稱	主 事 者	內 部 組 織	主 要 訴 求／事 件 活 動
二二八處委會新竹市分會	張式穀、何乾欽等	設總務、政務、糧食、治安等部	3月2日成立；3月5日作出十項提案，並派員向全省性之處委會提出；3月6日，處委會人員南下購糧以解決米荒問題，並募徵經費、組織治安隊
二二八處委會員林分會	張清柳、林朝業、詹春泉等	設自衛隊	3月2日成立，以維持地方治安
臺中地區時局處理委員會	林獻堂、黃朝清等	設執行委員	3月4日由臺中仕紳成立「治安本部」，以牽制臺共謝雪紅主持的「臺中地區治安委員會作戰本部」；3月5日提出七項主張，並派員協助各機關照常辦公
彰化市善後處理委員會		設總務、警備、傳另、消防、治安、宣傳、情報、救護等組	3月3日成立，成員包括市長、警察局長及市參議會議員，與市府同一立場處理事件善後
嘉義三二事件處理委員會	陳復志、盧鎰、蘇憲章等	設防衛司令部、參謀本部、宣傳、總務、外務、宣傳、治安等部與各區保安隊	3月3日三青團嘉義分團召開市民大會，並組成「嘉義三二事件處理委員會」及防衛司令部，由分團主任陳復志擔任主委兼防衛司令
大甲時局處理委員會	吳淮澄、王萬傳、郭金焜等	設總務、治安、宣傳、救護、民生等組	3月3日成立
二二八處委會新營分會	陳華宗、沈昆山、吳榮輝等	設總務、聯絡、治安、糧食、救護、青年等組	3月3日成立
二二八處委會斗六分會	吳景徽等	設治安維持會	3月3日成立

二二八處委會基隆分會	黃樹水、楊元丁等	設總務、治安、宣慰、調查、善後、糧食等組	3月4日成立，要求政治改革，並解決糧食問題；3月8日獲增援之憲兵第四團兩個營與基隆要塞部隊開始鎮壓；3月9日陸軍二十一師增援部隊抵達，基隆傷亡慘重
二二八處委會宜蘭市會	郭章垣、黃再壽、陳金波等		3月4日成立，推舉代理市長，並派代表赴臺北請願；3月5日接管武器與維持治安秩序逐漸恢復；3月6日向全省性之處委會提出五項要求建議
二二八處委會臺東縣分會	陳振宗、吳金玉、邱英等	設總務、指揮、情報、治安、經濟、救護、消防、宣傳等組	3月4日成立，發生零星武裝衝突；3月7日處委會代表至電台廣播，縣府恢復上班
二二八處委會鳳林分會	林茂盛、陳長明等	設總務、指揮、情報、治安、經濟、救護、消防、宣傳等組	3月4日成立，組織青年維持治安
臺南縣北門區事變處理委員會	吳新榮等	設總務、糧食、宣傳、治安、聯絡、青年、救護等組	3月4日成立時局對策擴大委員會；3月5日更名為北門區事變處理委員會
二二八處委會花蓮分會	馬有岳、鄭東辛、鄭根井等	設總務、宣傳、交通、治安、糧食、調查、交涉等組	3月4日成立；3月5日提出十二項要求，由縣長張文成廣播公佈，秩序恢復
二二八處委會臺南市分會	韓石泉、黃百祿、侯全成等	設總務、治安、宣傳、糧食、聯絡及救護等組	3月5日成立，組織「臺南市治安協助委員會」，與市政府共同提出解決事件之四項原則
二二八處委會高雄市分會	彭清靠等	設治安、宣傳、糧食等組	3月5日成立
二二八處委會朴子鎮分會	黃媽典、黃慎言等	設總務、糧食、宣傳、治安、聯絡、救護等組	3月5日成立
二二八處委會屏東分會	葉秋木、張吉甫、黃聯登等	設政治、交涉、財政、救護、宣傳、警備、聯絡、糧食等組	3月6日成立，提出有關政治、軍事、經濟等十三項要求

二二八處委會澎湖分會	許整景等	設總務、宣傳、糧食、維持等組	3月6日成立
二二八處委會板橋支會	王以文、游石虎等	設總務、糧食、治安、財務、救護等組	3月6日成立，支持省處委會所提出八項政治改革方案，並派代表參與省處委會
二二八處委會新竹縣分會	黃運金等	設總務、治安、糧食等部	3月7日成立，募徵經費、組織治安隊
二二八處委會臺北縣分會			3月7日成立
豐原時局處理委員會	林碧梧、羅安等	設總務、調查宣傳、保安、運輸、救護等組	3月7日成立
二二八處委會臺南縣分會	陳華宗、楊瑞雲等		3月9日成立
二二八處委會淡水分會	陳玉光、楊三郎等		決議搶奪槍械
二二八處委會羅東分會	陳成岳等	設總務、宣傳、糧食、維持等組	維持地方治安
二二八處委會中壢分會	張阿滿、林煥榮等		
二二八處委會北斗分會	林伯餘、林文騰等	設總務、保安、宣傳等部	維持地方治安

- 資料來源：參考整理自《重探「二二八事件處理委員會」的角色》（侯坤宏，2013）與《派系鬥爭與權謀政治－二二八悲劇的另一面向》（陳翠蓮，1995）。
- 説　明：由於當時情勢緊迫，數日內事件變化快速，許多二二八處委會未留下完整文字紀錄或資料缺漏待補。此外，由於見諸文字的資料不少來自於當時官方檔案或報告，因此在資料運用上需謹慎判斷，避免誤導。

■ 附　錄：

　　隨著近年新史料逐步挖掘，許多當時的史實得以完整呈現，並讓人們瞭解臺民的處境與心聲。以最近從彰化市警察局與員林區警察所發掘的警察機關檔案為例，3月6日，彰化縣田中地區的一群有志青年共同連署，對於二二八事件提出了十二條政治改革建言，此一訴求經二二八處委會彰化分會議決，並由蘇振輝、石錫勳起草條文，內容如下：（()為刪減或錯別字或註解對照）

　　彰化田中青年同志十二條訴求：

第一條：要求二二八事件的意義作文宣明。
解　決：為以下各點發生本事件，所以不改革各點者，本事件的示威對抗，續行繼續。
　　　　又該當第二條的死亡者，我們要表明另意。
第二條：本事件死亡的青年學徒及其他勇士要嘉獎，表現他們的（爭取民主精神的義士
　　　　、自由平等平和的戰士）行為有最後的美。
第三條：二二八事件之處理方法是實現臺灣自治政府，處委會不可落入老獪的外省人的
　　　　策略，不可解散，要繼續努力。
第四條：認識臺灣人民的特殊性。
解　決：臺灣人民的特殊性；對人的方面觀，臺灣人民絕對（不願）犧牲自己，作外省人
　　　　的奴隸，也不是被詐取的愚民。臺灣人民是文明國民，也具有一等國民的資格。
第五條：要求憲法的同時實施。
解　決：臺灣不是殖民地，是有前條的資格，也有體得民主立憲精神的人民。
第六條：要求行政長官制度的即刻廢止。
解　決：臺灣人不是被榨取階級，如殖民地行政的總督的行政長官制度一定即刻廢止，
　　　　調派體得民主立憲精神臺灣省人省長，要求實行縣市以下憲政。
第七條：要求行政長官的即辭職。
解　決：負政治責任的行政長官及各處長即時辭職，對中央政府交涉政治改革。他們過去
　　　　對省民說民主立憲不能改革，他們是虛偽省民的傲慢不遜的獨裁者，所以要求本
　　　　條主旨的貫徹。

第八條：民主政治在憲法實施以前也要各自治團體的徹底改革。

解　決：要求地方自治團體及其他民意機關的再選舉，要求一掃光復後乘機抬頭的無力政治家。

第九條：日常想昇官發財、榨油、無技術專門的外省公務員的排斥，官僚資本之絕滅，拒絕惡德商人之來臺。

第十條：以蔭（假借）民生主義的美名，凡國營之事業獨占，返以（反而）釀成貪官汙吏，要求這制度廢止。

解　決：專賣局、貿易局、臺灣銀行及其他工廠等等之殖民地的機構，即時廢止其事業，以歸復名營企業。現臺灣銀行制度及其紙幣亂發，使物價暴騰以致民生生活不安定，要掃清官僚資本及金融元之性質「金圓券發行方式」，同時並擊退吸血浸骨的惡鬼。

第十一條：要求處理委員會之處理狀況，以廣播電臺或各報紙以統一的正確明瞭公開報告。

第十二條：要求某某機關的地下工作之名義之下，施暗黑政治與危險政治即「刻」廢止。

解　決：基於此名義，叫令為虎作賑（倀）之輩，同胞互相互剋，擾亂民主精神反動派之輩，加以絕滅。

The Analysis of the 228 Incident Settlement Committee：Standpoints, Roles and the Demonstration of its Historical Status

5-1 Rehabilitation : The Essence of the 228 Settlement Committee

The 32 Demands, proposed by the 228 Settlement Committee, were later demonstrated to be advisedly framed up by the Intelligence Agency, which purposely added 10 additional clauses of radical political demands and accordingly brought a false accusation of treason against what the authorizes later denounced as the 42 Evidences of Guilt. Furthermore, from a historical point of view, the essence of the original 32 Demands and the directions it proposed cohered extensively with the course of democratization of modern Taiwan. In short, the 32 Demands, as the principle of the 228 Settlement Committee, was a significant achievement of democracy that came into view from the 228 Incident, hence the rehabilitation of the 228 Settlement Committee was eventually concluded.

5-2 Maintaining and Restoring Social Order and Resolving the Burden of the People

During the 228 Incident, the 228 Settlement Committee had played a crucial role in resolving the burden of the people, including materials and goods distribution, inflation control, and livelihood improvement. In addition, the 228 Settlement Committee also aimed at maintaining and restoring social order and restraining the spreading of violent disorder by mitigating the public's anger, protecting the Mainlanders from irrational revenges, pacifying the conflicts, preventing firearms abuse, and negotiating and intervening with local military agency.

5-3 The Voice of Taiwan's Democratic Autonomy

The 32 Demands, drafted and proposed by Wang Tien-Teng, extensively integrated the aspirations coming from the entire Taiwanese society. The 32 Demands were later passed by people, the Taiwanese elites, National Assembly members, provincial senators, and county and city councilors, who were considerably aware of the political corruption of the Kuomintang government. The 32 Demands not only proposed substantial advices regarding government reforms, but also unfolded the Taiwanese forerunners' collective goal of democratic autonomy since the Japanese colonization.

第六章／指路明燈—戰後臺灣第一民主高峰會
The Beacon Light : Taiwan's First Summit for Democracy

第六章／指路明燈— 戰後臺灣第一民主高峰會
The Beacon Light : Taiwan's First Summit for Democracy

二二八事件是臺灣近代史上意義重大的歷史事件，而要探究二二八事件的本質，以及二二八處委會所採取的立場和所爭取的目標，首先必須看到，從殖民時期開始，新文化運動帶來的教育啟蒙，增進了民眾對法治與民主精神的逐漸認識，而臺灣地方自治聯盟的設立，標誌著臺灣的社會運動從早期民族主義的立場，逐漸轉為對民主體制的追求，使得推動政治體制改革、爭取臺灣地方自治權利，成為臺灣人民的普遍追求。

其次，也要瞭解，臺灣在歷經半世紀的殖民壓迫，以及戰後經濟凋敝與省政弊端叢生等背景下，臺灣社會的民意代表、各界菁英、仕紳階級、群眾團體等，不分層級、不分職業的廣泛參與二二八事件，而非少數人「煽動」所能引發。由此可知，此一事件，不僅是單一私菸取締問題，而牽涉到臺民對於國府接收後省政的不滿，更是延續臺灣民眾長期以來對於爭取地方自治的一貫主張。

因此，此一事件參與者的路線或立場或有不同，但是提出的訴求卻是相同的，而二二八事件最重要的民主成果，就是歷經多次政治協商，廣納各界民意，由處委會通過、王添灯代表宣讀之《三十二條處理大綱》。此一大綱並非僅是政治改革的臨時芻議，也絕非當時官方羅織的「反叛罪證」，當中展現了臺灣民主先進一直努力不懈

追求的民主自治理想，不僅引領時代之先，時至今日仍是國際社會民主潮流。

由此可知，二二八事件的核心價值，並非顛覆性的武裝對抗，而是訴求依憲法保障人民權利與自由的一場民主改革運動，釋放了臺灣人民追求民主自由的蓬勃熱情，也影響了今日臺灣社會對於民主精神的堅定捍衛，因此，二二八處委會可視為戰後臺灣人民爭取自治的第一場民主高峰會！

二二八事件後，臺灣人民亟欲擺脫殖民地的心聲才開始被正視。在1950年針對地方自治與縣市長民選的行政院會上，院長陳誠指出，「我們要瞭解本省人民的性格，就是要能說到做到，說了不做，或做得不實在，均易引起人民

王添灯代表二二八處委會向中外廣播的《三十二條大綱》，高度整合了臺灣社會各界的心聲，說明了二二八處委會的主要訴求在於改革政治弊端

的不良反響」，因此，在陳誠的強力背書之下，1950年10月25日臺灣完成了行政區劃，地方自治也得以逐步實施。此後，不論是義務教育、農村建設、土地改革、交通建設等方面，地方自治制度都發揮了重要的影響力，更成為臺灣近代民主化的重要基石。

百年回首，二二八事件如同其他臺灣歷史上波瀾壯闊的民主運動一樣，留給我們最大的資產，就是堅決反對貪腐的專制體制，努力不懈爭取民主與維護法治精神。從1895年日本殖民統治到1996總統首次民選，不論是爭取設置臺灣議會、廢除行政長官公署改設省政府、人民直接選舉、解除黨禁報禁、本土化政策、保障自由人權等，一再證明當年二二八處委會的民主先賢不僅是善盡言責，更是指引臺灣朝向民主化的一盞明燈。

解嚴後，政府開始反省與平反二二八事件，對於受難者或其家屬頒發回復名譽證書，二二八處委會成員終於從當年被羅織的「叛亂」罪名，洗刷冤屈、恢復名譽。2001年，在臺北二二八紀念館入口大廳裡，豎立起了《三十二條處理大綱》銅匾及宣讀者王添灯的銅像，讓今日的參觀民眾得以重新看見二二八處委會民主賢們的身影，並見證67年前那個撼動人心的歷史時刻。

1. 2001年，王添灯塑像落成揭幕，家人終於能夠再睹其容顏
2. 二二八受難者王添灯回復名譽證書
3. 佇立於台北二二八紀念館大廳的王添灯塑像

《三十二條處理大綱》與臺灣近代民主政治發展

	《三十二條處理大綱》	臺灣民主政治發展
宗 旨	《三十二條處理大綱》宗旨為團結全省人民、改革政治及處理二二八事件	《中華民國憲法》之訂定，係為鞏固國權，保障民權，奠定社會安寧，增進人民福利
直接選舉與地方自治	■ 改專制之行政長官公署制度為省政府 ■ 縣市長於1947年六月以前實施民選，縣市參議會同時改選 ■ 制定省自治法，為本省政治最高規範，以便實現國父建國大綱之理想 ■ 省各處長人選應經省參議會(改選後為省議會)之同意廢止民意機關選舉辦法	■ 1950年全面實施地方自治，1951年在戒嚴體制下開辦縣市長選舉 ■ 1972年，第一次中央民意代表增額選舉 ■ 1987年，宣佈解嚴，開放黨禁與報禁 ■ 1991年，終止動員戡亂時期、廢止臨時條款 ■ 1992年，第二屆立法委員選舉，國會全面改選 ■ 1994年，臺灣省長、臺北及高雄直轄市長直接民選 ■ 1996年，總統直接民選
善用臺籍人才與澄清吏治	■ 省各廳處長三分之二以上須由在本省居住十年以上者擔任之(最好秘書長、民政、財政、工礦、農林、教育、警務等處長應該如是) ■ 警務處長及各縣市警察局長應由本省人擔任，省警察大隊及鐵道工礦等警察即刻廢止 ■ 法制委員會委員數半數以上由本省人充任，主任委員由委員互選 ■ 一切公營事業之主管人由本省人擔任 ■ 各地方法院院長、各地方法院首席檢察官全部以本省人充任 ■ 各法院推事、檢察官以下司法人員各半數以上省民充任	■ 1972年，蔣經國出任行政院長，大量拔擢臺籍青年才俊，推行本土化政策 ■ 1992年起，政府陸續修訂《貪污治罪條例》，並訂頒「公職人員財產申報法」、「公職人員利益衝突迴避法」、「政治獻金法」等陽光法案，以杜絕貪污，澄清吏治

| 人民基本權利 | ■ 非武裝之集合結社絕對自由
■ 言論、出版、罷工絕對自由
■ 即刻廢止人民團體組織條例
■ 除警察機關之外，不得逮捕人犯憲兵除軍隊之犯人外，不得逮捕人犯
■ 禁止帶有政治性之逮捕拘禁 | ■ 憲法第8條規定，人民身體之自由應予保障，除現行犯外，非經司法或警察機關依法定程序，不得逮捕拘禁
■ 1992年，通過修正刑法100條，取消「陰謀內亂罪」及「言論內亂罪」，同年，修訂《人民團體法》，讓臺灣的言論與結社自由獲更進一步保障
■ 1993年，《警察職權行使法》公布，規範警察依法行使職權，以保障人民權益
■ 2009年，簽署「公民與政治權利國際公約」及「經濟社會文化權利國際公約」批准書，送聯合國存放，以進一步保障民權 |

The Beacon Light : Taiwan's First Summit for Democracy

The 228 Incident was a significant event in Taiwanese modern history. To probe to the essence of 228 Incident, plus position and goal of 288 Incident Settlement Committee, it is necessary to realize the educational enlightenment of Taiwnese New Culture Movement during Japanese Colonial period. The public had developed attention to the spirit of the rule of law and democracy. In addition, the founding of Taiwan Local Self-Government League represented Taiwan's social movement had turned to pursue a democratic system. Thus, reforming political system and fighting for self-government right had become common goals among Taiwanese people.

Furthermore, we have to understand that Taiwan had been through half-century oppression under colonization. Based on the context of postwar economic depression and of massive corruption of provincial government, almost all level of social classes in Taiwan got involved with the 228 Incident. Only a few people couldn't evolve it. Therefore, this Incident must not only about banning smuggled cigarettes. This is because Taiwanese were very resentful of political corruption as well as kept fighting for local self-governance for a long time.

In this Incident, participants might have different approaches or standpoints; however, they have a common goal. The most significant democratic result of the 228 Incident is the "32 Demands."- after numerous political negotiations and public consultation, and passed by the committee, and announced by the representative Wang Tien-Teng. These demands were not merely temporary political claims for rebellion that declared by government. It not only shows the ideals of Taiwanese democratic pioneers' pursue-democratic self-governance-for all the time but also leads the way for the future generation.

Thus it could be seen: the core value of the 228 Incident was not to overthrow the authority, instead, it　was a democratic reformation movement of pursuing people's rights and freedom in the name of the constitution. The movement releases the passion of seeking democracy and freedom in Taiwanese people's mind and affects peoples's belief of defending democratic spirit in Taiwanese society nowadays. Overall, the 228 Incident Settlement Committee could be regarded as the first democratic summit of fighting for self-governance.

The truth is that Taiwanese were desperate to get rid of the status as colonial impression had not been taken seriously until the 228 Incident. In 1950, on the assembly that focused on the topic of local self-governance and of election of counties and cities, the speaker Chen Cheng pointed out that, "We understand the personality of our people. We have to keep our promises. If we break our promises or make them unfaithfully, people would have negative feedbacks." Moreover, administrative division had been passed in Taiwan with Chen Cheng's endorsement. Local self-governance was finally implemented gradually. After that, including compulsory education, countryside construction, land reform, and traffic construction, local self-governance system brought positive impacts on them and built a solid foundation for Taiwan's modern democratization.

Look back at the past century, the 228 Incident, like many other monumental democratic movements, its legacy is to fight firmly against corruptiive and autocratic government and to strive for democracy and to protect the spirit of rule by law. From 1895 (Japanese-Colonial Period) to 1996 (first time of direct election of President), many democratic events have happened, such as setting up Taiwan's Congress, abolishment of Taiwan provincial administrative executive office, establishment of Provincial Government, direct election, lifting the ban on newspaper publications or political parties, localization policy, protection of human rights, etc. By reviewing through these, it is clear that the 228 Incident Settlement Committee fully well implemented their responsibilities and played as a beacon light to show the way toward Taiwan's democratization.

After abolishment of the martial law, the government started to introspect and redress miscarriage of justice of the 228 Incident and rendered Honor Recovery Certificate to victims and their family members. The 228 Incident Settlement Committee members were finally redressed. On 2001, the "32 Demands" inscribed board and the statue of the representative Wang Tien-Teng were set up in the front hall of Taipei 228 Memorial Museum and to make the public rediscover the accomplishments of these democratic pioneers and witness the cirtical moment 68 years ago.

Taiwan's first session of the Taiwan Provincial Consultative Council on 1st May, 1946 (back row, 3rd from the right is Hahn Shyr-Chyuan, 7th from the right is Wang Tien-Teng)

人民導報 大明報 [illegible]是日報
臺北市民報 中外日報 重建日報
經濟日報 工商日報
上海大公報 新聞報 駐臺灣辦事處
臺灣 一同

號外

（民國三十六年三月二日下午八時）

此次省垣發生不幸事件，本省[illegible]職工[illegible]，進行[illegible]交通阻隔，消息隔絕，未能照常出報，殊為歉疚，本日戒嚴令業已解除，而市面秩序未甚恢復常態，本報記者[illegible]聯合[illegible]，[illegible]情形與讀民眾之瞭述，並站[illegible]輿論界之立場，向長官公署建議數項：

一，受傷者迅由各醫院收容治療，費用由政府負擔

二，傷亡及失蹤[illegible]集中報告於市政府俾便訪問調查

三，軍警巡邏隊即撤銷，並不必全列武裝以安人心

四，即時恢復交通「鐵路由國大代表簡文發氏負責」

五，食米即運市內供應民家

六，關于公案死者由政府撫卹

七，被捕民眾[illegible]交憲兵隊負責辦理保釋手續並將被捕者名單列後

鄭	[illegible]途	二十三	古亭町板溪里三二二番
吳	祖業	二十五	建成町三ノ三
[illegible]	靖熙	二十二	[illegible]里一五一
陳	茂生	三十四	新[illegible]新埔鎮三四四
鄭	天財	二二	古亭町一四一
張	火成	二八	樺山町一〇一
李	仍鴻	二〇	三張犁[illegible]景里圍六〇
周	途	二二	臺北市中[illegible]二〇九
許	兩全	一八	富田町三二六
李	添丁	一三	古亭町二四〇
陳	天和	二二	[illegible]町二ノ十一

特展開幕紀實與展場紀錄
Documentation of the Opening and the Exhibition

2014/8/21

特展開幕與展場紀錄 *2014/8/21*
Documentation of the Opening and the Exhibition

臺北市政府文化局主任秘書—李麗珠致詞

　　大家好，剛剛我們的館長跟黃老師已經一一的介紹今天出席的各位，我們的一些前輩、先進、還有受難者的家屬、以及很多位的老師，所以我想我就不逐一的跟各位唱名。首先，我代表臺北市文化局，因為我們劉局長剛好今天出國，所以由我來代表，歡迎大家出席今天紀念特展的開幕典禮。

　　二二八事件是我們臺灣最重要的歷史事件，臺北市政府為了紀念此一事件，所以成立了台北二二八紀念館。大家應該在二二八紀念館入口大廳，看到有呈現一個處理委員會當時撰寫的三十二條處理大綱的銅片，以及當時撰寫大綱的一位重要人士，王添灯先生，那時候撰寫時的一個塑像在那邊，剛剛我也特別又再進去感受了一下，真的彷彿我們重現了當時在67年前，那時候這些委員、先賢們為了我們大家、市民等等，為民喉舌，以及當時的一個服務奉獻的場景跟精神，讓我非常的敬佩。

　　王先生當時就在我們台北二二八紀念館，也就是當時的臺灣廣播電臺，對外宣讀了《三十二條處理大綱》，很多對於改革的主張、理念等等，逐一都在裡面，大家等下可以再去參觀。臺北市政府文化局為了將這樣一個事件的歷史以及《三十二條處理大綱》的歷史呈現出來，能夠讓市民更進一步的了解，所以我們特別舉辦了這次的紀念特展。

　　另外也跟各位報告一下，這次的展覽特別請謝英從館長把二二八紀念館裡最重要的館藏品，也就是當時在二二八事件發生的時候，很多的報章媒體所發行的號外等等一些刊出的物件，也會在這次的展覽裡特別的呈現，我想這是非常有意義的，也可以了解對我們臺灣民主的一些影響等等。

　　另外還有會把像王先生的懷錶，或者當時處理委員會的一些遺物、照片、書籍，在這次展覽裡同時呈現出來，我覺得這個是非常的珍貴也很難得，能夠在這次展覽裡面一併讓市民更深入的了解整個二二八事件，尤其是《三十二條處理大綱》當時的一些主張跟改革，對地方自治的影響等等，我想這是很重要的。

　　最後在這也謝謝剛剛提到的好幾位先進、前輩、以及黃秀婉老師、侯處長，還有我們各位前輩，給我們的展覽很多的指導與協助，讓我們能夠如期的展出。也在這裏預祝我們展覽能夠很圓滿順利，謝謝大家今天來出席，最後祝福大家平安幸福、健康快樂。

二二八處委會宣傳組組長王添灯先生長孫
　　　— 王贊紘致詞

　　今天非常謝謝主辦單位邀請我來，講一下二二八處理委員會的特展，對於二二處理委員會的一些事情。這個事情是發生在67年前，首先我想帶各位回到當時的狀況，二二八事件是發生在臺灣，但是他跟當時大陸的政權是有不可分割的關係，如果各位回去查一下歷史，我們可以發現到中華民國的憲法，是在1947年1月1號發佈，在1947年12月25號實施，也就是說在二二八事件發生的1947年那個時候，我們是處在所謂的國民政府的訓政時期。

　　那國民政府是怎麼來的？國民政府是從北伐以後的國民軍政府，然後變成國民政府，這個國民政府是由中國國民黨一手主持，也就是說在那個時間點，是處於一個中國國民黨的一黨專政的時期，相當於類似今天的中華人民共和國處於中國共產黨一黨專政的時期。這兩個政權在當時的時間跟在今天的中國來比較有一點差異，就是中華人民共和國除了政府的一黨專政以外，它設立的機構叫做政協（政治協商會議），在當時中國國民黨需要協商的時候，就是用國民大會來做一個協商機制。

　　簡單的說二二八事件的發生，跟中國國民黨是有不可分割的關係，我個人到今天還是有一個希望，我不知道中國國民黨的黨史裡面，寫二二八事件是怎麼寫的，但是我還是要提醒各位，當時中國國民黨對中國統治時採取一種政策，所有各省的省主席，包括臺灣省的行政長官公署都是由中國國民黨派任。在這個政治的架構底下，臺灣成立了一個叫做臺灣省政府參政會，它是一個民意的機構，作為與國民政府交通的橋樑，以及監督國民政府所做的一些行為。

二二八事變發生以後，臺灣的民意代表，包括參政議員或是當時國民黨出來的國民代表…等等，跟陳儀做一個協商，陳儀行政長官公署同意成立一個叫做二二八調查委員會，這個會是在政府機構同意下跟民意代表所一起產生的，以臺灣一個簡單的比喻來講，就是政府跟人民發生了衝突，我們組了一個委員會來做「公親(居中協調的人)」來調查這件事情。這個委員會正式開會是在3月3號，被行政長官公署下令解散是3月11號，所以前後只有9天的時間。很不幸的這個委員會由公親的角色，我們簡單的講就是說公親變成事主，它變成被歸類一個違法的機構，所以它原先的角色是希望協調民眾與政府之間的衝突，希望能夠化解、給政府做一個建議怎麼解決這個問題，可是在3月11號以後它變成是一個，應該講說當時認為是一個叛亂團體，這個是一個很奇妙的轉變。

3月3號開始以後有一些少數的民意代表做為主幹，隨著日子的演變，這一個委員會加入了相當多數當時在臺灣活耀的政治團體、公民團體、商業會、公會、學生通通加進去了，所以你如果說這個會是一個大雜燴那也不為過，但是你也可以說這一個會是聚集了臺灣所有的民意，它有一個非常大的代表性，因為各派人馬都在裡面。在這個從1945年的戰爭結束到1947年，兩年的時間，如果各位看以後的民主發展，我今天必須要說，這兩年臺灣的民主政治是急速的發展，非常非常快速，它這個會議所產生的效益，可以說從1949年到今天是最高的效益，而且從這麼多這麼複雜的各個派系的角力、各個不同組織的角力底下，取得了一個32條的共識，是一個非常有效率的組織。我想各位如果跟今天的立法院來比較，很難在9天、10天之中，能夠取得這麼大的一個共識，這個也是臺灣從光復以後，第一個全省性的會議，所以我想主辦單位定的標題是非常的好，這是一個臺灣的、民主的高峰會議，也展現出雖然在各個不同領域有不同的意見，但是這32條的共識是大家的共識。

這個委員會所做的貢獻在民主的歷史上來說，我想應該占了一席非常重要的地位，所以我之前也講過，我說二二八事件是臺灣民主運動的啟蒙事件，那這個會議是一個非常好的典範的一個結論，有這麼多黨派在裡面，包括親國民黨的、親共產黨的、商業的利益、公會的利益、學生團體的意見，都能夠整合成一個非常具體的32條，給做為執政者的一個參考。

　　當然我祖父在這32條裡面下了非常大的功夫，他在3月7號，也是就在這邊的電臺做了最後一個廣播，他所講的最後一句話是說：「二二八事件調查委員會，能夠做的就到這裡為止，能夠跟政府做的建議、跟臺灣老百姓做的建議就到此為止，剩下的就看各位臺灣的百姓怎麼處理這件事情。」我想這句話到今天還是成立，臺灣未來的前途、臺灣怎麼走下去，這件事還是需要看臺灣老百姓的智慧，我們臺灣的前途也應該由臺灣人民來做一個決定，到底臺灣該何去何從，未來我們希望有什麼樣的改革，我們希望有什麼樣的路，除了所有的競選員提出的建議藍圖以外，我們也應該督促政府應該怎麼做。

　　這個時候我認為應該回到一件事情，我也不相信人民的權利是天生的，我相信任何一個執政者都有他自己的想法，我們作為一個老百姓，不可能天天等待一個親民的政府，今天臺灣是一個民主政治的國家，人民是政府的組員，所有權利的爭取應該是靠全民參與，我們應該掌握我們自己的未來。

　　我話講到這邊，我想各位一定可以看得到，在這個展覽會場裡面有許多資料，告訴你說在當時是一個非常混亂的一個狀況，有各個不同擁護、各個不同主義的人，但是透過民主的制度、民主的機構讓它產生了一個共識，這個對臺灣的民主歷史是非常珍貴的，希望各位能夠好好的看一下，然後再去思考我們臺灣應該何去何從，謝謝各位。

臺南市二二八處委會主任委員韓石泉醫師公子
　　　　　—韓良俊致詞

　　主持人謝館長、臺北市文化局李主秘，各位貴賓、各位女士、先生早安！大家好！能夠受邀參加這一很有意義之特展的開幕式，我感到非常榮幸。

　　整整67年前發生的二二八事件中，臺灣省和各縣市的二二八事件處理委員會為維持秩序，並向官方爭取民眾的安全和民主、自治權益，曾做了很大、很多的努力。當時先父第一屆臺灣省參議員韓石泉醫師，曾於3月3日以揹負十字架的決心，接受臺南市長卓高煊和臺南市參議會黃百祿議長懇託，出面協助維護臺南市安寧時，即向卓市長提示和平處理四大原則，即：一、不擴大，二、不流血，三、不否認現有行政機構，四、政治問題用政治方法解決。

　　隔日3月4日上午八時，更與臺南市參議會議長黃百祿、參議員侯全成、高壽齡和民間人士臺南興文齋書局負責人林占鰲、中學教師李國澤等確認此四大原則，並馬上開始分頭勸導學生、民眾，請其切勿輕舉妄動，以免發生危險及不利事故。

　　其後數天，靠此四大原則，才能穩住臺南市，而使得臺南市在事件動亂當中，民眾的死傷是臺灣各大縣市中最少的。但之後的四十年間，這一和平的理念、價值竟完全遭到遺忘，幾無人提及，甚至遭到誤解。直到1987年2月13日，才又有陳永興、李勝雄和鄭南榕等人組成「二二八和平日促進會」，呼籲公佈真相、平反冤屈，發表「二二八和平日宣言」，展開二二八平反運動。

　　時至今日，一談到「二二八」，大家都會聯想到「和平」兩字，如「二二八和平日」、「二二八和平公園」、「二二八公義和平運動」等，因為和平已是全世界公認的普世價值，就連這台北二二八紀念館右前方樹蔭下，也立有一個漆成白色的木柱，上面有中(正體、簡體)、英、日共四種文字，如：「期望世界人類和平」、"May Peace Prevail On Earth"、「世界人類が平和でありますように」等。那麼，在事件大動亂當時的二二八事件處理委員會臺南市分會，從主任委員韓石泉醫師到多位成員，在那瞬息萬變、極度危險的關鍵時刻，就早已勇敢地主張、堅守並付諸實行的，這愛與非暴力的和平原則，今後是否在臺灣史中更該受到遲來的、應有的肯定與重視？

　　希望大家在參觀今天開始的特展之同時，也能一起思考這一個嚴肅的問題。

附錄：在2014年8月21日開幕（為期三個月）的「台灣民主高峰會—二二八處理委員會紀念特展」中，全國首度公開展出台北二二八紀念館館藏的，1947年3月7日《台灣新生報》報頁原件，其第一版有一則大標題的新聞是：「臺南市處理會成立 - 席上各界代表熱烈提供意見」。這則新聞的最後，接著有一則「又訊」。其原文完整內容照抄如下（原件參照 p109、p148）：

[又訊]臺南市於六日下午一時半，舉行學生遊行，是日全市中等以上男女學生全體參加，由韓省參議員，黃市參議會議長等引導下，工學院學生為先導，一齊步武堂堂，對社會及政府表示學生們之熱烈意氣，與神聖態度。（韓註：他們在遊行中手持的標語，以當年時、空之言論限制尺度而言，既敏感、又大膽敢言，如「確定民主政治」、「改革本省腐敗政治」、「促進地方自治之實施」、「建設新台灣」。雖然如此，最後幸賴韓石泉省參議員、黃百祿議長等和平誘導、維持秩序、因勢利導之功，在市內走完全程後，終告和平落幕，沒有發生任何暴力衝突。以上的「又訊」，是臺灣史上第一次，學生上街頭和平理性的遊行之最原始、真實紀錄。）

發行人 李萬居

社址 臺北市武昌街四段九十九號 十二號

電報掛號 二四五〇 中英文交

SIN SEN PO

社長室 二七一一號
編輯部 三〇二三號
總務處 二六一七號
營業部 二七一二號
營業部 二六五二號
新生印刷廠 二〇九六號

電話

本報日小半張

每月預售 一百元 四元

二二八事件處理委會

正式選出常務委員

派員監理臺灣銀行業

煤炭千噸運市廉價

【本報訊】臺灣省二·二八事件處理委員會，昨（六）日下午於中山堂補開正式成立大會，出席委員及民眾旁聽二百餘人，主席王添灯報告宣讀情形，即選舉常務委員，其名單如次：

到會報告宣讀情形

省參議員 王添灯、黃朝琴、黃純青、蘇維梁、林為恭、郭國基

國民參政員 林獻堂、陳逸松

國民大會代表 李萬居、連震東、黃國書

臺北市參議員 周延壽、潘渠源、簡檉堉、徐春卿、吳春霖

委員 洪火煉、吳國信，名單發表後，王添灯宣讀向中央及全國廣播真相，全文及事件處理經過，該文將以國語、閩南語、客語、英語

【本報訊】二、二八事件處理委員會宣傳組發表：（一）煤炭派員監理臺灣銀行，至五時許閉會云云。

價格以二月二十八日以前減百分之三十。（二）電話公司派員監理，並由象要加以保護。

宋子文
卜居滬濱

【中央社南京六日電】前任行政院長宋子文，六日晨十時乘蔣主席之美齡號專機飛滬，聞宋氏今後將居滬。

隊長二名。

第四條：同志之年齡，不論老幼，凡參加本同盟

開放糧倉以
尊重人民

監院關懷臺北情勢
電令楊亮功即來臺

【中央社南京四日電】臺北人民發生紛擾，並有死傷情勢，頗為嚴重，監察院聞訊，即電令閩臺監察使楊亮功，即日前往查辦。

六日上午十一時假市參議會議廳，召開第一次委員會，並擬討論此後工作方針，並提完強化各組織，組長各委員，欽市參議會議員等引導，提出關於各組當面重要任務及問題，然烈烈當意見下，工商院學生為先導，一齊步武登堂，對社會及政府表示歡生們之熱烈寫集，與神聖態度。

【文訊】臺南市於六日舉行學生遊行，是日全市中等以上男女學生全體參加，由韓省參議員下午一時始散會。

自治青年同盟
召開幹部會議

【本報臺中六日電訊】臺中地區二二八處理委員會，於三月五日下午四時，召開會議，討論結果，決議事項民權，保障

臺中處委

監察使楊亮功，即日前往查辦。
有死傷情勢，頗為嚴重，監察院聞訊，即電令閩臺

我们祝愿世界人类的和平

期望世界人類和平

May Peace Prevail On Earth

台北二二八紀念館建築物的左側壁上，貼有「臺
灣民主高峰會─二二八事件處理委員會特展」
(103/8/21-103/11/21)的大幅布幕廣告；照片右
下角大樹下可見寫有和平標語的白色木柱

站在台北二二八紀念館與白色木柱中間觀
看後者的兩面文字，寫的是日文和簡體字
中文的和平標語

國史館纂修兼修纂處處長—侯坤宏致詞

　　李主任秘書、謝館長，還有在座的各位朋友大家好。我剛剛是從長沙街辦公室走過來的，我在國史館已經服務了二十幾年，個人對於二二八持續關注，二二八史是我的研究領域裡面一個重要的部分。為什麼今天我會站在這裡，因為去年我曾經參加有關二二八檔案最後一批，至少我們所可以掌握的最後一批，還沒有完全對外公布檔案的解讀，就在中央研究院臺灣史研究所，去年我們在那裏舉辦了一個會議，我是以二二八事件處理委員會做為一個研究的題目，這次的展覽主題剛好就是二二八事件處理委員會，在展覽之前整個文案我已經都看過了，覺得寫得相當的平實、相當的不錯。

　　大家看過整個主題把它定位為臺灣民主高峰會，這樣的一個定位其實是需要進一步的理解。臺灣的整個政治民主運動其實是最近幾年比較有發展，如果要理解二二八事件處理委員會，為它做一個歷史定位，我們可以這麼說，戰後初期的二二八處理委員會具有一個民主高峰會的一個雛形，可惜後來沒有完全的發展成熟，而且在事件後，參與這些高峰會的人都被遭到追殺或者政治迫害。依個人研究，當時二二八事件處理委員會，除了在中山堂的總會外，其實在各省，有縣市層級的、也有鄉鎮層級的處理委員會，那我初步統計了一下大約有27個，參與處委會的這些人，可以說是當時臺灣政治的一批菁英份子，後來的下場我們都非常不幸。

　　今天我們在這裡辦這樣的一個展覽，我們要認定說這樣的一個展覽我們的意義是在哪裡。博物館的一個功能其實就是在推廣社會教育，站在這樣的一個立場、或者站在我們現在臺灣整個政治發展的一個脈絡來講，怎麼樣讓我們的社會大眾能夠走進這個博物館，透過這樣的一個展覽來了解當年所發生的這樣的一段不幸的歷史，做為我們思考未來如何發展的一個起點。

希望我們這次的展覽能夠順利成功，有很多人能夠走進這個一個展覽的場地，能夠了解到過去這段不幸歷史的一些遭遇、一些情況，透過這樣的展覽，為未來臺灣的民主發展能夠提供一些貢獻。在此，預祝展出成功，祝福大家身體健康，家庭和樂美滿，謝謝！

台北二二八紀念館 謝英從館長為與會貴賓介紹首次展出之重要館藏－二二八事件當時號外

臺灣民主高峰會
二二八事件處理委員會紀念特展

Taiwan Summit for Democr
——— The 228 Settlement Comm

臺北市政府文化局主任秘書李麗珠（左一）、臺南二二八處委會主任委員韓石泉醫生公子韓良俊（左二）、二二八處委會發言人王添灯先生之長孫王贊紘（右二）、台北二二八紀念館館長謝英從（右一）與首次展出之重要館藏－二二八事件當時號外合影留念

Chief Secretary of the Taipei City Cultural Affairs Department Director - Lee Li-Chu

Hello everyone, our curator and the presenter Mrs. Huang have already introduced all of today's guests one by one, some of our predecessors, seniors, as well as families of the victims, and a number of teachers, so I guess I won't do a roll call.

First of all, I am representing the Taipei City Cultural Affairs Department, because our director Liu just went abroad today, so I came as a representative. Welcome everyone to our Memorial Exhibition opening ceremony.

This 228 Incident is Taiwan's most important historical event and I believe that the Taipei City government in order to commemorate this event and to establish this 228 Memorial Hall. In our 228 Memorial entrance hall, everyone should be able to see the bronze plaque of the 32 Demands composed by the 228 Incident Settlement Committee as well as the important advocatorwho composed the Demands, Wang Tien-Teng. The statue of him at the time of composition is over there, and just now it made me feel like I had gone back a little bit. It really seemed as if we had returned to that time 67 years ago, when the committee members, those sages who for all citizens, became the spokesmen of the people. It is a picture and spirit of sacrificial service, and I admire them greatly.

Mr. Wang was in our Taipei 228 Memorial Museum which was the Taiwan radio broadcasting station at that time. His reading of the 32 Demands, and the many ideas and concepts about reform are all presented in the exhibition. I sincerely invite everyone to enjoy the show.

The Taipei City Government Department of Cultural Affairs, in order to present the importance of this historical event as well as the 32 Demands, and to help the public gain a better understanding of them, held this special Memorial Exhibition.

In addition I would like to inform everyone that this exhibition presents the most important documents of the 228 Memorial Museum from the time of the 228 Incident, such as the many published special edition newspapers and periodicals. I believe this is very meaningful for you to learn about their impact on our Taiwanese democracy.

Additionally, we will also be displaying Mr. Wang's pocket watch and also many artifacts, pictures, and books, from the 228 Incident Settlement Committee. I think it is really precious and rare to be able in this exhibition to join this with giving the citizens a deeper understanding of the whole 228 Incident, especially the reforms and ideas of the 32 Demands, about some of the influence for a local self-government and so on. I think this is really important.

Finally, here I would also like to thank the several just mentioned seniors, predecessors, as well as Mrs. Huang, director of the Academia Historica Editor and Compilation Department - Hou Kun-Hung, and all of our elders who gave our exhibition a lot of guidance and assistance, allowing us to be able to hold the exhibition on time. Also here I want to wish our exhibition to be smooth and successful. Everyone, thank you for coming out to the exhibition, and finally I wish everyone peace, happiness, health and joy.

228 Incident Settlement Committee Publicity Chief Wang Tien-Teng's eldest grandson – Wang Zan-Hong

Today I'm very thankful to the organizers for inviting me to come and speak a bit about the exhibition of the 228 Incident Settlement Committee and some matters related to them. The Incident occurred 67 years ago, and first I would like to take everyone back to the situation of that time. The 228 Incident happened in Taiwan, but it has an inseparable connection with the political regime of the mainland at that time. If everyone went and checked their history we would discover the Constitution of the Republic of China was written on January 1, 1947 and implemented on December 25, 1947. In other words, during the year of 1947, the time of the 228 Incident's occurrence, we were in the Republic of China's so-called period of political tutelage.

So how did the Nationalist government come about? The Nationalist government came after the national junta from China and afterwards it became the Republic of China. The R.O.C. was single-handedly held by the Nationalist Party-Kuomintang. That is to say that during the early period of the R.O.C. it was a one party dictatorship by the Nationalist Party. It is similar to the state of today's People's Republic of China being in a one-party dictatorship of the Communist Party. There are some comparative differences between these two regimes at that time and with those of today's China. In addition to the PRC's one-party dictatorship, they had established an organization called the CPPCC (Chinese People's Political Consultative Conference), during the time the Kuomintang needed to negotiate, and it used the National Assembly as a consultative mechanism.

To put it simply the occurrence of the 228 Incident, and the Kuomintang have an inseparable connection. Personally, even today I still have a hope, I don't know the internal history of the Kuomintang, or how the 228 Incident is recorded, but I still want to remind everyone. At that time the Kuomintang adopted a policy for ruling China that the chairman of every province, including the Taiwan Provincial Administrative Executive Office must be held by a Kuomintang member. Within this political framework, Taiwan set up a program called the Taiwan Provincial Government's Political Council, which was a public institution that acted as a communication bridge with the Nationalist government, as well as a monitor of the Nationalist government's actions.

After the 228 Incident, Taiwan's elected officials and political participants consulted with Chen Yi and Chen Yi's Administrative Executive Office agreed to set up a committee called the 228 Incident Settlement Committee. This committee was created in agreement with both the political framework and the elected officials. To use a simple Taiwanese analogy, the government and people had a conflict, so we formed a committee to be "the mediator" and investigate this Incident. This committee officially began on March 3, and was ordered to disband by the Chief Executive Office on March 11 and so from beginning to end was only nine days of time. Unfortunately, because this committee played the role of mediator it also turned into the victim, becoming classified as an illegal institution. In its original role it had hoped to harmonize the conflicts between the public and the government, to bring resolution, to give the government a recommendation on how to resolve this problem, but after March 11th, it became regarded as a rebel group. It was an strange development.

Beginning after the unfolding developments of March 3rd, there was a small core group of officials left and this committee accepted quite a few active political groups, citizen groups, commercial associations, guilds, and students. They were all accepted, so if you called this committee a hodgepodge that wouldn't be an exaggeration, but you could also say it was a gathering of Taiwan's public opinions. It was extremely representative because every faction had their men inside. If everyone looks at the period two years after the end of the war, from 1945 to 1947, we can see that these two years are the fastest period of Taiwan's democratic development. It was really, really, fast and with all of the gains produced by this committee, the greatest results were shown today. Futhermore it emerged with a consensus for the 32 demands from such a diverse and complex power struggle of every faction and various organizations. It was a very effective organization. I think that if you compare it with today's Legislative Yuan, it would be difficult for them to reach such an important consensus in just 9 or 10 days. This was also the first provincial conference after Taiwan's retrocession, so I think the organizers picked a very good title, as this was Taiwan's Summit for Democracy. It shows that although there are different opinions in various areas, the consensus on the 32 Demands was our consensus.

The contributions of this committee in the history of democracy, I think should occupy a very important place, so as I said before that the 228 Incident was Taiwan's democracy movement initiation, so this conference was a very good model of a conclusion. Having so many parties in it, including pro-communist, business interests, guild interests, and student bodies, integrating all of their opinions into the very specific 32 Demands given as a reference to the officials.

Of course my grandfather put a lot of effort into these 32 Demands. On March 7th, it was on this side of the radio station he gave a final broadcast and the final words he said were: "The 228 Incident Settlement Committee had done all it could do, and all it was able to suggest to the government and the Taiwanese people ended here. The rest is up to how the Taiwanese people handle this situation." I think these words still stand today. The future path of Taiwan, how Taiwan moves forward, this is a matter that still requires the wisdom of the people. The future of Taiwan should be decided by the Taiwanese people, the path that Taiwan should follow in the end, what kind of reforms we want to have in the future, the kind of road we hope to take and in addition to all of the proposed blueprints made by candidates, we also should urge the government on how to run.

At this point I think I should return to something and that is that I don't believe people are born with the right to rule. I believe each ruler has his own philosophies and we as ordinary people can't wait day after day for a people-oriented government. Today, Taiwan is a democratic country, citizens are members of the government, and all struggles for power should be done with public participation. We should take hold of our own future.

My speech is now finished and I think everyone will definitely be able to see the many materials on these exhibition grounds that inform us about the chaotic situation at that time. There were supporters and people of all kinds of different doctrines, but through the institution of democracy, it allowed them to come to a consensus. This is really precious for the history of democracy in Taiwan. I hope everyone really pays attentions to this and then thinks about where Taiwan should go from here. Thanks everyone.

The son of the 228 Incident Settlement Committee-Tainan Branch's Chairman Dr. Hahn Shyr-Chyuan-Hahn Liang-Jiunn

The director of the Taipei 228 Memorial Museum-Mr. Hsieh, Chief Secretary of Taipei City Government's Department of Cultural Affairs-Mrs. Lee, distinguished guests, ladies and gentlemen, good morning and hello!

I feel very honored to be invited to participate in this meaningful opening of this special exhibition. The 228 Incident occurred exactly 67 years ago. The Taiwanese provincial and county 228 Settlement Committees, in order to maintain order and to negotiate with the government officials for people's security, democracy and autonomous interests made a great effort. At that time, my father Dr. Hahn Shyr-Chyuan, was a Provincial Senator of Taiwan. On March 3, when he accepted the sincere plea of Tainan City Mayor Zhuo Gao-Xuan and Tainan City Senate Speaker Huang Bai-Lu, to come forward to help defend the peace of Tianan city, he also pointed out the four great principles of peaceful settlement to Mayor Zhuo. Namely :

1. Do Not Escalate
2. Without Bloodshed
3. Do Not Deny Existing Authority
4. Solve Political Issues with Political Methods

The next day, on March 4, 8 a.m., along with Tainan city's Senate Speaker Huang Bai-Lu, Senator Hou Quan-Cheng, Gao Shou-Ling, and private individuals of Tainan, Mr. Lin Zhan-Ao, owner of Xingwhenzhai bookstore, middle school teacher Lee Guo-Ze among others, affirmed these four principles of peace and immediately split up to persuade students and the public not to act rashly, in order to avoid dangerous and disadvantageous incidents from occurring.

Several days later, by relying on these four principles they were then able to stabilize Tainan city and ensured that Tainan even in midst of turmoil, had the lowest number of people killed and injured of all Taiwan's major cities and counties. However, in the four following decades, this concept of peace was utterly and completely forgotten, with almost no one mentioning it. Until February 13th, 1987, there was then Chen Yong-Hsin, Li Sheng-Hsiung and Cheng Nan-Jung among others who formed the "228 Peace Day Promotion Association" which called for the publication of the truth and a redress of injustices, publishing the "228 Peace Day Declaration," and launching the 228 Rehabilitation Movement.

Today as soon as you mention "228" everyone will think of the word "peace," like "228 Peace Memorial Day," "228 Peace Memorial Park," and the "228 Justice and Peace Movement," because peace is already a world recognized universal value. Even in the shade of the front right side of the Taipei 228 Memorial Museum there stands a white wooden pillar with four scripts, Chinese, (Traditional and Simplified) English, and Japanese written on it saying "May Peace Prevail On Earth." So during the time of the Incident, the 228 Incident Settlement Committee-Tainan Branch, from the chairman Dr. Hahn Shyr-Chyuan to many members, advocated adhering to and putting into practice these peaceful principles of love and non-violence. In the future, shouldn't it receive the belated attention it deserves in Taiwan's history?

I hope everyone visiting the special exhibition that started today would at the same time consider together this serious topic.

The Academia Historica Editor and Compilation Department Director - Hou Kun-Hung

Chief Secretary of Taipei City Government's Department of Cultural Affairs-Mrs. Lee, the director of the Taipei 228 Memorial Museum-Mr. Hsieh, and as well as all of you friends, hello.

I just came from the office. Because I've already served 20 some years over in the Presidential Palace's Academia Historica over on Changsha street, and have personally continued to pay attention to 228 Incident over these 20 some years, it has become a very important part of my entire field of research. So the reason I am standing here today is because last year I had participated in the last publication of archives related to the 228 Incident, at least the last batch of documents we could handle, as the interpretation of the archives has not been fully announced. At Academia Sinica's Institute of Taiwan History, where last year we held a conference, I had taken the 228 Settlement Committee as a research topic and the theme of this exhibition is also exactly the 228 Settlement Committee. Prior to the exhibition I had already read a copy of all of the documents, and I thought that it was written quite well and balanced.

Everyone saw that the entire theme is framing it as Taiwan's Summit for Democracy, but this kind of determination needs further understanding, because Taiwan's whole political democratic movement has really only developed in recent years. So if you want to understand this kind of meeting and then give the 228 Incident Settlement Committee a historical determination, we can probably say that the 228 Incident Settlement Committee in the beginning of the post-war period really possessed the embryonic form of a democracy summit and unfortunately afterwards did not develop fully. Furthermore, after the Incident, those who had participated in this summit were all hunted down and killed or were politically persecuted. According to my personal research, the 228 Incident Settlement Committee, in addition to the main meeting at Taipei Zhongshan Hall, there were county and city level ones and also township level Settlement Committees. So in my initial estimate there were approximately 27 and those people who participated in these Settlement Committees could be said to be a group of Taiwan's political elites and their later fate we don't need to talk too much about.

Today we are holding this kind of exhibition, and in fact we need to acknowledge that this kind of exhibition is significant of where we are. The function of the museum is to promote social education, whether taking such a position as this or the context of Taiwan's political development, how do we get the masses of society to enter this museum and through this kind of exhibition to understand this section of unfortunate history that happened in 1947. Then we can launch the direction of the development of our entire future history, with this as the starting point for our thinking.

We hope this exhibition will be smooth and successful, and that many people will be able to enter here and through this exhibition understand the experiences and circumstances of this past sad section of history, in order that it may offer some contribution to the future democratic development of Taiwan. I wish the exhibition success, wish for everyone to be in good health, and for your family to be full of peace, joy and beauty. Thank you.

台北二二八協會理事長　黃秀婉女士為與會貴賓導覽特展

◀ 二二八事件見證者、二二八處委會發言人王添灯表妹　高黃娥女士（圖左）

紀錄片訪談錄
Documentary Film's Interview

September, 2014

紀錄片訪談錄 —— *September, 2014*
Documentary Film's Interview

受訪者：陳重光

嘉義二二八處理委員會嘉義分會陳澄波長子

問題：二二八處委會嘉義分會的成立與演變經過？

陳：我首先介紹我自己，我是我先父陳澄波的長子。1947年二二八發生當時，我是臺灣師範大學一年級的學生，當時我是已經二十一歲，所以當時狀況我大概了解。嘉義頭一個三二處理委員會，應該是後來又改為二二八處理委員會，所以我簡單說明二二八發生的經過。二二八不能以一句話來表達，一開始臺灣人民是歡迎國民政府來臺統治，大部份的人歡迎，但是看政府亂七八糟，所以變成失望，失望、被欺負一年，不到一年半就變怨恨。所以1947年2月27日就發生緝私事件，就演變成整個臺灣反抗政府的運動，這政治問題應該是要用政治的手腕來解決問題，結果國民政府聽陳儀長官的一面之詞，就派軍隊二十一師及憲兵團來基隆登陸，一律以武力來解決問題，當然當時國軍有武器，臺灣人民沒有武器，所以一路被屠殺，從基隆，一路行經到新竹、臺中、嘉義、臺南、高雄用武力鎮壓之後就開始清算，所謂清鄉。以後接著是白色恐怖，白色恐怖之後，二二八事件四十年來，都不能談論。以一般的常識來想就知道，這件這麼大的事件，死亡人數根據行政院研究小組報告，死亡兩萬人以上，這麼大的事件，命令人不可以說，表示政府做見不得人的事才怕人說，所以一直四十年間，都不可以說二二八有關的事情。嘉義的第一件三二事變，二二八發生事件之後，隔天三月初一就有人到車站演講，因為一年多的時間被欺負，所以自3月2日就引起抗議行動，嘉義市政府無能來解決問題，所以他們會退至水上機場，所以無政府狀況之情形下，參議會負起責任和社會人士來參與組成三二事件處理委員會，因為臺北成立二二八事件處理委員會，這經過陳儀長官來認可的一個組織，所以嘉義也開成二二八處理委員會。當時，我爸爸陳澄波當市議員，是參議員，所以當然他會加入這組織裡面。

問題：陳澄波先生對於政治的理念，以及他與二二八處委會的關係？

陳：當然他知道人民的力量要對抗政府，提出了高度自治的要求會很困難被接受，因為他們經過了日本人五十年的統治，臺灣人不了解中國是一個專權、無人權的政府、國家，所以他以為他們可以講道理，結果道理都不講，市參議會是民意上要參加政治活動，但是它的決議沒有任何效果，市政府想怎麼做就怎麼做。所以不了解的狀況下，本來要選舉的時候，我家裡的人不太贊成，因為他當時日本時代就是很出名的畫家，大家都認識他，所以要選舉的時候，很多朋友都推他出來選舉，光只有印名片，朋友發一發就當選了，也沒有去左右鄰居拜託，也沒有辦演講，也沒有印海報，都沒有，只有朋友拿名片去拜託發一發就選上了。我爸爸原來就是一位很有正義感的一位畫家，雖然說想去上海教書，1929至1933年才回來，1933回來後前後五年的時間去教書，藝術家對政治本來就是不怎麼干涉的，雖然在藝專教五年的書，對中國政治也不了解，他會講北京話的情況下，他就被叫去做翻譯。我剛才說嘉義市政府及警察局外省族群沒辦法控制嘉義的抗議活動，所以他們就全部退去水上機場。為了要和解，就派了好幾次去往談判，他們都拖延時間，等到二十一師及憲兵團登陸臺灣後，他們就硬起來。我爸爸最後一次去水上，可以說是和平使節，他知道明天軍隊就要來嘉義接管，所以大家都想說是最後一次，要好好談，一邊安撫年輕人不要肇事趕快溜走，希望軍隊進來嘉義後也不要隨便抓人、殺人，所以兩部卡車，一部載油鹽水果去訪問，當時要派人進去，我爸爸當時因為在上海教了五年的書，國語多少會講一點，當時的國大代表一直推薦他要去，不得已之下只好去，去到北迴歸線還沒進去機場，就被軍隊攔下來，拿衣服給你蓋起來，手用鉛線綁起來，就被抓起來。根本就不重視和平使節的任務，沒談判就被抓起來，隔天就進來接管嘉義市，經過兩個禮拜後，三月十一號就被抓去，抓去機場，三月二十四號送來嘉義市警察局，隔日二十五號，都是聽別人說的，聽說在裡面被刑求，秘密的審判，甚至空手壓印，他們都不承認，沒有反叛的事實，所以硬抓著手去蓋章，造成很多反叛的理由，當時有四個議員，二十五號早上從警察局出發兩部卡車，一部是二十幾個帶槍的士兵，後一部他們四個議員，跪著插著好像清朝要斬首的牌子，在二月二十五號早上八點左右要槍決示眾，槍決之後，屍體也不讓人收埋，等到黃昏五六點的時候，才讓人抬回家。抬回家之後，我媽媽在很大的勇氣下，去請攝影師來照一張相，那時候正好是屍體抬進客廳的時候，我在一百週年我爸爸剛好一百歲的時候辦美展，百年美展，當時第一次公開這張相片，當時李登輝當總統，他有來看展覽，也看那張相片，看了約一分鐘才離開。因為這個相片，我媽媽的理念就是證據，就是國民政府來亂殺人的證據，很可惜的是，我在市面上發現的照片當中只有兩張，一張是我爸爸，一張是吳伯雄他伯父(指吳鴻麒)，當時當法官的樣子，他的屍體也有照相照起來，我只有看到這兩張。後來行政院郝柏村當行政院長時，有二二八研究小組，他們的研究結果是兩萬人以上的受難者，根據戶口人口的調查結果，因為當時實施戒嚴，所以殺死人無罪，所以到處去抓人，抓了人有金條就判生，沒金條就判死，這種情形到處都發生。

底片是玻璃底片，藏了將近四十年，第一次百年美展在1994年，在嘉義開百年美展的時候才第一次公開出來。之前在總統府，我們有當二二八受難家屬的代表去總統府和李登輝總統有討論過二二八的事情。我想說，和總統都可以說二二八，在社會也可以公開，所以我在百年美展時才公開。如果再早幾年，底片會被沒收，還會被判罪，當時還是白色恐怖的時代，郝柏村當行政院長有研究小組，分北區、中區、南區跟東區有研究小組，研究小組訪問很多人，訪問完後要做記錄，大家都不願意簽字，有的一千字一直消成剩一百字，有這種情形，當時還很驚慌，在這情形之下，所以1994年百年美展當時，也是很多事情都沒辦法說出來，很多人都不敢說都不敢承認。

問題：作為後代，您認為今後臺灣的民主發展，應如何從此一事件中學習教訓？

陳：臺灣人應該是還沒學到真正的教訓，常常出現對二二八事件模稜兩可的解釋，因為四十年來噤聲，所以在配合政府模稜兩可的政策之下，大家對二二八事件已經全部忘光光，而怎麼發生的，現在課本雖然有寫詳細一點，但是也是寥寥無幾，大部分都讀大陸的歷史地理，而臺灣的歷史地理都放一邊，到現在還是這種情形，所以臺灣人對自己本身認識不夠的情況之下，還是沒辦法達到民主的情形。所以當時沒有民主政治，威權、獨裁比日本的帝國主義還要厲害，所以要改變這種情形，要靠大家努力，所以沒辦法說用金錢、黑道，利用這些來辦理民主政治，本來就是很不公平的事情，這不公平要如何打破，就是今後我們要努力的目標。

Interviewee: Chen Tsung-kuang, the eldest son of the 228 Incident Settlement Committee-Chiayi Branch's Chen Cheng-Po, hereinafter referred to as Chen.

Question: What was the process of the 228 Incident Settlement Committee - Chiayi Branch's establishment and evolution?

Chen: First let me introduce myself, I am my father's, Chen Cheng-Po's eldest son. In 1947 when 228 occurred, I was a freshman at National Taiwan Normal University. At that time I was already 21 years old, so I probably understood the situation then. Chiayi's initial 32 Settlement Committee was later changed to the 228 Incident Settlement Committee, so I'll briefly explain how 228 occurred. 228 cannot be expressed in one sentence. In the beginning the majority of Taiwanese people welcomed the KMT to come and rule Taiwan, but they saw the government was in a hideous mess. So they became disappointed and were bullied for a year. And after less than a year and a half, they became resentful.

On February 27th, 1947 the anti-smuggling incident occurred and it morphed into a movement of the whole of Taiwan rebelling against the government. This political problem should have used a political maneuver to resolve the issue. What happened was that the Nationalist government only listened to Chen Yi's side of the story and then sent the 21st army division and the Military Police Corps to land at Keelung and without exception used force to solve every issue. Of course, in those days the National Army had weapons and the Taiwanese people didn't. So they were slaughtered all the way from Keelung and then after the military crackdown had passed through Hsinchu, Taichung, Chiayi, Tainan, and Kaohsiung began the purge, the so-called cleansing of society. Following the 228 Incident was the White Terror, and neither of them could be openly discussed up to 40 years.

Using common sense I know that such a huge event, the death toll according to the Executive Yuan Research Report Group was greater than 20,000 people, such a huge event, by ordering people not to talk about it, proves the government did horrible things and they were afraid of what people would say. So for forty straight years, no one could talk about anything related to 228. Chiayi's 32 Incident occurred after the 228 Incident. The next day on March 1st, people went down to the railroad station to give speeches because they had been exploited for more than a year. So from March 2nd, a protest movement arose and the Chiayi government was unable to solve the problem. So they would retreat to Shueishang Airport, and with circumstances of anarchy, the City Council took up responsibility and public figures came together to form the 32 Incident Council. Because Taipei set up a 228 Incident Settlement Committee, this passed through Chief Executive Chen Yi's approval, so Chiayi also opened its 228 Incident Settlement Committee. At that time, my father Chen Cheng-Po served as a city councilor, a representative, so of course he would join this organization.

Question: What were Mr. Chen Cheng-Po's political philosophies and his relationship to the 228 Incident Settlement Committee?

Chen: Of course he knew the power of the people to rebel against the government, and that putting forward demands of a high degree of autonomy would be received with great difficulty, but it was because Taiwanese people had experienced 50 years of Japanese rule, that they didn't understand that China was a dictatorship, a country and government without human rights. So he thought they could be reasoned with, but reason wasn't spoken of. The city council wanted to participate in the political movement of the will of the people, but its resolutions didn't have any effect, the city government just did what ever they wanted to do. So they didn't understand the situation, and at first during election time, my family didn't really support him. But because in the Japanese era he had been a very famous painter, and everybody recognized him, therefore at election time a lot of friends pushed for him to be elected. With only business cards, friends handed them out and chose. No door-to-door campaigning, no political speeches, no printing posters, nothing. He was elected with just friends campaigning by handing out business cards. My father had been a painter with a sense of justice. He went to Shanghai to teach art, from 1929 to 1933, and then he came back home. Artists, after all don't really meddle in politics and although he taught for five years at the art college, he didn't understand Chinese politics. But the fact that he could speak Mandarin, he was called to do translation.

I previously mentioned that Chiayi's mainlander city government and police department couldn't control Chiayi's resistance movement, and so they completely retreated to the Shueishang airport. In order to make a settlement they were sent back and forth several times for negotiations. They just stalled for time, waiting until after the 21st division of the Military Police Corp had landed on Taiwan and then they hardened. The last time my father went to Shueishang, you could say he was an ambassador of peace, he knew that the next day the military would come and take over Chiayi. So everyone wanted to say it was the last time and that they needed to speak really well. On one side they were appeasing young people to not make trouble and to leave quickly and on the other hoped that when the military entered Chiayi they wouldn't randomly arrest people, kill people.

So two trucks, one carrying oil, salt, and fruits went in to visit. At that time they wanted to send someone in, and because my father had taught for five years in Shanghai, and he could more or less speak Mandarin, the council members at the time recommended him to go. Reluctantly he went, he got to the Tropic of Cancer monument, he still hadn't entered the airport yet and then he was stopped by the army. They grabbed his clothes and covered his head, tied his hands up with lead wire and arrested him. They simply didn't pay attention to the mission of a peace ambassador; no talks just tied him up.

The next day came and they took control of Chiayi city, after the next two weeks, on March 11th he was arrested, and taken to the airport. On March 24th, he was sent to the Chiayi police station and on the following day, March 25th, and this is what I heard from other people, I heard inside he was tortured and that he was held at secret trials. They even forged his seal, they wouldn't admit that there was no evidence of rebellion, so they forced his hand to place his seal, manufacturing a lot of reasons for rebellion. At that time there were four Senators. On the morning of the 25th they set off in two trucks, the first had twenty-some gun-carrying soldiers and the one behind it had the four representatives, kneeling with their heads sticking out, like the Qing Dynasty was going to give the order to behead them.

Around 8:00 a.m., on the morning of February 25th, they were publicly executed by firing squad and they didn't let anyone collect the bodies. They waited until 5 or 6 pm in the evening and then let people carry them home. After he was carried home, my mother with a great deal of courage went to get a photographer to come and take a picture. At that time, it was just when his corpse had been carried into the living room. At my father's centennial, when my father was one hundred years old, I set-up an art exhibition. At the time Lee Teng Hui was president and he had come to see the exhibition. He also saw that photo; he looked at it for about a minute and then he left, because this picture, my mother's idea was proof, proof that the National Government had indiscriminately killed people. It's a pity however that in the market, I discovered that among the photos there were only two, one was my father and the other was Wu PoHsiung and his uncle (Wu Hong Qi). His body also had a picture taken of it. I've only seen these two photos.

Later when the Executive Yuan, when Hau Pei-Tsun was premier, the 228 Research Report Group, and their research results were that there were more than 20,000 victims, the investigation findings were according to the registered population records. Because martial law had been imposed during that time, so killing people wasn't a crime, and they grabbed people everywhere. If you had gold your sentence was life and if you didn't have it then your sentence was death. This kind of situation happened all over.

The negatives are glass plate negatives, hidden for almost 40 years. The first centennial art exhibition was in 1994, and when Chiayi held it's centennial art exhibition was the first time it came out publicly. Ealier at the Presidential Palace, we had a representative of the families of the 228 Incident go to the Presidential Palace and discuss with President Lee Teng-Hui about the 228 Incident. I would like to say, that you can even talk about the 228 Incident with the president, you can also talk about it openly in society, so during the centennial art exhibition, I too was open. If it was a few years ago, the negative would have been confiscated and I would've been convicted, as at that time it was still the era of White Terror.

With Hau Pei-Tsun serving as premier there were a Research Report Groups divided into north, middle, south and east Research Report Groups. The Research Report Groups interviewed a lot of people and after they finished interviewing they would make a record. Everyone was unwilling to sign their names, and some record thus deleted from a thousand words to only a few hundred left. It was that kind of situation, and that time is still so frightening. So with this kind of situation in 1994 and at the time of the centennial art exhibition, there were a lot of matters that were unable to be expressed and a lot of people who didn't dare speak and didn't dare admit.

Question: As his descendant, how do you think the future development of Taiwanese democracy should learn from this Incident?

Chen: I suppose that the Taiwanese people still haven't learned the real lesson and frequently have an ambiguous interpretation of the 228 Incident. Because of four decades of silencing and in compliance with the government's ambiguous laws, everyone has completely forgotten about the 228 Incident and how it happened. Now, even though textbooks write about it in more detail, it's still very sparse. Most of them read about the Mainland's history and geography and Taiwan's history and geography are set aside. That is still the case today and so if Taiwanese people have a lack of understanding about themselves, there is still no way they will reach a democratic state. There was no democracy at that time, but an authoritarian dictatorship that was even more severe than Japan's Imperialism. Therefore the situation had to be changed, we had to rely on everyone's efforts. So we should not use money or the underworld force, to take advantage and to guide in democracy. It was originally a very unfair situation, and this is how we broke the unfairness, and it is the future goal we strive for.

受訪者：韓良俊
二二八處委會臺南分會主任委員韓石泉之四子

問題：請介紹韓石泉醫師在二二八處委會臺南分會裡的角色？他的理念與臺灣民主發展的關係？

韓：我父親韓石泉醫師，他當過臺灣省參議會第一屆的參議員，他擔任的任期是從1946年的4月到1951年的12月，大概五年八個月左右。二二八事件是1947年的2月27日從專賣局緝私員傅學通以槍托打傷賣菸的女販林江邁頭部開始，所以也就是在他省議員期間發生的。在事件發生之前，其實他也已曾在省議員任內注意到、看到有很多使他覺得很驚異、很訝異的現象，就是說他發現帶槍的警員跟士兵特別多，所以常常會發生事端，比方說士兵跟警員會衝突時，民眾跟警員衝突時，甚至法警跟自己警局裡面的人衝突時，還有夫妻口角時也都拔槍來威嚇，甚至對拒捕的嫌犯也常常直接就擊斃的也有，也就是攜槍跟槍支使用非常浮濫，所以他就認為這個就是惹起二二八的導火線，對此都沒有其他人講過，其實這個可以算是遠因，也是很重要的原因。

所以他在第二次省參議會大會的時候，曾經正式提案說，「非依法不能攜帶槍械」，曾經提這樣很重要的案，很可惜沒有獲得負責當局的重視，結果影響到後來二二八的發生，成為它的遠因。所以他覺得很感慨、很可惜，這是在二二八發生之前的情形。

談到處委會的話，他是擔任臺南市分會，也就是二二八處理委員會臺南市分會的主任委員，所以他在任內就有非常重要的角色發揮，主要都是擔任主任委員的關係。

　　至於有關臺灣民主發展，我想提兩點事情來說明。他在接任主任委員以後的3月6日，發生一件事就是，臺南市的各級學校包括大學、高中等中等學校以上學生，一起來要求說要上街遊行，要在臺南市遊行，條件當然是沒有武裝的遊行，沒有帶什麼武器。所以我父親就跟黃議長，去替他們向軍方，特別是要塞的項台長，還有警察局長他們交涉，並獲得許可。後來就由我父親跟黃議長，還有李國澤先生他們，負責維持秩序，讓這些當時臺南工學院也就是現在的成大的學生帶頭，遊行臺南市街道。那個時候他們手持的標語，第一個就是「擁護國民政府」，還有「確定民主政治」、「改革本省腐敗的政治」、「促進地方自治實施」，還有「建設新臺灣」。可見這些標語除了第一個，以當時時空的狀況來說，都是很敏感、很大膽的題目，雖然是大膽，但是因為我父親他們負責維持秩序維持得好，所以遊行完全程，還好結果和平落幕，沒有發生任何暴力的衝突。所以這個就是一個非常重要的民主發展特例，在那麼早的時期，就提出那麼敏感的標語來遊行，居然都沒有發生什麼衝突。這件事是在1947年發生的，最後居然能和平落幕，所以這事對民主發展，應可說有一個啟蒙作用，並有相當的貢獻。

　　另外一件事我要提的就是，他在省參議員任內，因為那個時候的省參議會可以說是臺灣最高的民意機關，立法院還沒有搬遷過來，所以臺灣省參議會是當時臺灣最高的民意機構。他在臺灣省參議會做了很多事、提了很多案，特別是有關醫藥衛生、有關教育、有關經濟交通都有很多提案。所以最近的今年5月，臺灣省諮議會出版的這本《台灣省參議會省參議員小傳》裡面，有關我父親的部分，有提到他的提案非常多元。所以由此可以知道，韓參議員對於議會事務的認真與負責態度，以及韓參議員為民服務之雄心壯志，這個當然都是最早期的民主發展中，為台灣做到一個很好的開始。我特別要提的是，我也看到這本小傳才知道，他有那麼多、重要的提案，比方說，在教育的部分裡面，他曾經提案說，鑑於我國醫療人才的缺乏，提案請政府籌設「藥學齒科專科學校」，齒科就是牙科，還建議在臺南市設立「省立臺南醫學專科學校」，在我看這本書之前，都不知道他有這樣的建議。這事很特別也很重要，也可以說是很有先見之明，會注意到在1984年政府在臺南成大設立醫學院，之前這麼早(至少三十多年前)，他就建議說應該設立「臺南省立醫學專科學校」，而且就在他提案的數年內，1950年代初期台大也先後成立藥學系和牙醫學系，這些都是非常好的遠見，非常了不起的遠見。

問題：說明二二八處委會台南分會成立經過及事件和平處理原則

韓：我父親擔任台南處委會主委的經過是這樣子的:1947年3月2日晚上八點，台南市長卓高煊請臺南市的警察局陳懷讓局長直接來家裡，請他出來協助維護臺南市的安寧、治安。所以，他就到市長的官邸，那個時候有卓市長，還有高雄要塞的項台長，還有憲兵營的廖營長，加上陳警察局長，跟臺南市各中學的校長都在那裡，那個時候，他們當面請我父親協助事變的處理，以保持臺南市的安寧，所以他就在那個時候答應了，同時也提出了他的四個和平處理原則。到了3月4號的上午八點，我父親就去找當時的臺南市參議會參議員的侯全成，他也是一位內科醫師，在侯全成議員家裡，那時正好也有議員的張壽齡，加上議長黃百祿，跟民間人士興文齋書局的負責人林占鰲先生，就又和大家確認說，如果要進行二二八的處理跟維護臺南市的安寧的話，他希望有四個和平的原則。到了3月5日夜間，二二八處理委員會開會的時候，他就被推舉當主任委員。

我父親在臺南市分會從事或者進行二二八處理特別是維持臺南市的安寧、平安，最重要的是有那四個他提出、堅持，而且後面更有實踐的和平處理原則。第一就是「不擴大」，第二就是「不流血」，第三是「不否認現有行政機構」，第四個就是「政治問題要用政治方法來解決」。我想這些對維持和平都可以說都是非常必要，也是明確抓到重點的原則。當時的台南名律師沈榮即曾說:這四大原則「合乎溫和、正當，民眾及政府之利益、威信，均有兼顧」。比方說「不擴大」，這個當然重要，否則你一直擴大的話，當然不可能維持和平。而「不流血」之重要性更不用講，因為他從日治時代就已經參加的抗日，是非武裝非暴力的抗日，不使用暴力，不是用武裝，因為這樣會造成流血，付出的代價太大，這是當然的，如要和平的話，就要維持不流血的原則。又，「不否認現有機構」的話，你才能跟政府，跟行政單位來對話，因為對話是最重要的。衝突的任何雙方，一定要經由對話才能溝通，才能達到解決，所以不否認現有行政機構，這是對話的一個先決條件，要不然就不可能對話。那麼，第四點的「政治問題用政治方法解決」，這個更是到現在，任何政治問題都是可以行得通的方法，到現在都可以說是適用的。所以，這四個和平原則，可以說是達成臺南市能夠比較和平落幕，也沒有遭受較大的鎮壓，可以說這四條是很重要的關鍵要件。

不管是臺南市整體，整體的官民，包括公務員或者是官方的人士跟民眾，還有我父親本身，比較少的傷亡，最主要的還是一開始有正確的方向，採取這和平的四大原則，而且真的去努力和民眾溝通。有這些原則一開始在臺南實行，才能有這樣的，可以說，和平的成果。

但是，一開始的時候，其實我父親，比方說提出有關二二八處理的意見的時候，在臺南市議會，其實也有一些人士有帶槍械在那裡，所以我父親剛剛提出這和平四大原則的時候，也曾經有些激進的民眾威脅他、恐嚇他，因為那個時候有一些民眾堅持非用暴力的方式來抗爭不可。所以，就威脅我父親說要對他的生命不利，使得不少親戚朋友很替我父親憂心，擔心他會遭到不測的生命危險，不過他還是以他不動的信念加上以他作為基督徒的禱告，克服了這些危險的場面，最後安然度過。後來的溝通上比較大的危險，就在軍隊方面。因為，軍方當然也有那些強硬派，鷹派，所以他們認為你怎麼一天到晚替民眾講話，或者替民眾爭取他們的權益。所以這點，軍方也可能會有不滿，所以結果當然也就須去冒這些危險。我父親說，在這樣的事態漩渦中，勇氣竟不知從何而來，而且他還能坦然處之，到後來想一想，也算是很驚險的經歷。而這個「坦然處之」當中，他有經由靠他的宗教信仰禱告，還有由此得到的那些很強的信心，去做他認為是做對的事，他一直有這樣的信念。

問題：談一談韓石泉醫師的『和平』理念

韓：講到我父親的和平理念，除了那些他在二二八處委會臺南市分會提出，而且堅持的那四大和平處理原則以外，其實，其根柢就是「愛與非暴力」。我想，他本身從立志學醫，還有一直四、五十年從事醫師的工作，當然最重要的出發點就是「愛」。因為醫師的工作就是要助人、要救人，這都是要從愛心出發的。所以，當然，即使在那樣嚴重的衝突情況下，他提出了「不流血」原則，這就是以醫師的立場，不忍心也不願看到不管任官、警、軍、民任何一方，有流血受傷甚至死亡的，這都是作為醫師不能接受或者忍受的事，所以出發點的愛心，是他最主要的理念。

所以在1963年他逝世時，《中華日報》有如下的評語：「韓石泉博士本於基督的博愛精神，以醫學服務人群，愛人如己。」當然，這還包括「非暴力」。剛剛講過他在日治時代參與的不管是臺灣文化協會也好，還有前面的臺灣議會期成運動，爭取臺灣的議會，還有後來那擔任重要職務的臺灣民眾黨，都是從「非暴力」之理念出發的。因為他也在日治時代，抗日初期看到太多的武裝抗日、暴力抗日，付出了很大的傷亡的代價。同樣，到二二八的時候，還是延續這種「愛與非暴力」的理念與這樣的原則。我想，這事對大家看來應是很自然的，也是他本來就認為應該這樣做的。因為，這就是他根深柢固的、不可動移的理念。

問題：作為後代，您認為今後臺灣的民主發展，應如何從此一事件中學習教訓？

韓：我想，其實大家也看到在二二八事件裡面，有很多抗爭方法，有很多人認為一定要以武裝的或者暴力的方式抗爭，這個也可算是他們的看法，我們也尊重。但至少我們可以講說，暴力的抗爭不應是唯一的做法。應該有很多種不同的選擇，不同的方式來分工，來殊途同歸。所以我認為非暴力的抗爭也非常重要，而且也不要誤解，有些人曾誤會說，好像講和平就不用抗爭，但並不是這樣子。和平有和平抗爭的做法，像前面提到的很多在臺南市的做法，包括學生的和平遊行，還是有提出很敏感的標語出來，結果也是很成功地抗爭了。

所以我認為，大家要知道，抗爭並不一定非要用暴力的方式不可。雖然有些人認為，暴力有暴力的，或者武裝有武裝的需要或者價值，但是如果要採取武裝，或者暴力抗爭的話，一定要好好評估要付出多大的代價。特別是當自己要登高一呼說，一定要採取武裝抗爭的時候，對你的那些夥伴、同伴，或者民眾會造成多大的傷亡，你要負責任地，好好事先評估好。而且最好是一次就能成功，不要進行好多次，然後會有好多、很大的傷亡的話，我想，像現代這樣各種武器都很先進的時代，要非常小心慎重的決定。

所以，我們也可以了解，比方說諾貝爾獎金，為何就設有有關和平的諾貝爾和平獎。他們也並不鼓勵說一定要用革命、武裝的方式來做抗爭，或者爭取不管是人權也好，自由民主也好，他們還是強調要用和平的方式。所以我們從這件事來講，來了解就知道，和平其實是一個最高的普世價值，應該在做任何抗爭的時候，還是要作為最優先的考慮，萬不得已一定要採取暴力或者武裝抗爭的話，我剛剛講過，一定要好好評估須付出多大的代價，如果代價太大的話，就不要隨便採取暴力或者武裝的抗爭。

在我父親所撰《六十回憶－韓石泉醫師自傳》的第194頁，有特別寫到說事件以後，他得到一個深刻的教訓，就是在這樣的事件或者緊急的事態當中，一定要有正確的指導原則，而且要有誠心合作的同志，還要有置生死榮辱於不顧的精神，才能處於急難之中也不至發生動搖，才能保有不可動搖的信念。如果畏首畏尾、躊躇不前的話，不但會一無所獲，而且反而災害會臨到身上，這是他自己從二二八事件得到的一個很深刻的教訓。所以他也提到，在他後來的檢討裡面，他自己也有提到說，在事變或者這些緊急的狀況下，除了要有正確的指導原則，實際上還要強力去推動，才能達到真正預期的效果。

最後，我想強調的就是，我父親雖曾提出那四大和平原則，而且後來大家再提到二二八事件的時候，都會聯想到「和平」這兩個字，所以才會有「二二八和平公園」、「二二八和平日」或者「二二八和平公義運動」，這些都是二二八跟和平已有的密切關係，後來都讓人聯想在一起。那麼，既然這樣的話，我們關心臺灣歷史的人士，還有臺灣的一些有識之士，是不是應該把我父親在當年，還有當時二二八事件發生的當下，就提出了和平這個理念，而且努力地、認真地實踐這一段史實，這段歷史，是不是大家應該要重視它更要肯定它，而且在以後未來，萬一又有類似情況的話，應該還是以和平的方式作為優先第一個考慮的選項。這是我在看到我父親冒很大的危險，甚至以背十字架、赴湯蹈火的精神去保護了臺南市民眾的生命、財產的安全這段史實，所得到的最大的感想跟獲得的教訓，那就是，和平應該是最高的理念，這本來就是普世的價值，應該受到更多的人的重視。

問題：前述的和平原則，是如何在二二八處委會臺南分會的討論中通過的？過程中是否發生意見分歧與爭執？

韓：當然如要做到和平，第一個就是以「不擴大、不流血」是比較重要，特別是「不流血」就是最大原則。至於在商量當中，如果有一些爭執，這個就民主的立場來講，是可以接受而且難免的，只要最後能達到大家中比較多數的人的共識，而得到一個結論。像我父親提出的那四大原則，也是除了我父親強力的去提倡、推動以外，還是曾經在二二八處委會臺南市分會裡面有得到共識說，就要用這四個原則來進行，有這樣好的、和平的原則，才能在會裡面獲得討論通過。

問題：除了臺南市之外，他那時候有去別的縣市推廣他的和平理念嗎？

韓：別的縣市據我所知，是沒有，因為他在臺南市就可以說已歷盡千辛萬苦，分身乏術了，沒有辦法再兼顧到別的地方。但是真的，看臺南北部的嘉義有一千多個民眾死亡，高雄死亡則有三千多人，臺南後來統計是一兩百名，所以雖夾在較嚴重的南部嘉、高中間，但是看起來台南的死亡人數是少了很多。這個就是可以見到的客觀的事實，可以證明說，在臺南市有發生效果，所以才能有這樣的情形。我在我編著的一本《二二八事件與和平－台灣近代史中被遺漏的一頁》小冊，好像是第18頁，我有參考幾本二二八有關的專書，整理成一個表，就可以看出來，在臺灣的各大縣市裡面，臺南市是死傷(包括外省人被毆傷者)最少的。特別夾在嘉義跟高雄之間，能夠是較少的一兩百人，雖然也都是寶貴的生命，但是比起嘉義、高雄就少那麼多，可以說少十分之一以下，所以這是很難得、很寶貴的事實，也可以說是愛好和平的台南人士努力的成果。

問題：同樣作為與政府談判的民眾代表，相較於其他遭逮捕處決的受難者，您父親最終得以倖免的可能原因是什麼？

韓：我父親除了在事件當中領導二二八處理委員會的臺南市分會，實際做到維持和平的原則以外，後來在1947年3月30日版出的臺灣省行政長官公署的紀錄裡面，有提到說我父親，還有其他別人也有，提到他們有「救護外省人員、保全公物、宣撫臺民、協助處理事變」，這些在臺灣省行政長官公署，在事件平息後的1947年3月30日編印的紀錄裡面有寫到這點。可見我父親這些努力維持和平的原則與做法，曾受到當時政府單位的認知與肯定。當然也有人會認為說，是不是因為很軟弱或者怎麼樣才沒有被追究。其實，事件結束以後，軍隊的指揮官也曾經要求他要寫自白書，自白書就是認為我有錯，我才要寫自白書，來認為我有怎樣怎樣的錯，那才是自白書。他有很明白、堅決的拒絕軍方指揮官，告訴他說：「我沒有做錯什麼事，你如果要我寫的話，我就寫處理書給你，但我不寫自白書」，而向他拒絕。

　　像這樣，他並不是軟弱，反而應該說，該堅強、該抗爭的時候，他還是有抗爭，也可算是義正詞嚴，所以連軍隊也軟化、接受了，所以後來就是只有讓他寫處理書而沒有寫自白書。所以，從這些也知道，為何他後來沒有被追究而受難。關於這事，前面提到的沈榮律師更曾寫道：「....但當時之極端份子，卻以為無能、柔弱，表示不滿。於平靜之後，地方當局未能理解中央之德意，而檢舉很多人士，對韓先生亦欲索取自白書以便核辦，韓先生不僅嚴詞峻拒，並為被控人士設法營救。其為國家、民族、正義、合理，不怕權勢之真面目，由此可見。」

　　其實也有一份二二八的資料，好像是辭典，曾經寫說他後來「反正」了，才沒有去追究他。我想那是錯誤的，並不是事實。因為他並不是沒有抗爭，他從頭到尾就是維持他一貫的原則，不管對官方或者對民眾，他主要是既為民設想，而且也替民眾跟官方溝通，但不是完全偏向一邊。因為這樣的關係，他立得正，所以後來沒有被追究或者處分，我想這些原因是都有的。不過，他也曾經在3月11日於臺南市議會開會的時候，被軍方士兵用刺刀，裝刺刀的長槍，逼著他上軍車，押到軍方的南區指揮部那裡去訊問。他也曾經遭受這樣的對待，但是他還是主要就因為是立場公正，而且也沒有做錯什麼事，所以後來都能化險為夷，才沒有遭受逮捕、處決。不僅如此，在二二八事件後，同年六月召開的省參議會第三次大會質詢時，他還大膽地明言二二八事件「官民均有責任」，並且批評中央事後的處理，「省民均有不夠寬大之感」，更曾下結論指責官方謂：「主其事者(按，暗指最高當局)昧於先機，疏於防範」，有以致之。請記得，這樣的言論，是在二二八事件之後已開始的白色恐怖時代，是以白紙黑字正式公開發表的，這不算是非常大膽、敢言嗎?凡此種種，哪裡可說是「軟弱」?

　　但是這裡還要再強調一點，並不是說主張和平就不會有危險。比方說，我整理的那本《二二八事件與和平－台灣近代史中被遺漏的一頁》裡　就有提到，也同樣有主張和平的人士，這些人士就比較沒有那麼幸運，例如在嘉義市有參議員陳澄波，這位大家都很認識，還有三民主義青年團嘉義分團主任的陳復志、嘉義市參議員潘木枝、盧炳欽、柯麟，他們在嘉義水上機場交涉和平事宜，但是卻馬上遭到逮捕，而在嘉義火車站前公開被槍決，令人感到很痛心、很不幸。還有岡山教會的牧師叫蕭朝金牧師，也是一樣，因為勸阻青年人抗爭的當中，反而受到士兵的逮捕，然後也是受到屠殺。

　　所以並不是說，主張和平而且為和平交涉的話就沒有危險。還是可能遭受很大的危險，但是我父親還是去做了，不管向軍方交涉，或者跟民眾溝通。常常因為他們幾位同志，特別是侯全成先生、李國澤先生他們都是基督徒，所以他們也曾經一起跪在臺南市議會的地上禱告，然後問上帝說，是不是應該背負這個十字架，禱告的結果大家有共識，才以甘冒非常大的生命危險的精神，去跟民眾溝通，或者到軍營交涉。可見，並不是主張和平就沒有危險，看嘉義那些不幸的例子就知道。而在臺南市，幸好可能一開始就採取和平的原則並且很快實行了，可能讓軍方也比較放心，所以才沒有遭遇那麼大的不幸。但是仍有湯德章律師遭受槍決，這是很大的不幸，是臺南市菁英中的受難者之一，對臺南市來講這是很可惜的。

Interviewee: Hahn Liang-Jiunn, is the fourth son of the 228 Incident Settlement Committee-Tainan Branch's Chairman Hahn Shyr-Chyuan, hereinafter referred to as Hahn.

Question: Please describe Dr. Hahn Shyr-Chyuan's role in the 228 Incident Settlement Committee-Tainan Branch. How did his ideas affect Taiwan's democratic development?

Hahn: My father, Dr. Hahn Shyr-Chyuan, served as a senator in the Taiwan Provincial Legislature's first session and the term he held office for was from April, 1946 to December, 1951, about five years and eight months. The 228 Incident started on February 27th, 1947, when the Monopoly Bureau agent Fu Hsueh-Tung used the butt of a gun to hit and injure Lin Chiang-Mai, a female tobacco trader, in the head. So it happened during his term as a provincial senator. Prior to the incident, actually, during his time as a senator, he had already noticed a lot of startling phenomenon. Namely, he found that the number of armed police officers and soldiers was especially numerous, resulting in frequent disturbances. For instance, gun overuse occurred at clashes between soldiers and police, between the public and police, between the bailiff and his fellow officers, or even between the officer and his spouse. Even more exaggeratedly, suspects resisting arrest were often immediately shot dead. The carry and use of guns was extremely excessive, so he believed that this was the fuse that incited the 228 Incident. No one else has ever talked about this before, but in fact this could be regarded as an underlying cause, a very important reason.

Accordingly, when he was in the Second Provincial Senate General Assembly, he made a formal proposal called "Ban on the Unlawful Bearing of Arms." Unfortunately, this important proposal did not receive the attention of the responsible authorities and as a result, it affected the later 228 Incident, becoming its underlying cause, for which he felt lamentable and a great pity. This was the situation preceding the 228 Incident.

Speaking of the committee, he held office in the Tainan branch. My father, as the 228 Incident Settlement Committee Chairman of the Tainan branch played a very important role in the office.

As far as Taiwan's democratic development is concerned, I would like to mention two events as illustration. After he took over as chairman on March 6, an event occurred where the students at all levels of school including university, high school, and other secondary schools etc. in Tainan city, came together and requested to march in the streets, to march in Tainan. A condition, of course, was that it would not be an armed march and they would not bring any kind of weapon. So my father and Prolocutor Huang went to the military on their behalf, especially negotiating and obtaining permission from both Xiang, head of defense, and the police chief. Later it was my father, Prolocutor Huang and also Lee Guo-Ze who took the responsibility for maintaining order, letting the students from, at the time, Tainan Institute of Technology, which is now National Cheng Kung University, take the lead marching on the streets of Tainan.

At that time they held up banners, the first one was "Support the Nationalist Government," "Establish Democracy," "Reform Taiwan Province's Corrupted Politics," "Advance the Implementation of a Local Self-Government," and also "Build a New Taiwan." These banners, except for the first one, in the prevailing conditions of the time were all very sensitive, very bold topics. Even though they were brazen, but because my father and other fellows maintained order well, the demonstration completed its entire route and had a peaceful ending. No violent conflicts of any kind occurred. So this is a special and important example of democratic development, at such an early period, raising and marching with such sensitive slogans, and yet surprisingly having no conflict. This event occurred in 1947, and ultimately was able to have a surprisingly peaceful resolution. So, in regard to democratic development, this event could be considered to have an enlightening role and a considerable contribution.

Another event I would like to mention is him serving as a provincial senator, because at the time the Provincial Council could be said to be Taiwan's highest legislative body, since the Legislative Yuan had not yet moved to Taiwan. So Taiwan's Provincial Council was then Taiwan's highest representative body. He did a lot of things at Taiwan's Provincial Council, and he proposed many bills, particularly with regard to medicine, health, education, economy, and transportation. The volume, "Taiwan's Provincial Legislature and Provincial Senator's Biographies," recently published by the Provincial Consultative Council this May, also mentioned the diversity of my father's proposals in the section about him. So from this we can see Senator Harn's conscientious and responsible attitude toward Council affairs, and moreover Senator Hahn's great ambition to serve the people. These of course were the very earliest stages of democratic development, achieving a good start for Taiwan. I really want to mention that I too, only after reading this biography knew that he had so many important proposals. For instance, regarding the education at that time and also in view of Taiwan's lack of medical personnel, he once proposed a bill requesting the government plan and construct a "College of Pharmacy and Dentistry." He also recommended the establishment of a "Provincial Tainan Medical College" in Tainan. Before I read this book, I had no idea he had these kinds of proposals. This is something very special and very important. It could also be said to be prescient, considering his suggestion of a "Tainan Provincial Medical College" occurred much earlier (at least 30 plus years earlier) than the establishment of a medical college in Tainan's National Cheng Kung University in 1984. Furthermore, within a few years of his proposal, in the early 1950's NTU (National Taiwan University) had set up a Department of Pharmacy and then a Department of Dentistry. These are all great amazing foresight.

Question: Describe how the 228 Incident Settlement Committee-Tainan Branch was established and its principles for peacefully handling the incident.

Hahn: My father's experience serving as committee chairman at Tainan was like this: At 8 p.m. on March 2nd, 1947, as requested by Tainan City's mayor, Cho Gao-Xuan, Tainan's police chief, Chen Huai-Rang, came directly to my father's house and asked him to help maintain the peace, law and order in Tainan city. So my father went to the mayors' official residence, which at that time Mayor Zhuo, Kaohsiung Defense Station Chief Xiang, Military Police Chief Liao, together with Police Chief Chen and all of the secondary school principals were all there as well. At that time they asked my father to assist them in handling this unforeseen event, and to protect the peace of Tainan city. He promised them and put forward his four principles for peaceful resolution. On March 4th, 8 a.m., my father went to find Tainan city's council senator, Hou Quan-Cheng, who was also a physician. At Senator Hou Quan-Cheng's house, where Senator Zhang Shou-Ling, Prolocutor Huang Bai-Lu, and Mr. Lin Zhan-Ao, owner of the Xingwenzhai Bookstore are there as well. My father reiterated with everyone, that if they wanted to make progress in resolving the 228 Incident and maintain the peace of Tainan city, he hoped that they would follow the four principles of peace. Then on the night of March 5th, when the 228 Incident Settlement Committee opened session, he was elected to act as committee chairman.

My father at the Tainan branch carried out the managing of the 228 Incident, particularly to maintain the peace and tranquility of Tainan city. The most important thing is having those four principles of peace that he proposed upheld and then later put further into practice. The first is "Do Not Escalate", the second is "Without Bloodshed", the third is "Do Not Deny Existing Authorities", and the fourth is "Solve Political Issues with Political Methods." I think these are all very essential for peacekeeping, and also clearly define the main point of the principles. A well-known Tainan lawyer at the time, Shen Rong, once pointed out, "These four great principles are in line with moderation, justice, prestige and give equal consideration to both the peoples and governments interests." For example, "Do Not Escalate", of course this is important, otherwise if you keep escalating, eventually the peace will not be kept. Secondly, the importance of "Without Bloodshed" goes without saying. The anti-Japanese movement, which he had participated in during the Japanese colonial era, was an unarmed and non-violent anti-Japanese resistance. They did not use violence or weapons because otherwise it would obviously cause bloodshed, and the price to be paid was too great. If you want peace, then you must support the principal of no bloodshed. Also, only if you "Do Not Deny Existing Authorities", then you could have a dialogue with the government because dialogue is most important. Any two parties in conflict must go through dialogue and then they can communicate, then can reach a solution. So not denying existing political institutions is a prerequisite for dialogue. Otherwise it is impossible to have dialogue. Then, the fourth point, "Solve Political Issues With Political Methods," remains applicable today. Any political problem has a workable solution; this is still applicable today. Therefore, these four principles of peace have enabled Tainan to reach a more peaceful conclusion, and not suffer a larger crackdown. You could say that these four provisions are important key elements.

No matter the whole of Tainan, the whole of the body of government officials, including civil servants or public figures related to the government and the public, even my own father, had relatively few casualties, the key point is that we started in the right direction, adopting these four principles of peace and really working hard to communicate with the people. Implementing these four principles at Tainan in the beginning enabled it to achieve, what we might call, a peaceful result.

However, when it had just begun, actually, when my father proposed his views on handling the 228 Incident at the Tainan City Council, there were also armed people there to threaten him because at that time there were some activists who could not adhere to the way of non-violent protest. They threatened my father, saying that they were going to take his life, making many relatives and friends worry about him. They were worried that he would suffer an unexpected dangerous situation. However, because of his unmovable faith coupled with his prayers as a Christian, he overcame these dangerous scenes and safely passed through. The subsequent talks with the military side became even more dangerous. Because, of course, the military also has its hardliners, hawks, questioning how one could speak on behalf of the people or fight for their rights all the time, So on this matter, the military could also be discontent, and of course the consequence is that my father just had to take these risks. My father said, that in this kind of situational maelstrom, courage unexpectedly came out, and he was still able to be fully at ease. Only later when he reflected on it, considered it to be a life-on-edge experience. It was his religious faith and prayers that get him through these situations, and furthermore, from which he obtained a very strong confidence to do what he thought was right. He always had this kind of faith.

Question: Talk about Dr. Hahn Shyr-Chyuan's concept of "peace."

Hahn: To talk about my father's concept of peace, in addition to those proposed at the 228 Incident Settlement Committee-Tainan Branch, and also the adherence to the four principles of the peace process, really, the foundation for it is "love and nonviolence." I think that his personal determination to study medicine, as well as having 40-50 years engaging in physicians work, of course, the most important starting point is "love". Because a doctor's work is to help people, to save people, and this needs to come from a heart of love. So, of course, even with a backdrop of serious conflict, he proposed the "Without Bloodshed" principle, this was based on the standpoint of a doctor. He could not bear and was not willing to see, no matter if it was an official, police, military, civilian or any party, to have blood shed in injury or even death. As a physician this was something unacceptable or intolerable, so love as the starting point, this is his most important idea.

Therefore, when my father passed away in 1963, "China Daily News" had the following comment: "Dr. Hahn Shyr-Chyuan, in the spirit of Christ's love, used medicine to serve the people, and loved his neighbor as himself." Of course, this still includes "non-violence." I just talked about his involvement during the Japanese colonial era, no matter it was the Taiwanese Cultural Association, the Taiwan Council Petition Movement or later holding important positions in Taiwanese People's Party, his participation began from "non-violence." Because in the Japanese colonial era and in the beginning of the anti-Japanese movement, he saw too many armed and violent resistances pay a heavy price in casualties. Similarly, at the time of the 228 Incident, he still continued on in this kind of "love and non-violence" concept and principles. I think this is something natural, something that he originally believed to do it this way, because this was his deeply rooted and unmovable philosophy.

Question: As his descendant, how do you think the future development of Taiwanese democracy should learn from this incident?

Hahn: I think, well, actually everyone can see that within the 228 Incident there were a number of different ways to fight and that a lot of people thought that it must be by armed or violent conflict. This can be considered their view and we respect them. But at least we can say that violent resistance is not the only approach. There should be a variety of different options; different ways to divide up the task, while arriving at the same destination. Therefore, I think that a nonviolent struggle is also very important. Some people misunderstand and say that when speaking of peace it seems to mean there is no resistance, but it is not like that. Peace has its peaceful fighting methods, like the ones mentioned earlier that were used in Tainan. The peaceful student protests, with their raising of very sensitive banners, can still result in a very successful protest.

So I think everyone needs to know that we need not necessarily use methods of violence to protest. Some people might advocate that violent resistance has its value and is necessary. However, if you want to take up arms or protest violently, you must carefully assess how large of a price you are willing to pay. Especially when you are certain you want to make a public call to arms, how many casualties will be caused among your partners, companions or the people? You must take responsibility and carefully consider it beforehand. It is preferable to succeed at once, and not repeatedly undertake actions, to avoid a great number of casualties. I think this is a decision that needs to be made with great prudence.

So we can also understand then, for instance, why the Nobel Peace Prize was established with regard for peace. They also do not encourage an armed revolutionary approach to protesting. Whether fighting for human rights, freedom or democracy, they still emphasize using peaceful means. So we can learn and know from this incident that peace is actually one of the highest universal values, and before undertaking any struggle, should consider it as the top priority. And if as a last resort that we must make a violent or armed struggle, as I just mentioned, we need to carefully assess how much of price we would pay. If the price is too high, then we must not just casually take up violence or arms and fight.

In my father's book, "Sixty Memories—Hahn Shyr-Chyuan's Autobiography," on page 194, he wrote in particular that after the incident he had learned a profound lesson. That it is in the midst of these kinds of events or emergency situations, that it is imperative to have right guiding principles, the sincere cooperation of comrades, and to have a spirit with no regard for personal life, death, glory, or shame and only then, when in the midst of disaster be unwavering, be able to hold onto an unshakable faith. If you are too timid or hesitant, not only will this not do anything, but also disaster will befall you yourself. This is the profound lesson he learned from the 228 Incident. So he brought up in a later self-criticism, he himself mentioned it, that in these unforeseen circumstances or states of emergency, aside from having the right guiding principles, things still needed to be powerfully pushed forward to achieve the expected results.

Lastly, something I want to emphasize is that both those four great principles of peace my father once proposed, and the way we now address the 228 Incident with the word "peace," for instance, the "228 Peace Park," the "228 Peace Day," or the "228 Justice and Peace Movement," they all demonstrate a close relation between peace and the 228 Incident. Then since this is the case, shouldn't we pay attention to my father's concept of peace and his earnest efforts to put them into practice during this historical moment, and affirm it more? So that in the future, if by chance there is any similar situation, we could still first consider the path of peace, as the option with the highest priority. This is the lessen I learned when I encountered the history of my father taking on great risk, even bearing his cross, having the courage to walk through hell fire to protect the lives of the people and the safety of the property in Tainan City. Peace should be the greatest concept of all of the impressions and lessons gained from this history. This, after all is a universal value and it deserves more attention.

Question: How were the aforementioned principles of peace pushed through the discussions in the 228 Incident Settlement Committee-Tainan Branch? Were there any disagreements or disputes during the process?

Hahn: Of course, if you want to achieve peace, the first principles, "No Escalation and Without Bloodshed" are rather important. The most important part is "Without Bloodshed." As for, if during the discussions there were disputes, and this is speaking from a democratic standpoint, they were acceptable and inevitable, as long as we attained a consensus majority and reached a conclusion. Like the four principles put forward by my father, in addition to his strong advocating and promotion, he had attained a consensus in the 228 Incident Settlement Committee-Tainan Branch saying that they would implement these four principles. Only with the principle of peace, the four principles were able to pass at the meeting.

Question: In addition to Tainan City, at that time did he go to other cities and counties to spread his ideas of peace ?

Hahn: As far as I know he did not go to any other cities and counties, because he was already tied up and had already experienced untold hardships in Tainan, and had no way to give considerations to other places. But really, just look north of Tainan at Chiayi, more than 1,000 people died, and then in Kaohsiung more than 3,000 died. Later the statistics in Tainan were 1-200, so even though it was sandwiched between the more severe Chiayi and Kaohsiung, it seems like the number of deaths in Tainan is a lot less. This can be seen as an objective fact and can be proved by the resulting effect in Tainan that my father's ideas of peace were effective at that time and played an important role leading to such an outcome.

In a booklet I authored, "The 228 Incident and Peace—A Missing Page in Taiwan's Modern History," I think it was on page 18, where I had referenced several books related to the 228 Incident and with everything laid out in a table that you could then see, that in every major city and county of Taiwan, the Tainan casualties were the least (including the Mainlander victims of battery). That it lost 100 or 200 people, and while those lives were precious, compared to Chiayi and Kaohsiung it is just so much less, arguably less than a tenth. So this is a very rare and valuable fact. It could be described as the fruit of the peace-loving efforts of Tainan's people.

Question: Acting the same as other public representatives who negotiated with the government, compared to those victims of arrest and execution, what might be the ultimate reason your father was spared ?

Hahn: In addition to my father leading the 228 Incident Settlement Committee-Tainan Branch and personally maintaining the principles of peace, it was later printed in the Taiwanese Provincial Administrative Executive Office record, mentioning my father, as well as others, saying that they had "rescued mainland officials, protected public property, pacified the Taiwanese people, and helped handle the incident." The records were compiled and printed by the Taiwanese Provincial Chief Executive Office, on March 30, 1947, after the incident subsided, and had that written in them. My father's efforts to maintain these principles and practices of peace had acquired acknowledgement from the government agencies. Of course, some people might ask, "Wasn't it because he was too soft or for some other reason that he wasn't investigated?" Actually, after the incident ended, the army commanders had asked him to write a confession. A confession is when you think that you have made some mistake and then you have to write it out, believing you have made this or that kind of mistake. That is a confession. My father clearly and resolutely refused the military commander and told him, "I did not do anything wrong, and if you want me to write, then I will write an official report, but I will not write a confession."

As such, he was not weak, but instead should be said that he was strong. When it was time to fight, he would fight and speak with a righteous sense of justice, so that eventually the military softened, and became accepting an official report rather than a confession. Therefore, we may understand why later he was not investigated or suffered from the incident. Regarding this matter, the aforementioned lawyer, Shen Rong, also wrote, "the extremists of that day thought he was incompetent, weak and they expressed their dissatisfaction. After it was settled, the local authorities, failing to understand the virtues of the central government, prosecuted many citizens, and wanted to obtain a confession from Mr. Harn so that they could treat him accordingly. Mr. Harn not only sternly refused, but tried to rescue those people who were accused. Thus it can be seen that for his country, people, justice, and rational, he was not afraid of oppression from local authorities."

Actually, there is some other document of the 228 Incident, which seems to be a dictionary and it has written in it that he received "rehabilitation," and so they did not continue to pursue him. I think that is a mistake and far from being the truth. Because he was not without protest, from start to finish he consistently maintained his principles, whether towards the officials or the people. He was mainly concerned with having considerations for the people, as well as communicating with the officials on behalf of the people. But it was never completely one sided. Because of this relationship he had a positive standing and so later was not prosecuted or punished. I think these reasons are all there is to it. As a matter of fact, on March 11th during a Tainan City Council meeting he was forced onto a military vehicle by army soldiers using bayonets, the bayonets of long rifles, escorting him to the military's southern district headquarters for interrogation. He too was subjected to this kind of treatment, but because he was mainly impartial and did not do anything wrong, and so that is why afterwards he was able to emerge safely from danger and not be arrested or executed. Moreover, after the 228 Incident, in June of the same year when the Provincial Legislature convened the third investigative meeting, he boldly stated that "the officials and the people both share an equal responsibility," and he also criticized the central government handling of the process "made people feel lacking of generosity." He even once drew a conclusion that criticized the officials, saying, "The ones in charge (A reference that implies the highest authorities) were ignorant of decisive opportunities, and failed to take precautions," and this was the result. Please remember that these kinds of remarks are in the White Terror era, which in the aftermath of the 228 Incident, had already started. And this was officially published in black ink on white paper. Doesn't this constitute being bold, outspoken? In any of this, where can he be said to be "weak?"

But, here I would like to stress again that it does not mean advocating for peace will be free of danger. For example in the book I compiled, "The 228 Incident and Peace—A Missing Page in Taiwan's Modern History," it mentions public figures who also advocated for peace, but these people were not so fortunate, such as in Chiayi City there was Senator Chen Cheng-Po, whom we are all very familiar with, Chen Fu-Zhi, director of the Three People's Principles Youth League Branch of Chiayi, and Chiayi senators Pan Mu-Zhi, Lu Bing-Qin, and Ke Lin. They had negotiated peaceful arrangements at the Chiayi Shueishang Airport, but instead were immediately arrested and in front of Chiayi's train station were publicly executed, causing everyone to be very grieved and sad. Then there was the pastor of Gangshan Church named Xiao Chao-Jin. It was the same with him. While he was in the middle of young people, discouraging them from fighting, he instead was arrested by the soldiers and also later executed.

So it does not mean that there is no danger in advocating for peace and peaceful negotiations. It was still possible to be subjected to very great danger, but my father still went to do it. No matter if it was negotiating with the military, or communicating with the people. They often, because several of his comrades, especially Hou Quan-Cheng and Lee Guo-Ze, were Christians, knelt together in prayers on the floor of the Tainan City Council. There they inquired of God, whether or not they should carry the weight of this cross. The result of praying was that everyone had consensus, and then had the courage to risk their very lives, to communicate with the public, or go to the barracks to negotiate. Thus it is clear that advocating for peace is not without its dangers, just look at those unfortunate examples in Chiayi and then you will know. Fortunately, in Tainan City, the principles of peace were probably adopted and implemented quickly as soon as it began, so this probably allowed the military to be more at ease, and therefore people did not encounter so much misfortune. But there was still Lawyer Tang De-Zhang who executed by the firing squad. This was a great misfortune. He was not the only person among the elite of Tainan to have suffered. It was a great pity for Tainan City.

受訪者：廖繼斌
臺灣省政治建設協會參與二二八處委會代表
廖進平之孫、二二八國家紀念館館長

問題：事件爆發前後臺灣人民做了什麼努力？

廖：二二八事件爆發前，事實上很多有遠見的臺灣人以及精英份子，他們就已經透過很多管道，用盡各種方法，希望能夠幫助當時的陳儀政府能夠實行實踐，馬上憲法頒布後，所應該做的一些比較民主法治的一些措施。陳儀政府那時候並沒辦法做到，所以就已經埋下了所有的這些種子。可是事實上事件爆發後，我們可以看到當時的臺灣的這些社會精英、這些社會的士紳，也是想盡辦法希望能夠跟當時的陳儀政府合作，也是完全配合陳儀政府來成立二二八處理委員會，把事件的這個暴力性降到最低，希望能夠用比較和緩的、和平的民主法治的方式來解決當時整個臺灣人積壓一年多來的這個不滿與憤怒。使整個埋在民間的仇恨的種子，不安的種，不安的這些情況能夠降到最低。他們希望能夠用最小的犧牲、最平和的方式，讓臺灣能夠徹底地實施地方自治。可是當時的陳儀政府也沒有辦法做到這一點，導致這個事件以悲劇性來收尾。

問題：廖進平在事件與處委會裡的角色？他的理念與臺灣民主發展的關係？

廖：先祖父進平公，事實上在日治時代的時候，他就參加文化協會、臺灣民眾黨，跟許許多多的先進一起做所謂的非武裝抗日的一些活動。臺灣民眾黨在1927年成立，1931年被解散，一直到二次大戰結束有十幾年的時間，事實上先祖父並沒有放棄所謂從事社會改造運動的這些努力。所以二次大戰一結束陳儀政府過來，他馬上跟一些以前的同志組了臺灣省政治建設協會，這個臺灣省政治建設協會事實上是等於一個黨。在戰後到二二八發生的短短一年多，事實上，臺灣省政治建設協會是非常活躍的政治組織。在二二八事件發生，陳儀要求官民合組所謂的二二八處理委員會，臺灣省政治建設協會有好幾個人很積極地參與。先祖父就是參加這個處委會，也當重要的幹部。事實上，先祖父的政治理念是非常的簡單，以大家現在的觀念都能理解，他是希望一個政府、一個社會應該有最基本的民主法治。當時，南京政府在1947年的1月1日也公佈了中華民國憲法，打算1947年12月25日實施。所以先祖父他們就以中華民國南京政府公佈的這部憲法為藍本，他們也單純只要求說，希望臺灣省能夠建立成一個三民主義的模範省，可惜因為當時政治環境的關係，先祖父的願望並沒有達成。

問題：廖進平在二二八事件的受難經過？

廖：因為在參加二二八處委會前，先祖父就曾經參與了一兩次所謂的大型的遊行活動，像支援日本涉谷發生的涉谷事件的臺灣人民的權益也好，當時在大陸發生的沈崇事件也好，先祖父都非常活躍，當遊行主要的策動者。所以陳儀政府早就把先祖父看成眼中釘，在二二八處委會成立沒有多久，先祖父從一個特殊管道很早就知道，蔣介石已經派兵從上海出發了，所以先祖父大概在3月6號、7號左右，就開始逃亡到八里去。可惜的就是，因為先祖父常常在街頭演講，那麼很多的、不管白道或黑道的人，對他都很熟稔，他在逃的時候，又被這個政府，應該是有透過各種管道懸重賞來緝拿他。所以他從八里打算到淡水，淡水打算看有沒有機會，從淡水或著基隆，坐船逃到日本去。在這個計劃中，很可惜的在八里淡水中間，就被當時的流氓去密報、被憲兵隊緝獲。照我們事後輾轉得到的消息，應該是在淡水河口的海邊被密裁丟到海裡面去，那麼他從1947年的3月中旬，我們知道他被抓以後，就一直到現在，也沒有他的蹤跡，我們大概是知道說已經早在被抓沒多久就被密裁掉了。

問題：作為二二八國家館館長，對於二二八處委會的看法，以及二二八國家館如何透過歷史教育讓民眾瞭解二二八處委會的理念與影響？

廖：我們從事後來看，當時二二八處委會所主張的一些，不管三十二條也好、四十二條也好，他們那些主張，事實上都是一些很基本的民主法治的一些理念。那麼，1947年處委會主張以後，到現在也六十七、六十八個年頭了，我們回顧來看，事實上，都是我們這幾十年來臺灣在各界的精英、各界的民主人士奮鬥，都是朝這個目標在努力。簡單講，司法要獨立，政治要清明，要有真正全民深入的、深化的民主法治，這個都是其實我們今天耳熟能詳，我們可以想看看，當時我們的先烈先賢在六十七、八年前就能主張，這個實在是令人非常的欽佩。我們二二八國家館，是國內第一個中央政府層級的人權館，我們也肩負著人權教育的使命，所謂的記住歷史教訓、不要再重蹈覆轍。怎麼把民主法治的種子來傳承下去，我們是負有非常重大的深責大任。我們國家館從民國一百年二二八開館以後，現在快三年多了，邁入第四個年頭，事實上，我們也跟很多的學校，尤其是相關的科系系所合作，辦了很多的講座、專題演講，我們甚至已經規劃進入第三年的人權影片的系列放映，透過多媒體多元的媒介，吸引各種不同階層、不同喜好的朋友能夠踏進我們二二八國家館，只要他們能夠願意進來，我們就有機會把二二八的這種先賢先烈的這種對臺灣民主奉獻的精神，能夠傳播出去。我想我們還有很多改善的空間，我們是臨淵履薄，我們會全力以赴。

Interviewee: Liao Chie-Ping, the grandson of Liao Jin-Ping the Taiwanese Provincial Political Construction Association representative who participated in the 228 Incident Settlement Committee, and the director of the National 228 Memorial Museum hereinafter referred to as Liao.

Question: Before and after the incident's outbreak, what efforts did the Taiwanese people make?

Liao: Actually, before the outbreak of the 228 Incident, many far-sighted Taiwanese people and elites had already gone through many different channels and used up all available options in the hope of being able to help Chen Yi's authority at the time implement and put into practice all of the more democratic measures it should've made immediately following the enactment of the constitution. At that time, Chen Yi's authority had no way to do it, but all of the seeds had been planted. But truly, after the outbreak of the incident, we can find that the Taiwanese elites of the day, the gentry of society also left no stone unturned in hopes of being able to collaborate with Chen Yi's authority. They also completely cooperated with Chen Yi's authority by setting up the 228 Incident Settlement Committee to minimize the violence of the incident, hoping to be able to use a gentler, more peaceful democratic method to resolve the accumulation of more than a year's discontent and anger from the entire Taiwanese population. They wanted to minimize all the seeds of hatred, and discord buried among the people, these conditions of unrest. They hoped to be able to use the smallest sacrifice, the most peaceful method, so that Taiwan could thoroughly implement local self-government. But Chen Yi's authority at the time couldn't do this, and they let this incident end in tragedy.

Question: What was Liao Jin-Ping's role in the incident and in the Settlement Committee? What were his ideas regarding Taiwan's democratic development?

Liao: Actually during the period of Japanese rule, Grandfather Liao Jin-Ping had joined the Taiwanese Cultural Association, the Taiwanese People's Party, together with many unarmed anti-Japanese movements.

So, the Taiwanese People's Party was formed in 1927 and disbanded in 1931. Straight up until the end of World War II there were ten plus years but grandfather really did not abandon his efforts in engaging social reform movements. Then as soon as World War II ended Chen Yi's authority came over, and he immediately with some of his former comrades organized the Taiwanese Provincial Political Construction Association, which was in fact equivalent to a political party. From after the war it was just over a year till the 228 Incident occurred, and the Taiwanese Provincial Political Construction Association was, in fact a very active political organization. When the 228 Incident occurred, Chen Yi asked the officials to joined the 228 Incident Settlement Committee, and the Taiwanese Provincial Political Construction Association had a good number of people actively participating. My grandfather participated in this Settlement Committee, and he also served as an important officer. Actually my grandfather's political ideas were very simple, and everyone can understand them through our modern concepts. He wanted a government, a society that would have the fundamentals of a democratic rule of law. At that time, on December 31, 1946 the Nanking Government also announced the Constitution of the Republic of China, intending to implement it on December 25, 1947. So my grandfather and those with him then used the Republic of China's Constitution published by the Nanking Government, as a blueprint. They also just simply requested that they wanted Taiwan to be established as a Three Principles of the People model province. But, unfortunately because of the political environment at the time, grandfather's aspirations were not achieved.

Question: What was Liao Jin-Ping's experience in the 228 Incident ?

Liao: Because before participating in the 228 Incident Settlement Committee, my grandfather had already participated in one or two so-called large-scale demonstrations, such as supporting the Taiwanese peoples rights in the Shibuya Incident that occurred in Shibuya, Japan, or then at that time the Shen Chong Case occurred in the mainland. My grandfather was very active, serving as the main instigator for these demonstrations. So the Chen Yi government had long looked at my grandfather as a thorn in their side, and it wasn't long after the establishment of the 228 Incident Settlement Committee that my grandfather had been Informed through a special channel that the troops Chiang Kai-Shek had sent for from Shanghai had departed. So probably around March 6th or 7th he started fleeing to the Bali district of Taipei. The unfortunate thing was that because my grandfather often gave speeches in the streets, there were so many, no matter law-abiding or part of the underworld, people that recognized him. So when he was on the run, this government, who probably through all sorts of channels offered a generous reward, again captured him. So he planned to go from Bali District to Tanshui, to see if there were any opportunities at Tanshui to escape by boat from Tanshui or Keelung to Japan. Unfortunately during this plan, in between Bali District and Tanshui he was seized by the military police who were tipped-off by a gangster. According to information we received indirectly after the event, it was probably on the shore at the mouth of the Tanshui River, where they secretly dispose of him into the ocean. So from mid-March 1947 after he was captured up until now we know that there hasn't been any sign of him. We probably know that shortly after he was arrested it wasn't long before he was disposed of.

Question: As director of the 228 National Museum, what are your views on the 228 Incident Settlement Committee and how does the 228 National Museum through history education allow the public to understand the concepts and impact of the 228 Incident Settlement Committee?

Liao: When we look back in hindsight at some of the things the 228 Incident Settlement Committee advocated, no matter if it was 32 or 42 Demands, their propositions in fact were some of the most fundamental ideas of democratic rule of law. So 67 or 68 years after the propositions of the 1947 Settlement Committee until today, we look back and see that it truly was the Taiwanese elites and democratic personages from every circle and all walks of life that struggled over these decades, working towards a common goal. In short, we wanted judicial independence, political transparency and to have a real, further deepening in the development of the universal democratic rule of law. In fact today we are so familiar with these things that we can speak of them in great detail, but we might want to look at our martyrs and sages, who 67 or 68 years ago were able to advocate for them. This is really very admirable. Our 228 National Museum, is the first central government level human rights museum in the country. So we are also shouldering the mission of human rights education, the so-called remembering the lessons of history, so that we don't repeat the same mistakes again. Then how should we pass on the seeds of democracy and rule of law? We bear a very great, profound and important responsibility. Since the opening of our National Museum on 2-28, the one hundredth anniversary of the Republic to now, it's been almost more than three years and it's entering into its fourth year. We actually also collaborate with many schools, especially with related departments and majors and have held many lectures, and special seminars. We have even planned to enter our third year of screening a series of human rights films. Through multimedia and various mediums, attracting a variety of different levels of society, people of different tastes can step into our 228 National Museum. As long as they are willing to come in, I think, we have an opportunity to take the kind of spirit of dedication that those martyrs of 228 had for Taiwan's democracy, and are able to spread it on. I think that we still have a lot of room for improvement. We are walking on thin ice and we are going all out.

受訪者：王贊紘
二二八處委會宣傳組長暨三十二條大綱主撰者
王添灯之長孫

問題：請問王添灯先生參與二二八處委會的背景？

王：我祖父一直是相信民主政治的。那他從日據時代在臺灣還沒有光復以前，就是常常參加很多民主的社團，也參加很多的活動，也常常被日本警察抓去，那個時候一抓去，就是拘留十九天。我也聽家裡的人講過，好幾次因為參加民主運動，在日據時代就被日本的警察抓走。臺灣光復以後，他相當積極地參加政治運動，所以他也當選了臺灣的參議員。二二八事件發生以後，他也參加了二二八事件的調查委員會，因為這個對他來說是一個可以替人民服務的機會，可以讓人民跟政府之間能夠取得和平，所以他也參加。

問題：請介紹王添灯先生在二二八處委會裡的角色？他的理念與臺灣民主發展的關係？

王：那當時他被委任的是作為二二八調查委員會的宣傳組組長，所以在很多的會議記錄跟對臺灣的全民的廣播都是他負責做的，所以在三十二條通過後，他也在今天的台北二二八紀念館，當時的電台對全省做了一個廣播。那在廣播，他在最後告訴全臺灣的人民說，二二八事件的調查委員會能夠做的就到這裡為止，那剩下的事情就是靠臺灣的人民的決定。我個人是一直覺得說，這幾句話到今天還是成立的，臺灣的前途還是需要靠臺灣的人民來做決定。

問題：你認為二二八事件處理委員會的定位是甚麼？

王：二二八這件事情，如果講遠一點，應該是臺灣人民對中華民國政府到臺灣來以後，他的期望值與他實質發生的事情有個落差。當然派來的這些官員很多在那個時候有貪污等等的狀況，有一部分把臺灣的物質送到中國去，所以在戰後以後，在國民政府的管理之下，臺灣的很多物質是相當的缺乏，人民的生活也是相當的痛苦。從私煙的事情發生了以後，組了一個私煙血案的調查。經過兩三天，應該在三月大概三號左右，就成立了一個二二八事件的調查委員會。這個調查委員會是由我祖父等四個人去跟陳儀報告以後，跟陳儀商量，最後他們決定成立了一個二二八事件的調查委員會。在這個調查委員會裡面，有一部分是政府的官員，也就是說這個調查委員會是在政府的允許之下，所產生的一個委員會。整個事情是因為臺灣人民跟政府之間有些不同的意見，在私煙的這件事情上有不同的意見，所以他們組了一個這個團體，簡單的說，以臺語講說就是「做公親」，就是一個公親的團體，希望能夠站在一個客觀的立場，替兩方面的人都可以尋求一個大家都可以接受的事情。那二二八事件調查委員會，後來又經過政府的要求，也就是說當時國民政府的要求，陳儀長官他們的要求，加入了一些商會、工會、學生團體，還有一些政治建設委員會等等，也就是說把這個編制加以擴大，所以他的成員是比較複雜的。因為在那個時候的政治狀況，除了臺灣的一些本土的一些政治勢力外，還有包含了很多商會或是工會，加上也有擁國民政府的，有擁共產主義的等等，是一個相當複雜的環境。

問題：您認為三十二條大綱所代表的精神是什麼？

王：在二二八事件調查委員會成立以後，經過了幾天的商量，應該是在三月七號，由我祖父所草擬的三十二條提出來，希望能夠獲得大家大多數的同意。當場的開會是相當的混亂，後面也有人提了十條，加起來說叫做四十二條，事實上，原先只提了三十二條，裡面最重要的有幾樣事情，幾樣基本的原則，就是說希望臺灣的事情能夠由臺灣的人民來處理，很多官員的任命等等，希望能夠多加一點臺籍當時的立場，然後他也希望說能夠因為這個樣子，兩邊可以取得一個比較大家都可以接受的狀況。很不幸的，這個事情一直大概到了三月八日左右，當國民政府開始「平叛」，二二八事件調查委員會被宣布是非法的，反正就是認為說是把它解散掉，最後因為當時所提的後來加的這十條裡面，然後做一個藉口把很多委員會裡面都抓了。我們講說，本來是說做公親的，現在變成事主，那麼這些人都被抓去了。那在這個二二八事件調查委員會，雖然短短大概差不多一個禮拜的時間，那在這麼一個各方面的勢力，就是本土的勢力、共產黨的勢力、國民黨的勢力等等這些勢力之下，還是能夠很快地取得一個共識，就是應該是朝民主的這個方向走。所以，可以說，二二八調查委員會是臺灣回歸中國以後所舉行的一個民主的一個高峰會議，也可以講說是臺灣第一個由老百姓等各個不同派別、各個不同思想、各個不同想法、各個不同主張，然後大家能夠取得一個共識而產生的這個三十二條。

那二二八事件調查委員會是一個在臺灣，是第一個真正民主制度的一個事件，也是一個委員會，也是臺灣第一個民主的開的會議，簡單的說。因為在當時有各個不同的黨派，各個民眾、商會、學生，有這個擁國民黨，反國民黨，擁共產黨等等不同團體，聚集在一起的一個會議，可以說是一個民主的盛會。所以在會中，也有相當多不同的各個意見，但是最後我祖父整合的三十二條，大家都覺得這三十二條是大家應該要努力的方向，即使有對於政府，或者是其他的想法有不同，但是大家都同意以民主的方式來取得最大的共識，這三十二條是一個大家的一種共識。所以我說在這一個會議裡面，展現了相當多的民主，大家的協調，大家用英文說 compromise 後所產生的結果，從臺灣的歷史上來看，那是一個非常成功的一個民主制度的會議。

Interviewee: Wang Zan-Hong, the eldest grandson of the 228 Incident Settlement Committee Chief Publicity Officer and primary author of the 32 Demands Wang Tien-Teng, hereinafter referred to as Wang.

Question: What is the context of Mr. Wang Tien-Teng's participation in the 228 Incident Settlement Committee?

Wang: My grandfather had always believed in democracy. Since the era of the Japanese occupation of Taiwan, and before the retrocession, he was often involved in many democratic societies, and would also take part in many activities. So, he was also often captured by the Japanese police, and during that time, when he was caught, was detained for 19 days. I've also heard from family members that he was arrested several times because of his participation in democratic movements in the era of Japanese occupation. After Taiwan's retrocession, he quite actively participated in political campaigns, and so was elected as a Senator of Taiwan. After the 228 Incident occurred, he also participated in the 228 Incident Settlement Committee, because for him this was an opportunity to serve the people, allowing peace to be achieved between the people and the government.

Question: Can you explain Mr. Wang Tien-Teng's role in the 228 Incident Settlement Committee? What is the relationship between his ideas and Taiwan's democratic development?

Wang: At that time he was appointed to act as the Chief Publicity Officer of the 228 Incident Settlement Committee, so a lot of meeting records along with Taiwan's national broadcasts were all things he did. So after the 32 Demands passed, he was also in today's Taipei 228 Memorial Museum, at that time a radio station, making a province-wide broadcast. At the very end of the broadcast, he told the whole Taiwanese people that the 228 Incident Settlement Committee had done all it could do, and that now the rest depended upon the Taiwanese people's decision. Personally, I've always thought that these words still stand today, that Taiwan's future still requires the Taiwanese people to make a decision.

Question: What do you think the 228 Incident Settlement Committee's position is?

Wang: The 228 affair, if we take a step back farther, would be about the discrepancy between the Taiwanese people's expectations for the ROC government and the essence of what happened after they came to Taiwan. Certainly, many of those officials sent at that time were corrupt etc. They took a chunk of Taiwan's material wealth and sent it back to China so that later, after the war, under the management of the Nationalist government, Taiwan had a serious shortage of many material goods. The people's lives were quite hard.

Then after the contraband cigarette incident happened, a 227 Tobacco Seizure and Murder Case Investigation Commission was formed. After two or three days, probably around March 3rd, a 228 Incident Settlement Committee was formed. This 228 Incident Settlement Committee was formed after my father and four others went and reported the situation to Chen Yi, discussed it with Chen Yi and then finally decided to establish a 228 Incident Settlement Committee. In this investigation committee, there were some government officials, so in other words, this investigation committee was completely sanctioned by the government. The whole Incident was caused because there were some different views between the government and the Taiwanese people. There was a different opinion on the contraband cigarette matter and so they formed this group, "to play mediator," as we say in Taiwanese. It was an arbitration group hoping to be able to take an objective standpoint on behalf of both sides and to seek a mutually acceptable solution.

Afterwards, the 228 Incident Settlement Committee at the behest of the Nationalist Government, or in other words a request from Chen Yi, again enlarged the membership to include some commercial associations, trade unions, student groups and also some Taiwan Provincial Political Construction Association members etc. Because of the political situation at that time, expanding the staff to include all these different groups created quite a complex environment.

Question: What do you think the spirit of the 32 Demands represents ?

Wang: After the 228 Incident Settlement Committee was established, and after several days of discussion, probably on March 7th, was when the 32 Demands drafted by my father were proposed. He hoped to be able to gain a majority approval. The scene of the meeting was quite chaotic and that's why someone could put forward 10 more Demands later, combining them together and calling them the 42 Demands. In reality, there were only 32 original Demands. The couple of most important basic principles in these 32 Demands were those that wanted the matters of Taiwan to be handled by the Taiwanese people and to appoint more Taiwanese as local officials and so forth. He wanted to add a little bit more Taiwanese perspective, because he hoped that then the two sides could achieve a more acceptable state of affairs for everyone.

Unfortunately, this state-of-affairs continued until around March 8th, when the Nationalist government started "counterinsurgency operations," the so-called pacification of the countryside. So, the 228 Incident Settlement Committee was denounced as if it were illegal or something. In any case, I believe that it was disbanded because of the ten Demands that were proposed and added later. Afterwards, they were used as an excuse to arrest many of the those in the 228 Incident Settlement Committee. We say that 'they who were meant to be mediator have now have become the victim'. These people were all arrested. So although the 228 Incident Settlement Committee was around for just a few short weeks time and was under such a diverse power base, with local forces, Communist Party forces, Nationalist forces etc., it was still able to quickly attain a consensus and that was to head towards democracy. So it could be said that the 228 Incident Settlement Committee was the democracy summit held after Taiwan's retrocession to China. It could also be said to be the first held by every faction, every kind of thought, every kind of philosophy, and every kind of viewpoint of the Taiwanese people with everyone coming to the consensus that produced these 32 Demands.

So the 228 Incident Settlement Committee was the first real democratic event in Taiwan and simply put was Taiwan's first democratic and open meeting. At that time there was every different kind of political party, and the different groups gathered together in a meeting that could be called a grand democratic meeting.

During that meeting, with all of these different opinions, my father finally consolidated the 32 Demands, and everyone thought that they needed to make an effort towards these 32 Demands, even if it was different with regard to their own philosophy. Everyone agreed to use the democratic method to achieve a majority consensus and these 32 Demands are a kind of consensus of everyone. Therefore, I say that quite a bit of democracy, cooperation and the kind of results that compromise produces were discovered in this meeting. Looking at Taiwan's history, that is a very successful democratic meeting.

受訪者：侯坤宏
國史館纂修兼修纂處處長

問題：多年來，國史館做了什麼努力，讓臺灣民眾更加了解二二八事件與處委會歷史？

侯：關於國史館在二二八事件方面的成果，與國史館在政府部門的定位有關係。國史館是國家最高的史政單位，當然史政單位還有很多，比如說像臺灣文獻館、臺北市文獻會，以前的高雄市文獻會，這些都算。解嚴前後，為了要平反二二八，所以朝野各方人士就在這方面做了一些努力，國史館也做了一些，在這個過程裡面，大概可以分作三個方面來談。

　　第一、在1997年出版三本《國史館藏二二八檔案史料》，這其實是為了要因應立法院對史政單位的要求與監督，所以當時就編了三本，蒐錄國史館當時所典藏二二八事件相關史料。等到2000年，陳水扁擔任中華民國總統以後，在張炎憲館長的帶領努力之下，與檔案管理局、二二八事件紀念基金會，共同合作出版了十八冊的《二二八事件檔案彙編》。前後經歷的時間大概從2002年一直到2008年，期間大概有六、七年的時間。這裡面的資料相當的多，如果要研究二二八事件，這套資料是不能忽略的。另外，我剛剛講的說有三個工作，另外一個就是出版《二二八事件辭典》，花的心力更多，參與規劃及撰稿的學者都對二二八事件下過功夫，這項工作前後花了大概有三年多的時間，後來出版了上、下兩冊。辭典裡面的辭條都是經過特別篩選，每一個辭條撰寫人員也經過特別的選擇。這部書，到目前為止，對於想要了解二二八事件，還是很有參考價值。當然如果站在比較嚴格的要求，可能其中有一些人的生平或許還可以再增補，部分錯誤當然難免。以上所談就是國史館在這十幾年來所做，有關二二八事件的一些努力。

問題：請問二二八相關的史料來源包括哪些？

侯：前面所談到已出版的書，其史料有一些是本來就是國史館所典藏的，在進行編輯前先從目錄去尋找相關的條目，然後再調出原件來閱讀，從中選出擬用檔案經過整編再出版，這是一部分。另外比較大的那部分，其實現在不是典藏在國史館，而是在檔案管理局。檔案管理局當初成立的時候，因為是一個新成立的機構，所以就先借用國史館的地方上班，透過一些專家學者，幫忙從政府各單位蒐集有關二二八事件的檔案。我們出版的最大宗史料來源，就是這一批檔案。這一批檔案現在存放在檔案管理局。

問題：回首百年多來臺灣追求民主之路，二二八處委會在臺灣民主發展過程中的定位是什麼？

侯：這回台北二二八紀念館所辦的一個展覽，就是以二二八事件處理委員會為主題，標題為「臺灣民主高峰會議」。為什麼會定這樣的一個會議？這是主辦單位的一種認定，也可以說這是一種解釋的方式，對處委會的一種詮釋的方法，這也是可以的，但以此來訂題，理解時要考慮到前後的歷史脈絡與其發展。比如說，之前在日本統治時代的臺灣，當時的臺灣人是不是也有做過類似的活動，比如說議會請願的運動或者相關的運動等等。戰後臺灣，整個民主政治的發展，尤其是最近一二十年來，如果站在一個比較長的歷史脈絡來看的話，把二二八處委會看成是一次「臺灣民主高峰會」，也是可以。但是，我們應該要進一步來考慮，對二二八處委會這樣的認定，有沒有不足或不恰當的地方。因為二二八處委會成立的時間很匆促，雖然說在全省各地大概有二十幾個單位，存在的時間很短，可以講說曇花一現，其出現也是一個歷史的一個偶然。任何一個事件都有其特定的時空背景，我們現在研究二二八處委會，要把它的時空定位好，才比較好去評價它。

問題：事件初期，二二七緝煙血案調查委員會轉為二二八處委會的原由？

侯：二二七緝煙血案調查委員會，是為了處理民國36年2月27日晚在臺北爆發的事件。當時，邀請了一些像臺北市的參議會、臺籍的國大代表、省參議員、國民參政員等等來參與，決議推派代表跟行政長官公署提出一些要求，包括解除戒嚴，釋放被捕的民眾等，陳儀也做出一些回應，但後來整個事件發展的很快。緝煙處理委員會很快的就轉成二二八事件處理委員會，只是一個名稱的轉換，牽涉到整個這些處委會的委員跟行政長官公署的一些溝通、一些磨合。

問題：說明二二八處委會由臺北地區擴大到全省性最高民意機構的過程？

侯：從緝煙血案處委會轉為二二八處委會，在隨後的過程中，也開了很多次的會議。因為事件很快的就擴散到全省。為了因應這樣的一個局面，在中山堂的二二八處委會就鼓勵各地都要成立類似這樣的處委會。隨著事件在各地的風起雲湧，各地就有處委會的產生。其實在中山堂的二二八事件處委會在下令要各地成立處委會之前，在臺灣各地有些地方，就已經自主的陸陸續續成立一些二二八處委會。

問題：那麼照您剛剛所說，在二二八處委會還沒呼籲全省成立處委會之前，就陸陸續續已經有些地方有成立這些機構，主要原因是甚麼？

侯：為什麼會在全省各地都會有二二八處委會的組織？，應該說為了處理動亂，當地不同的動亂。其中有一些是自發性的，發生動亂就要有人要起來維持治安、維持秩序。這又要牽涉到二二八事件的起因問題，比如說對長官公署施政的不滿，對外省人的不滿等等。

問題：您認為各層級的二八處委會共同的理念與訴求是什麼？

侯：如果我們反過來問：各層級的二二八處委會，有沒有共同的理念跟共同的訴求？這樣的話，我們才能來說這樣問適不適當。在全省各地的二二八處委會，它的組織看起來好像是由上至下的關係，但其上下附屬關係不是那麼明顯。它不是一個很嚴密的結構，上面可以去指揮或者控制下面的單位。

所以說談到二二八的理念，其實應該以臺北市中山堂這個地方的處委會來說，會中所提出來的三十二條要求，或者四十二條要求，很難說有一致的看法，因為這牽涉到處委會成員的問題。臺北二二八處委會其成員也都相當複雜，而且裡面成員也有情治人員滲透進來的，譬如許忠義服務隊的德輝。

問題：三十二條或是四十二條大綱的提出，對於事件本身的演變，尤其是軍隊鎮壓，會有什麼不同嗎？

侯：有一種說法是原來有三十二條，後來變成了四十二條，當然這裡面還有一些爭論，還要去釐清。也有學者認為說，沒有四十二條，就是三十二條。針對軍隊的鎮壓來講，為什麼會有鎮壓，主要的原因是，處委會踩到了統治者的底線、紅線，統治者認為提出政治要求，已經不是屬於自治的範圍，已經是要推翻原來政權，所以才會引來當時南京政府派兵來臺鎮壓這個事實。

問題：那您覺得二二八處委會真的有踩到底線嗎，還是只是雙方的認知不同？

侯：如果在處委會，或者比較屬於強調臺灣自治、要實行民主的這些人來講，他們一定認為沒有，只是一個民主的訴求。但是就統治者言，即行政長官公署的領導人來講，他們會認為處委會已經踩到這個底線。

問題：二二八處委會從法理上來看，屬於什麼樣的組織定位？所提出的"大綱"，指的是什麼？是民眾陳情的提案，或是法案、政策的決議？

侯：這裡提到了幾個名詞，就是說，民眾陳情的提案，或者法案，或者政策的決議。如果用只能三選一，並不是那麼適合，但是可以用「政策的提案」來說。它不是決議，也不是屬於陳情的案件，因為陳情的案件大概不會，也不需要透過處委會這樣的一個機構來運作、來向長官公署提出來，所以它有一點類似政策的提案。這是把其中剛剛提到的陳情的提案，或者法案，或者政策的決議，做一綜合。如果就組織定位來講，二二八處委會比較屬於是一種政治性的團體。政治性的團體在民主發展的過程中，尤其是在剛開始萌芽階段，有時候會受到統治當局的打壓，因為想要奪取統治者的權力。

問題：如果從提案的角度來看，許多處委會成員本身就是參議員，這與他們平時的質詢提案有何不同？

侯：當時他們所提的案子，沒有說像處委會提的這樣尖銳，讓當時的行政長官公署沒有辦法接受。所以剛剛講的說已經踏到政治的紅線、底線，使得行政長官公署沒有辦法忍受。

問題：這樣說來，當年處委會的成員，為何會提出這些提案，又為何認為可以被行政長官公署所接受？

侯：因為有二二八事件的發生，才成立了二二八處委會。在二二八處委會中，這些人都是當時的臺灣精英，很多人都是有受過很好的教育，都有相當的理想，也關心臺灣未來的發展；再加上對政府已經積壓的很多不滿，在那個情境底下所提出來這些政策建言，希望能夠看看有沒有機會做到，但就是沒有那個機會。

問題：您覺得從歷史研究來看，二二八事件的重要性為何？是否被過度的政治炒作？

侯：二二八是戰後臺灣史上一個很重要的歷史事件。從日本統治臺灣的五十年，1945年由中華民國政府來接收，到1949年，國民黨一敗塗地，整個中國大陸都丟了，中華民國政府遷移到臺灣，在這個歷史的轉折過程，1947年就發生了二二八事件。為什麼我們會覺得是一個很重要的事件？因為它對於後續臺灣政治發展發生了相當大的影響。因為這個二二八事件，很多臺灣人對政治冷感而不敢去碰，二二八事件接下來就是白色恐怖，整個臺灣的政治完全處於一黨獨大的狀態，受到特務的控制。

　　您剛剛提到說，是不是有政治人物炒作這個議題。這就跟二二八事件之後，尤其是解嚴前後的發展很有關係了。因為在解嚴之前，二二八事件或者白色恐怖政治案件，是一個禁忌的話題，沒有人敢去碰觸，也沒有人敢研究。即使要研究，也沒有足夠的資料可以運用，研究條件還不具備。解嚴前後剛好發生二二八事件平反運動，然後開放黨禁、報禁，整個臺灣社會就變得很開放。在這個過程裡面，有很多的二二八檔案史料就被陸陸續續地公佈了。就前面所談的，比如說國史館的出版品，還有其中史政單位，如中央研究院近代史研究所、臺灣省文獻委員會也出版有關二二八事件的檔案資料，還有就是大量有關於二二八事件人物的口述訪問。因為這樣的關係，所以二二八事件的研究才比較有可能。但是，由我個人這一、二十年來對二二八事件的研究就發現，這是一個歷史事件，但是他又跟當代臺灣的歷史發展有密切的關係。很多政治人物會利用這個事件去操作利用。二二八國家紀念館或者臺北二二八紀念館，其實都是政治磨合、政治操作的產物，為什麼會有這個紀念館，就跟誰當臺北市長，誰當總統有關係。在這個過程裡面，不同理念的人，比如說比較屬於統派或比較屬於獨派的歷史學者，或者不是歷史學者但對於這個議題有興趣的人，他們在研究這個議題的時候，都有他們的一些基本立場，會用他們的色彩去處理或去解釋這個事件。不同角度、不同立場的人，比如說二二八受難者的家屬，或者受難者當事人，或者說不同政治理念的人，他會有不同的解讀，到現在，還是存在這樣的現象。

問題：那您覺得希望未來的小朋友，他們會用什麼樣的角度來理解這樣的事件比較好？

侯：當然是用比較客觀的、比較公平的角度來理解比較好。沒有任何黨派色彩，純歷史來論歷史。但是很難，不同的黨派他有不同的考慮。不同的家庭、不同的父母，有不同的政治理念，他對他的小孩也有影響。我們很難期待，在臺灣的每一個人都能夠超離越政治色彩、黨派色彩，用完全公正客觀的角度來理解這個事件。只能說，我們儘量努力地去做。

Interviewee: Hou Kun-Hung, the Academia Historica Editor and Compilation Department Director, hereinafter referred to as Hou.

Question: Over the years what efforts has Academia Historia made to deepen the Taiwanese people's understanding of the history of the 228 Incident and the Settlement Committee ?

Hou: The Academia Historica's achievements with regard to the 228 Incident are in relation to its position in the government departments. Academia Historica is the nation's top political history unit. Of course, there are many other political history units, like Taiwan Historica, Taipei City Archives and the former Kaohsiung City Archives. These are all included. After martial law lifted, people from all walks, inside and outside the government made some efforts for the rehabilitation of the 228 Incident and the Academia Historica made some as well. We can probably talk about it by splitting it into three aspects.

Firstly, are the three volumes published in 1997, the "Academia Historica's Collection of 228 Historical Archives." Actually, this was done in response to the requirements and oversight of the Legislative Yuan for the political history unit. Therefore, at that time there were three volumes compiled, searching all of the records Academia Historica had collected at that time for all historical data related to the 228 Incident. After the year 2000, after Chen Shui-Bian was serving as the ROC President, and under the leadership efforts of director Chang Yen-Hsien and the Archives Administration Council, the 228 Incident Memorial Foundation, jointly published 18 volumes of the "228 Incident Archives Compilation." The time line probably spans from about 2002 to 2008, during which were about six or seven years. There was a considerable amount of data in it and if you want to research the 228 Incident, this data cannot be ignored.

In addition, I just said that there were three works, and another one would be the publication of the "228 Incident Dictionary." The effort spent on this was even greater. The scholars involved in the planning and writing of it all put in a lot of effort with regard to the 228 Incident. This work took roughly more than three years from beginning to end and it was later published in two volumes. The entries inside the dictionary all went through a special screening, every entry's technical writer also went through a special selection process. This book, for those wanting to understand the 228 Incident, even now is a valuable reference. Of course, if you stand on more stringent requirements, it is possible that within it, there are a few people's lives that perhaps could still be supplemented and some errors are inevitable. What was referred to above were some of the efforts made by the Academia Historica with regard to the 228 Incident in the last ten years.

Question: What are included as the relevant historical data sources of the 228 Incident ?

Hou: The previously mentioned published books, some of their historical data was originally in the Academia Historica collection, and before editing we started with the directory and searched for relevant items. Afterwards we would bring up the original copy for reading, from which we would propose an archive to compile and then re-publish it. This is one part. Another larger part, is in fact not stored at the Academia Historica, but is in the National Archives. When the National Archives Administration Council was first established, because it was a newly established body, they borrowed the Academia Historica's workspace at first and via a number of experts and scholars helped collect relevant information for the 228 Incident from every government department and unit. We published the largest group of historical data sources, and it was this group of files. This group of files is now stored at the National Archives.

Question: Looking back at more than a century of Taiwanese pursuit of the democratic path, what is the 228 Incident Settlement Committee's position in Taiwan's process of democratic development ?

Hou: This exhibition put on by the Taipei 228 Memorial Museum took the 228 Incident Settlement Committee as its main theme, titling it as, "Taiwan's Democracy Summit." Why would they designate this meeting as such? This is a kind of belief held by the organizers, you could also say it is a way of explaining, or a possible way of interpreting the 228 Incident Settlement Committee. But to use that as the title, you must understand how to consider the historical context around its development. For example, earlier during the period of

Japanese rule of Taiwan, didn't the Taiwanese people of those times also do similar activities? Take for example the Parliamentary Petition Movement or related movements and so on. In postwar Taiwan, in the whole of its democratic development, especially the last decade or two, if you view it in a little bit of a larger historical context, could take the 228 Incident Settlement Committee as one of "Taiwan's Democracy Summits." However, we should take further consideration about whether or not such a designation about the 228 Incident Settlement Committee has any inadequacies or inaccuracies. This is because the establishment of the 228 Incident Settlement Committee was very short-lived, and although there were twenty-some units across the province, the time they existed was very short. You could call them a 'flash in the pan,' and that their appearance was just an accident of history. Every event has its own specific space-time context and we are now researching the 228 Incident Settlement Committee's. We want to give it a good temporal and spacial orientation and then we will be better able to evaluate it.

Question: In the Incident's early moments, what was the original reason the 227 Tobacco Seizure and Murder Case Investigation Commission was converted into the 228 Incident Settlement Committee ?

Hou: The 227 Tobacco Seizure and Murder Case Investigation Commission was to handle an incident on February 27, 1947 in Taipei. At that time, they invited some people like the Taipei City Councilmen, Provincial Senators, National Political Assemblymen and more to come participate and choose representatives, along with making some demands for the Taiwan Provincial Administrative Executive Office, including the lifting of martial law, the release of arrested civilians etc. Chen Yi had also made a response, but afterward the incident developed very quickly. The Committee very quickly transformed into the 228 Incident Settlement Committee.

Question: Can you describe the process of the 228 Incident Settlement Committee's expansion from being a regional Taipei authority to being the highest public provincial authority ?

Hou: Through the Tobacco Seizure and Murder Case Settlement Committee changing into the 228 Incident Settlement Committee, and during the following period there were many meetings held, because the Incident soon spread to the entire province. In order to respond to such a situation, the 228 Incident Settlement Committee in Chungshan Hall encouraged localities everywhere to set up similar types of Settlement Committees. Following the Incident's storm-like rage over the land, there was the rise of the local Settlement Committee. Actually, before the 228 Incident Settlement Committee in Chungshan Hall gave the order to set up a Settlement Committee in every locality, there were some places all around Taiwan that had already one by one, independently established 228 Incident Settlement Committees.

Question: Then, according to what you just said, that before the 228 Incident Settlement Committee had called for the establishment of a provincial Settlement Committee, there were some places that had already one after the other been setting up these institutions. What were their main reasons ?

Hou: Why would there be an organization of the 228 Incident Settlement Committee in all the province's ¡ocalities? It should be said that it was in order to deal with the unrest, the different unrest of each area. Some of them were spontaneous and when the unrest happened there needed to be people who would rise up and maintain law and order, to maintain peace. This again touches on the question of the original cause of the 228 Incident, for example, dissatisfaction with the Executive Office's administration, grievances against mainlanders and so on.

Question: What do you think were the common ideals and aspirations of all levels of the 228 Incident Settlement Committee ?

Hou: Let's ask the question in reverse: Are there any common ideals and aspirations at all levels of the 228 Incident Settlement Committee? Like this we are then able to see if this kind of question is correct or incorrect. Throughout the province, the 228 Incident Settlement Committee in its organization seems to be a top-down structure, but this top-down affiliated relationship is not always obvious. Its structure was not very strict, an upper unit could go and command or control a lower unit. So when talking about the concepts of the 228 Incident Settlement Committee, we really should talk about the Settlement Committee held in Taipei Zhongshan Hall. In that Committee the 32 Demands or 42 Demands were proposed, but it's difficult to say if there was a unified vision, because this question involves the Committee members themselves. The Taipei 228 Incident Settlement Committee's members are all quite complex, and also there were intelligence officers who had infiltrated among the members, for example, Xu De-Hui of the Loyal Service Brigade.

Question: What difference would a proposal of the 32 Demands vs. the 42 Demands have made on the evolution of the Incident itself, especially the military crackdown ?

Hou: One way of saying it is that originally there were 32 Demands and later they morphed into the 42 Demands. Of course, there is still some debate and we still need to clarify it. There are also some scholars who think that there were not the 42 Demands, but only the 32 Demands. Focusing on the topic of the military crackdown, why was there a crackdown? The main reason is that the Settlement Committee stepped over the ruler's bottom line, their red line. The rulers thought that to propose political demands was not within the scope of their autonomy and that they were already trying to overthrow the regime. Thus it led to the Nanjing government sending troops to Taiwan to suppress this movement.

Question: Do you think that the 228 Incident Settlement Committee really crossed the bottom line, or was it just that the two side's perception was different ?

Hou: If it were someone in the Settlement Committee or someone that was more part of the group that stressed Taiwanese self-government, and wanted to implement democracy, they wouldn't think so, it was just a democratic appeal. But then speaking of the rulers, namely the leaders of the Executive Office, they would think that the Settlement Committee had already crossed that bottom line.

Question: From a legal perspective, the 228 Incident Settlement Committee belonged to what kind of organizational category ? What do their proposed "Demands," refer to? Are they popular petition proposals, or are they bills, or policy resolutions ?

Hou: We've mentioned a few nouns here, that is, popular petition proposals, bills and policy resolutions. If you can only choose one of the three, then it is not so fitting, but you could call them "policy proposals." They are not resolutions, nor do they belong to popular petitions, because a popular petition probably wouldn't nor does it need to go through such an organization as the Settlement Committee to operate. They would be proposed to the Executive Office, so it also has some similar policy proposals. They are a combination of the just mentioned popular petitions, bills, or policy proposals. If we are talking about an organizational category, then the 228 Incident Settlement Committee is more closely related to a kind of political group. A political group in the process of democratic development, especially at the beginning of its embryonic stage, will sometimes be suppressed by the ruling authorities, because you are trying to seize their power.

Question: If we look at it from the viewpoint of the proposals, many of the 228 Incident Settlement Committee members themselves were Senators. How do these differ from their usual inquiry proposals ?

Hou: All of their proposals at that time were not as pointed as those of the Settlement Committee, causing the Executive Office to be unable to accept them. So what I just said is that they had already crossed that political red line, the bottom line forcing the Executive Office to be unable to bear them.

Question: In this light, why would the 228 Incident Settlement Committee members put forward this kind of proposal that year, and why would they think the Executive Office could accept it ?

Hou: Because the 228 Incident occurred and then the 228 Incident Settlement Committee was established. Those in the 228 Incident Settlement Committee were the elites of Taiwan at the time, many of them had received a very good education, were quite idealistic and were concerned about the future development of Taiwan; coupled with a lot of discontent that had already accumulated against the government, in that kind of situation they proposed these policy recommendations, hoping to see if there was any opportunity accomplish them, but there wasn't such an opportunity.

Question: Judging from your research, what do you think the significance of the 228 Incident is? Has it been excessively hyped politically ?

Hou: The 228 Incident is a very important historical event in Taiwan's post-war history. From fifty years of Japanese rule of Taiwan, to the retrocession to the ROC in 1945, to the Kuomintang suffering a crushing defeat in 1949, losing the whole of mainland China, to the ROC government migrating to Taiwan, in this process of historical transition, in 1947, the 228 Incident occurred. Why do we think it is a very important event? Because it produced a considerable impact regarding the subsequent political development of Taiwan. Because of this 228 Incident, many Taiwanese people are apathetic towards politics and do not dare touch it. Following the 228 Incident was the White Terror, and all of Taiwan's politics were in a state of one-party rule, controlled by the secret service.

You just touched on whether or not there are any political figures hyping this subject. This has a close relationship with after the 228 Incident, especially with the developments around the lifting of martial law. Because before the lifting of martial law, the 228 Incident or the White Terror political case was a taboo topic, no one dared touch it nor did anyone dare research it. Even if you wanted to study it there was insufficient usable data and the conditions for research were still not there.

Right around the time of the lifting of martial law, the 228 Incident Rectification Movement happened and afterwards they lifted the ban on political parties, newspapers and the entire Taiwanese society became very open. In this process there were many 228 historical archives being released in droves. Like what was talked about earlier, for example the publications of the Academia Historica, the Institute of Modern History Academia Sinica, and Taiwan Historica have also published historical archives about the 228 Incident. There were also a large number of oral interviews from figures related to the 228 Incident. So because of this relationship the research on the 228 Incident then became more possible.

However, from the last ten to twenty years of my own research on the 228 Incident, I realized that this was a historical incident, but that it also had a close relationship with the development of modern Taiwanese history. Many political figures use this Incident for a manipulative purpose. The 228 National Memorial Museum or the Taipei 228 Memorial Museum, are in fact a product of the political harmonization, of political action. Why is there a Memorial Museum? It had more to do with who was Taipei Mayor or who was President.

In this process, people with different ideas, for example those historians, or maybe not historians, but people who are interested in this topic that belong more to the pro-unification or the pro-independence parties, when they are studying this subject all have their own basic position, and will use their own bias to process or to explain this Incident. People of different perspectives and from different positions like the families of the victims of the 228 Incident, or the parties concerned with the victims or people with different political ideas, they will have different explanations. Even today this phenomenon still exists.

Question: What perspective do you hope that children in the future will use in order to better understand this kind of incident?

Hou: Of course it's better to use a more objective, fairer approach to understand it, without any political partisanship, just plain history to explain history. But this is difficult and different parties have different considerations. Different families and different parents have different political ideas and they also have an effect on their children. It's hard for us to expect that every person in Taiwan will all be able to transcend above their political colors, partisanships and use a completely impartial and objective perspective to understand this incident. I can only say that we try our best to do it.

受訪者：陳翠蓮
國立臺灣大學歷史學系教授

問題：二二八事件爆發前後臺灣人民做了什麼努力？

陳：1945年10月國民政府來臺灣接收，到1947年的2月就發生全島性的反抗行動；在很短的時間之內，臺灣民眾就已經發現到統治政權的問題，統治失敗。事實上，在這一年十個月的過程裡面已經有很多的行動、抗議行動，包括對政府的無能，譬如說違反法治的問題、米荒、日產接收等等，已經有過種種的抗議行動，人們有不斷進行集會、座談來]集思廣益、提出建議。大概到了1946年的年底，當時臺灣社會其實已經對新的政府的統治深深感到失望，他們開始去設想臺灣未來的可能性，要往哪些方向去發展。也就是說，在二二八事件發生前，臺灣的精英們就已經努力針對臺灣的未來的方向進行各種討論。那時候大概主要有三種主張，第一個主張認為可能中華民國憲法制定之後開始行憲，會讓地方有比較大的權限，所以行憲可能是一個契機、讓臺灣可以有自治的機會，這是第一種比較樂觀的想法。第二種主張，有一些人，譬如廖文毅，他就主張美國的聯邦制，他建議政府以美國聯邦制的方式授與地方比較大的參政權利，就是中央主要是管軍事、外交，而內政讓臺灣人自己來，「臺人治臺」，把他叫做「聯省自治」。所以這種主張包括林獻堂他也支持，這是第二個路線。第三個路線，有人的主張更積極一點，認為應該照大西洋憲章的規範，讓殖民地人民透過住民自決的方式決定自己的前途，例如廖文奎就持這種看法，他們主張應該透過公民投票、臺灣住民自決、是不是要獨立，透過這樣的方式決定台灣前途。

　　所以二二八事件之前，臺灣社會已經有非常多方面的討論，或者是說也進行了各種的努力。可是很不幸地，政府並未接受，反抗的事件還是全面的爆發了。

問題：回首百年多來臺灣追求民主之路，二二八事件在當中扮演發生了什麼作用？

陳：過去臺灣社會，或是說臺灣人這個群體，他們沒有過自己統治自己的經驗，幾百年來都是由外來的政權在國際政治的角力下，安排了臺灣的命運。所以沒有自己國家的經驗，沒有想像過可以自己可以統治自己。甚至因為長期的殖民統治，對自己的能力沒有信心，因為殖民者有一套論述，講臺灣人貪財、怕死、愛面子，臺灣人落後；在這種殖民論述影響之下，臺灣人對自己沒什麼信心。所以1945年戰爭結束的時候，那時候沒有提出自己當家作主的主張。事實上很多的殖民地在二次大戰之後獨立，臺灣變成一個比較特殊的例子。那當時認為說我們成為大國的國民，因為中國在戰爭結束的時候，被世界認為是世界四強之一，當時有這種依賴大國的想法。在臺灣追求民主的道路上，二二八事件最重大的意義就是，讓臺灣的人民對依附大國這種幻想破滅--即使依附大國，不是透過自己的力量，仍舊很難獲得政治權利，很難成為國家的主人，很難推動民主政治。

　　所以二二八事件最大的影響，讓臺灣人覺悟到自己的命運要掌握在自己的手裡，不能再依賴大國，譬如說不能依賴日本、依賴中國，甚至後來的美國。所以二二八事件之後，有臺灣獨立運動的興起，跟這個覺悟有關。二二八事件在整個臺灣歷史上，占了非常重要的地位，有關自己做自己的主人，要怎麼樣進行，起了一個覺醒的作用。

問題：您認為二二八處委會在臺灣民主發展過程中的定位是什麼？

陳：我們如果去分析他所提出來的三十二條處理大綱，或者是後來再加上十條，有人叫做是四十二條處理大綱，就會發現處理委員會的主張大概可以分成三個重點：第一個重點是臺灣人高度自治，因為在三十二條處理大綱裡面，有關在臺灣的政府機關中重要的職位，幾乎都反對由外來者擔任，主張臺灣人要佔半數以上的比例，三十二條大綱中與高度自治的條文是最多的，也就是臺灣人樣自己統治自己。第二個重點是有關基本人權的保障，包括臺灣人的思想、言論、集會、結社等等這些基本權利，基本人權的保障，這是相當進步的，就是有關臺灣作為一個民主自由的社會，應該建立這種人權保障的觀念。第三個部分，就是合理的經濟、社會制度的建立，例如廢除專賣局貿易局，認為那是政府剝削民眾的制度；例如要求要實施照顧勞工的法律、保障原住民等等，見李這些制度。也就是說，一個合理的社會，一個具有對所有的民眾合理照顧的制度，在當時已經有考慮到。所以我們大概可以知道二二八處理委員會提出來的主張，有相當的進步性。臺灣如何建立成為一個民主公平的社會，他們已經有一些具體的構想。

問題：三十二條或是四十二條大綱的提出，對於事件本身的演變，尤其是軍隊鎮壓，會有什麼不同嗎？

陳：一般史料上顯示，三十二條要求是處理委員會通過的，後來追加十條，部分口述、有些史料上提到說最後增加的十條，有些是特務人員加上去的。確實我們會看到，當時在政府的檔案裡面有提到，四十二條要求裡面主張取消警總、主張軍隊繳械，後來成為叛國的證據，官方用這樣子的藉口，軍隊進來鎮壓。但是事實上在中國政治文化裡面，民眾的反抗、地方的反抗，通常中央政府處理的手段就是武力鎮壓。所以四十二條要求或三十二條要求，是不是因為這樣子，所以引來鎮壓，我認為是沒有必然的關係。在中國政治文化裡面，對於民眾的抵抗行動，他所採取的慣有方式，就是鎮壓或屠殺，甚至栽贓一些罪名。我認為四十二條要求裡面說的撤銷警總、或是軍隊繳械，所謂的叛國證據，只是藉口或是罪名而已。當臺灣社會全面的反抗的時候，招致的中國政府的鎮壓，這樣子的命運，其實就已經決定了。

問題：從二二八處委會發展的脈絡來看,所謂的"大綱"，指的是什麼？是民眾陳情的提案，或是法案、政策的決議？

陳：二二八事件處理委員會當時集合臺灣主要是各地方的民意代表還有各縣市的精英，十七個縣市都成立了處理委員會，所以基本上是民眾的代表或是各地精英。他們負責去把民眾的改革意見集合起來，最後在臺北市的全省性的處理委員會做成決議，要求政府進行改革，名稱叫做「處理大綱」，所以基本上是二二八事件的處理原則，其中又分為當前必須要立即處理的，還有比較長遠的政治改革的具體構想。所以處理大綱基本上是一種改革的原則、改革的方向，要求政府應該往這個方向去推進，它不是一個法案，也不是單純民眾的請願案，也不是政府的政策，而是臺灣民眾對民主改革的要求。

Interviewee: Professor Chen Tsui-Lien of the National Taiwan University's History Department, hereinafter referred to as Chen.

Question: Before and after the outbreak of the 228 Incident, what had the Taiwanese people been striving for ?

Chen: In October 1945 the Nationalist government came to take over Taiwan, in February of 1947 there was an island-wide revolt and within a very short time, the Taiwanese people realized the ruling regime to be the problem and the rulers lost. In fact, in the course of these twenty-two months there had been a lot of movements, protest movements, including those about government incompetence, like the problems of violating the rule of law, rice shortages, the nationalization of Japanese industries and so on. There had been all sorts of protest actions, and people were continually holding meetings and symposiums to brainstorm and come up with suggestions.

Probably by the end of 1946, when Taiwanese society had completely lost hope in the new government, they began to think about Taiwan's future possibilities and which direction they wanted to develop in. In other words, before the 228 Incident occurred, the elites of Taiwan had already held numerous discussions aimed hard at the future direction of Taiwan. At that time there were probably three main proposals. The first view thought that maybe after the Republic of China framed a constitution it would start to implement it and this would allow the local government to have a relatively large range of powers. Thus, the implementation of a constitution would be a turning point, allowing Taiwan to have an opportunity at self-government. This is the first kind of idea; it's relatively optimistic.

This second view, there were some people, like Liao Wen-Yi, who promoted the U.S.'s federal system and suggested that the government use the U.S.'s style of federal system, granting local government larger political participation rights. Then the central government would primarily control military matters, foreign affairs, and the domestic government would allow the Taiwanese to rise up for themselves, "Formosa for the Formosans," and called it "Provincial Autonomy." Therefore, this view included Lin Hsien - Tang, who also supported it. This was the second route.

The advocates of the third route were a little bit more aggressive, believing they should adhere to the standard of the Atlantic Charter, allowing colonized peoples to determine their own future through self-determination. For example, Liao Wen-Kuei held this kind of view. They argued that it should be through referendum that Taiwan's self-determination and question of independence, that Taiwan's future, should be decided through this kind of method.

So before the 228 Incident, Taiwanese society had already held a wide range of discussions, or to say it another way, made a number of efforts. But unfortunately, the government had not yet accepted them, and the revolt had completely erupted.

Question: Looking back at more than a century of Taiwan pursuing the path of democracy, what role did the 228 Incident play ?

Chen: In past Taiwanese society, or to say, that group of Taiwanese people never had the experience of governing themselves. For hundreds of years, Taiwan's fate has been decided by foreign regimes in an international power struggle.So they had never experienced a country of their own, and they never imagined that they could govern themselves. And because of a long period of colonial rule they didn't even believe in their abilities, because the colonists had a treatise saying that Taiwanese people were greedy, feared death, face-saving, and that Taiwanese people were backward. Under the influence of this kind of colonial commentary, Taiwanese people didn't have much confidence in themselves. So in 1945 when the war ended, at that time we didn't advocate to be the masters of our own house. In fact, many colonies became independent after World War II, Taiwan however, became a rather exceptional example. At that time we thought to become citizens of a world power, and because after the war ended China was considered by the world to be one of the four strongest in the world, then at that time we had this kind of idea,to rely on a world

world power. On the road of Taiwan's pursuit of democracy, the great significance of the 228 Incident was in shattering the Taiwanese illusion of dependence on great powers - even if we depended on a world power, and not on our own strength, it was still just as difficult to obtain political rights, to become masters of our country, and to push for democracy.

Therefore, the biggest impact of the 228 Incident was in making the Taiwanese people realize that they need to grasp their destiny with their own two hands and no longer rely on world powers, for example, not relying on Japan, not on China, and not even on the United States. So after the 228 Incident, there arose a Taiwanese independence movement that was connected with this awareness. The 228 Incident holds an extremely important position in the whole of Taiwanese history, it's connected with being one's own master, how to advance forward, it's the role of an awakening.

Question: What do you think is the 228 Incident Settlement Committee's position in Taiwan's process of democratic development ?

Chen: If we analyze the 32 Demands it proposed, or the ten it added later that some people call the 42 Demands, then we will discover that the ideas of the Settlement Committee can probably be divided into three main points: The first main focus is on a high degree of autonomy for the Taiwanese people, because within the 32 Demands, those demands related to important positions in the Taiwanese government were almost all opposed to outsiders holding them and argued for a ratio of more than half to be Taiwanese people. In the 32 Demands the most numerous provisions are those about a high degree of autonomy, which is a style of Taiwanese people governing themselves.

The second main point is related to the protection of fundamental human rights, including the ideas of Taiwanese people, freedom of expression, assembly, association and so forth, these basic rights. This notion that it should establish these kinds of fundamental human rights protections, which was fairly advanced, is related to Taiwan being a free and democratic society.

The third part was the establishment of fair social and economic systems, like the abolishment of the Monopoly Bureau and the Board of Trade, believing that they were a system of government exploitation, like requiring the implementation of protective labor laws, including for indigenous people and so on. It was to establish these systems, or in other words, a fair society, a system that shows fair consideration for all of her people. They already had this in mind at that time. So we can probably know that the ideas put forward by the 228 Incident Settlement Committee were quite progressive. On how to build Taiwan into a democratic and fair society, they already had some specific ideas.

Question: What difference would a proposal of the 32 Demands vs. the 42 Demands have made on the evolution of the Incident itself, especially the military crackdown ?

Chen: Generally our historical evidence shows that the 32 Demands were passed by the Settlement Committee and then afterward ten more were appended. A portion of the oral accounts, some of the historical data mentioning it, say that the ten were added at the very end and some others say that a secret agent added them. And indeed we see mentioned in the government archives of the time that the 42 Demands call for the abolishment of the secret police, and the disarmament of the military. Later these became evidences of treason and the officials used these kinds of excuses to call in the military for the crackdown. But really, within Chinese political culture, popular protest, and local resistance is commonly handled by the central government through means of violent suppression. So, it wasn't because it was either way, the 42 Demands or the 32 Demands that lead to a crackdown. I don't think that there is necessarily a causal relationship. The customary methods taken by Chinese political culture for popular resistance movements is repression or slaughter, even planting a few false charges.

I believe those within the 42 Demands, which call for abolishing the secret police, or disarming the military, these so-called evidences of treason are nothing more than excuses or allegations. When all of Taiwanese society revolted, incurring a Chinese government crackdown was the kind of fate that was really, already sealed.

Question: Looking at the context of the 228 Incident Settlement Committees development, what do their so-called "Demands" refer to ? Are they popular petition proposals, or are they bills, or policy resolutions ?

Chen: The 228 Incident Settlement Committee at that time mainly assembled each local representative as well as each counties elites, and seventeen counties established a Settlement Committee, so basically it was the people's representatives and each areas elites. They took the responsibility of assembling the people's views on reform together, and then in the provincial Settlement Committee in Taipei finally turning them into resolutions, demanding the government to conduct reforms. It was called the "Settlement Outline," and was essentially the principles for managing the 228 Incident, which were divided between those in current need of immediate management, and those more long-term ideas on political reform. So the Demands (Settlement Outline) are essentially principles for reform, the direction of reform, demanding that the government should advance in this direction. They are not a bill, nor are they simply a popular petition, nor are they a government policy, but are the Taiwanese people's demands for democratic reforms.

附件—日文摘要
Annex - Exhibition Content (Japanese)

台湾民主の最高議会－二二八事件処理委員会

附件—日文摘要 台湾の民主的最高議会 – 二二八事件処理委員会
Annex - Exhibition Content (Japanese)

▌前書き：何の為に二二八処理委員会が有ったのか？

　二二八事件が発生した際、二二八処理委員会が成立した。それは違法煙草取り締まり事件の調査や、官民対立の協調だけで無く、更に台湾人民が長年ずっと追求してきた民主自治の意思表示という重要な役割を果たす為であった。言い換えれば、事実上、二二八事件の核心価値は、自治と民権の要求と獲得にあった。それ故に二二八処理委員会の役割と立場の進展動向は二二八事件探求の貴重な手掛かりだけで無く、更に台湾地方自治と民主化の過程を理解する最も重要な一環である。

▌王添灯の銅像、台北二二八記念館の入り口前

▌『台湾市街庄政之実』
1931年、王添灯による出版物

▌半世紀にわたる追求：台湾人民の民主自治取得奮闘の道

　日本植民統治時代、台湾人民は抗争や嘆願書等の方式で民主自治を追求した。第二次世界大戦後初期、中国は台湾に行政長官公署を設置し、日本植民統治時期の総督府専制統治をそのまま延用して、特殊な行政管理と全面的な経済統制を行い、その結果、経済は衰退し、政府の職権乱用や汚職が頻発して、人民は期待を裏切られて失望した。その為、民主憲政の実施や地方制度改革の推行が当時の台湾人民の差し迫った願望であった。

■台湾民眾党により1928年に第二回党員会議が台南
で開催された

■蔣渭水によって創設された台湾文化協会は
林献堂により初回議会が開催された

■二二八事件と二二八処理委員会

　1947年2月27日の夕暮れ、専売局の役員が違法煙草取り締まりの際に、煙草行商人林江邁を傷つけ、市民陳文渓を射殺したので、台北民衆が抗争を引き起した。28日、行政長官公署の前で抗議デモ中、群衆が機銃で掃射され、四方に逃走した民衆は怒りを抑えきれず、中国大陸から来た外省人を探し出しては殴打し、台北街頭は混乱状態に落ち入った。この消息は直ぐに台湾全島に伝わり、反政府抗争活動が各地に広がり、二二八事件が勃発した。

　事件勃発後、官と民で共に処理委員会を立ち上げて解決すべきだとの当時の社会的共識に基づいて、数多い社会エリート達が、危険千万な時局下でも、危険を顧みず事件解決に乗り出した。しかし行政長官陳儀は意図的に「二二七緝煙血案調査委員会」を「二二八事件処理委員会」に改名し、そして殊更に事件の起因を当局の職務失策から民衆抗争による官民衝突にすり替えたので、その後の事件処理に不安定な要因が埋伏された。

　この事件はただ単に地方の治安や違法煙草取締りの単一問題ではなく、人民の行政長官公署専権体制に対する改革訴求にも関連している。二二八事件処理委員会は単純な単一争議事件を処理する組織から転じて、社会秩序の維持、延いては当時緊迫した食糧、交通、電力等の民生問題の緩和にも関与し、ただ単に民衆が依頼する対象だけでなく、当時の政治改革訴求の最高民意機関でもあった。

　二二八事件処理委員会で決議され、王添灯が代表として読み上げた【三十二条処理大綱】は事件処理の提案と省政改革の抜本的解決方針を提出している。しかし陳儀と政府情報機関の計画的な手配りで、【三十二条処理大綱】は特務達によって更に十項目の要求が追加され、最終的に当局が「陰謀反乱」の罪をきせる「四十二条罪状」になり、軍事鎮圧や民主自治改革の呼びかけを弾圧する口実になった。

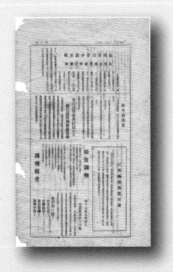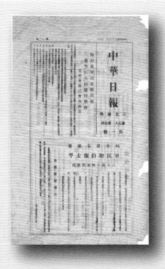

■ 中華日報は二二八事件処理委員会が台北の中山堂にて議会開催した旨を伝えた。
　1947年3月4日

■二二八処理委員会の重要な成員と受難した先賢達

王 添 灯
1901－1947

　　台北安坑の生まれ、日本領治時期に地方自治連盟理事、台北支部主任を歴任、著書『台湾市街庄政之実』は台湾で如何に地方自治を施行するかを論じた初めての専門書である。終戦後、三民主義青年団台北分団主任、【人民導報】新聞社社長、省参議会議員を歴任。平素は「最大多数の最大幸福を謀る」を座右の銘とし、その強権を畏れない表象は「鉄面議員」と讃えられた。二二八事件中、二二八事件処理委員会で談判代表と宣伝組長に推挙され、【三十二条処理大綱】を代表として読み上げた。其れ故に当局に睨まれ、中国の鎮圧軍隊が大陸から台湾に上陸した途端に、当局から勝手に罪名を羅列され非法逮捕の後、司法審判も経ずに殺害しされた。2007年、（二二八事件処理及賠償条例）に基づいて、政府は王添灯の冤罪を一掃し、遂に名誉を回復した。

■ 王添灯の書。「最大多数の最大幸福を謀る」

■ 王添灯と家族

林連宗
1905－1947

　彰化生まれ。日本領治時期は台中州弁護士公会会長、台湾新聞社法律顧問を務めた。戦後台湾省弁護士公会理事長、台湾省参議会議員、国民大会代表を歴任した。民意代表を担任している時、特に台湾の司法、教育、警察制度の弊害改革に献身した。二二八事件発生後、台中，彰化県市参議会と弁護士公会等が合同会議を開き、林連宗が代表に選ばれて、台北に赴き、二二八処理委員会の活動に参加した。その後間もなく、何の証拠も無いまま、林連宗は秘密裡に逮捕され、司法審判無しで殺害された。2007年、（二二八事件処理及賠償条例）に基づいて、政府は林連宗の冤罪を払拭して賠償し、名誉を回復した。

廖進平
1895－1947

　台中縣葫蘆墩（現在の豊原）生まれ。日本領治時期は台湾文化協会に参加、同志らと台湾民衆党を立ち上げ、抗植民地政権の長期運動に投入した。戦後、蔣渭川や黄朝生等と台湾省政治建設協会を設立し、二二八事件中は二二八処理委員会に加入、子息の廖徳雄もその「忠義服務隊」で学生隊隊長を担任して台北治安の維持に協力した。廖進平は事件後憲兵隊に逮捕され、生死不明になった。子息の廖徳雄は幸いにも逮捕を免れたが、その後の所謂白色テロ時期で政府の「ブラックリスト」に載せられ、長年家族と共に監視された。2007年、『二二八事件処理及賠償条例』に基づいて、廖進平は名誉を回復し、其の家族たちにも賠償金が払われた。

■ 林連宗と彼の娘

■ 廖進平と彼の子どもたち

■ 黄朝生と安生病院の同僚

■ 張義雄の描写
による演説するときの廖進平

黄朝生
1904-1947

　台南下営の生まれ。日本領治時期は蒋渭水等の抗日志士達と親しく、台湾文化協会に加入し、抗植民地政権の長期運動に参加した。戦後、台北市参議会議員に当選し、台湾省政治建設協会にも加入して、その常務理事兼財政組長を担任した。二二八事件発生後、二二八処理委員会の委員兼治安組長を担任し、王添灯や呉春霖等と代表に選ばれて、南京に出向き中央政府に陳情と事件の真相を説明する段取りをした。その間黄朝生は治安維持だけでなく、中国大陸から来た無害な外省人達が襲撃されないようにいろいろと手を打った。それにも拘わらず、3月12日憲兵に逮捕されて、それ以来生死不明になった。2007年、政府は『二二八事件処理及賠償条例』に基づいて、黄朝生の名誉を回復し、其の家族たちにも賠償金が払われ、冤罪が洗除された。

李仁貴
1900-1947

　台北県人。戦後台北市参議員に当選し、台湾省政治建設協会理事長を担任。二二八事件発生後、二二八処理委員会の委員と調査組長を兼任、事件の調査に専念した。3月2日、李仁貴は他の五名の代表や各新聞社の記者たちと一緒に軍法処に赴いて、違法煙草取り締まり事件の殺人犯の拘留状況を調査した。3月11日午前、突如に普段着の軍警が李仁貴を強引に連れ去り、その後、生死不明。戒厳令が解かれた後、国家安全局が公表した『台湾省二二八事変正法及死亡人犯名冊』で李仁貴の殺害が立証された。戒厳令解禁後、政府は『二二八事件処理及賠償条例』に基づいて、李仁貴の名誉を回復し、其の家族たちにも賠償金が払われ、冤罪が洗除された。

徐春卿
1895－1947

　台北錫口（松山）の生まれ。日本領治時期、教職や松山庄協議会員を歴任し、一時は警察の虚偽の告発で投獄されて刑に服した。戦後、行政長官署諮議に招聘され、その後、台北市参議員に当選。二二八事件発生後、徐春卿は積極的に二二八処理委員会の運営に参与し、常務委員に推挙された。3月11日、軍警に連行されてそのまま帰って来なかった。その長男徐世通が記憶を辿って、徐春卿が密かに捕らわれた原因は、日本人遺留の財産を陳儀が官商結託して競売りしたことに反対したのか、或いは人権保障に携わった為に密告されたのか、どちらかだと証言している。戒厳令解禁後、『二二八事件処理及賠償条例』に基づいて、政府は徐春卿の冤罪を洗拭して賠償し、名誉を回復した。

韓石泉
1897－1963

　台南市出身。日本植民統治時代、台湾文化協会に参加、そして地方自治制度の改革運動に投入した。戦後、台湾省参議員に当選し、長年台湾の教育や医学衛生等の議題に関与した。二二八事件が発生して、台南市の治安は一時混乱に陥ったが、各業界の推挙で韓石泉は事件紛争の協調に乗り出し、「不拡大、不流血」等の平和処理原則を打ち出して、台南市の死傷犠牲者を最少限に抑えた。事件の間、主任委員として湯徳章、侯全成と共に二二八処理委員会と協力折衝し、民衆をなだめ、流血衝突を避けると同時に大陸系外省人負傷者の救護、公共資財の保護、事件の沈静化、台南市民の保護など、多々重要な貢献をした。

台湾省参議会の出版物『台湾省参議会の
初回開会時の上院議員』（韓石泉の端的な紹介）

1959年に胡適が韓石泉の自叙伝『60の記憶』
を読んだ後に書いた手紙

1946年、台湾省参議会の初回開会（後列右から3番目、韓石泉、
右から7番目、王添灯）

二二八処理委員会による告知
『すべての人々へ』
（台灣新生報 1947.3.7）

▌処理委員会の核心立場と汚名の払拭

　　二二八事件処理委員会が提出した【三十二条処理大綱】には、当局の特務らが扇動して新たに十条の過激な政治要求が付け加えられたが、当局がそれを「四十二条叛国罪状」にでっち上げたことが後日実証された。しかし政府側からの事後の宣撫や処置、及び台湾近代民主化の過程などを併せてみると、【三十二条処理大綱】の精神と合致している。これは【三十二条処理大綱】が二二八処理委員会の核心立場であり、更にこの歴史的事件の重要な民主成果である事を立証している。そして間接的に二二八処理委員会の汚名を払拭した。

▌1947年、二二八事件処理委員会

▌二二八事件処理委員会の腕章

■ 3月3日、二二八事件処理委員会は再組織後、第一回会議を開き、
王添灯が陳儀と交渉する代表者として選出された
（1947年3月3日発行 新生デイリーニュース）

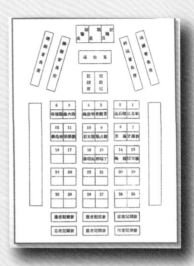

■ 二二八事件後、台湾省参議会はその
第3回の会議を開催したがほんの16
人の議員しか残っていなかった。台
湾のほとんどのエリートが失われて
いた

■ 防衛本局は罪なき人々を落としいれ、最重要指名手配の反逆者として名を載せた

▌安定した社会秩序の維持と民需困難の解決

　　事件の間、物資の調達分配、物価の抑制、及び人民生活難題の解決など二二八処理委員会は重要な役割を担った。それ以外にも、少数の地方の衝突を除いて、二二八処理委員会と同会が設立した地方治安維持団体は昂ぶる民衆情緒の鎮静化、大陸系外省人の集中保護、対立の緩和、軍警銃器が乱用されない様に看守、地方軍政機関との談判などなど、動乱蔓延の阻止に努め、台湾各地の治安の維持に協力した。

▌台湾民主自治の時代の声

　　王添灯が読み上げた『三十二条処理大綱』は台湾社会各階層の内心の声を高度に統合し、当時の台湾各界のエリートや台湾省政治の深刻な弊害に詳しい多数の国民大会代表、参政員、省県市参議員などが共同決議して通過した提案であり、当時の政務の弊害に対する具体的な改革要求を提出しただけで無く、更に植民地時期以来、台湾民主の先駆者達がたゆまず努力して求めてきた民主自治の理想でもある。

▌中山堂 - 二二八事件処理委員会の開会場所

■道しるべとなった明灯：戦後台湾民主の最高議会

　二二八事件の核心的価値は転覆性の武力抗争では無く、一回の民主改革運動によって、憲法に依る人民の権利と自由の保障を要求している。それによって台湾人民は民主自由を追求する旺盛な情熱を放出し、現在の台湾社会の民主精神を守るように影響を及ぼした。それ故に、二二八処理委員会が断固として戦後台湾人民が自治を勝ち取る為の初の民主的な最高議会である。

■ 二二八事件の間、地方自治の実施は台湾人エリートたちの共通の願望であり、改革要求でもあった

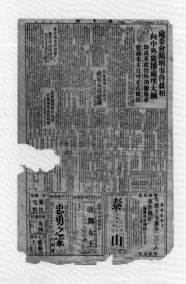

■ 王添灯らによって草案された『三十二条処理大綱』には台湾社会全体にみなぎる願望を広範囲にわたって統合され表現されていた

新生報 外號

（民國三十六年三月七日）

長官公署將改稱省政府
各廳長儘量任用本省人士
縣市長訂七月一日實施民選

陳長官昨晚廣播

【本報訊】陳長官于昨（六）日下午八時三十分在臺北廣播電臺向全省同胞廣播，發表省公署已向中央請示改為「臺灣省政府」，各縣長盡量任用本省人士，並縣市長亦訂于七月一日實施普遍民選，表示政府俯順民情，實現民主自治精神，茲將其廣播詞文譯之如次：

臺灣同胞：

自從二月二十八日臺北事件發生以後，我曾兩次廣播，宣布和平的解決辦法。臺北方面，過幾天，秩序已安定。曾經有過問題的各縣市，想不久可恢復原狀。不過各位所關心的，還有一個問題，就是如何改善政治的問題。但要善政治，須先調整人事。關於這一點，我也考慮到。此刻將我的意思，和你們開誠布公的說一說。

第一，省級行政機關，我已考慮將改為省政府，向中央請示。一經中央核准，即可實行政組，歐組等，省政府的委員各廳長或各處長要盡量任用本省人士。希望省參議會及其他可以代表民意的合法團體，推舉人格高尚，思想正確，能力卓越的本省適當人遞，以便向中央推薦。

第二，縣市級行政機關，我已預定在預備手續能完成的條件之下，縣市長於七月一日民選。在本年六月三十日以前，須擬定選舉法，選出各縣市長。至於縣市長未民選以前，現任縣市長之中，當地人民認為有不稱職的，可以更換其稱職。另由當地縣市參議會（各公法團體，要這如，不可以，可同意選出，（法），……候選人之選定，選舉法語……縣市長，……

中央核准。七月一日開始，辦好普遍直接的選舉。

參考書目
● References
參考文献

年代	書名	編著者	出版者
1946	臺灣省參議會第一屆第一次大會特輯	臺灣省參議會秘書處	臺灣省參議會秘書處
1946	臺灣省參議會第一屆第二次大會特輯	臺灣省參議會秘書處	臺灣省參議會秘書處
1947	臺灣省參議會第一屆第二次大會決議案辦理情形報告書	臺灣省參議會秘書處	臺灣省參議會秘書處
1994	二二八事件研究報告	賴澤涵	時報文化
1995	派系鬥爭與權謀政治：二二八悲劇的另一面相	陳翠蓮	時報文化
1997	國史館藏二二八檔案史料上冊	侯坤宏 編	國史館
1997	國史館藏二二八檔案史料中冊	侯坤宏 編	國史館
1997	國史館藏二二八檔案史料下冊	侯坤宏 編	國史館
1998	台北二二八紀念館文物展示圖集	莊永明	台北二二八紀念館
2001	臺灣省參議會資料彙編－行政區域規劃	何鳳嬌 編	國史館
2002	二二八事件檔案彙編（一）	侯坤宏、許進發 編	國史館
2002	二二八事件檔案彙編（二）	侯坤宏、許進發 編	國史館
2002	二二八事件檔案彙編（九）	侯坤宏、許進發 編	國史館
2004	二二八事件檔案彙編（十六）	侯坤宏、許進發 編	國史館
2004	彰化縣二二八事件檔案彙編	呂興忠 編撰	彰化縣文化局
2005	韓石泉醫師的生命故事	莊永明 著	遠流出版社
2005	王添灯紀念輯	張炎憲 主編	台灣史料中心
2007	紀念二二八事件60週年學術研討會論文集	國立高雄師範大學	高雄市文獻委員會
2007	二二八事件對臺灣省參議會的衝擊《以國家檔案局保管二二八事件檔案為基礎》	臺灣省諮議會 編	臺灣省諮議會
2008	二二八事件檔案彙編（十七）	侯坤宏 編	國史館
2008	消失在二二八迷霧中的王添灯	藍博洲	INK印刻文學生活雜誌社有限公司
2009	六十回憶－韓石泉醫師自傳	韓石泉 著　韓良俊 編	望春風出版社
2009	二二八事件臺灣本地新聞史料彙編－第一冊	林元輝 編註	二二八事件紀念基金會
2009	二二八事件臺灣本地新聞史料彙編－第二冊	林元輝 編註	二二八事件紀念基金會
2009	二二八事件臺灣本地新聞史料彙編－第三冊	林元輝 編註	二二八事件紀念基金會

2009	二二八事件臺灣本地新聞史料彙編－第四冊	林元輝 編註	二二八事件紀念基金會
2010	二二八現場：劫後餘生	曹慶國	台灣書房出版有限公司
2010	二二八現場：檔案直擊	曹慶國	台灣書房出版有限公司
2011	切切故鄉情：陳澄波紀念展	高雄市立美術館	高雄市立美術館
2011	台灣民主先聲與228－王添灯110週年紀念特展	純純文創 編著	臺北市政府文化局
2012	我是油彩的化身：原創音樂劇	嘉義市政府	嘉義市政府
2013	新史料與二二八研究－學術研討會會議資料	中央研究院臺灣史研究所	中央研究院臺灣史研究所
2013	百年追求：臺灣民主運動的故事（卷一 自治的夢想）	陳翠蓮	衛城出版

其他參考資料

《人民導報》

《中華日報》

《自由報》

《台灣新生報》

《臺灣新民報》

《民報》

《華盛頓郵報》

《新生報》

特別感謝
● Acknowledgements
感謝

■ 依中文筆劃順序排列　敬稱略

王添灯先生家屬
韓石泉醫師家屬

千鳥藝術有限公司
吳三連史料基金會
青睞影視製作有限公司
秋惠文庫
科億印刷股份有限公司
恁 | 藝 | 門 當代藝術
財團法人陳澄波文化基金會
財團法人蔣渭水文化基金會
國立中央圖書館台灣分館
國立臺灣博物館
國史館
國家電影資料館
國家檔案局
彰化縣文化局
臺北市文獻委員會
臺灣省諮議會
韓內兒科

反町真理香
何佳諭
李奇瑾
林信貞
林品貝
洪維健
高黃娥
張滄漢
黃紫青
陳建全
陳重光
陳翠蓮
楊孟倫
葉綺玲
廖德雄
蒲子超
蒲浩明
鄭乃瑋
韓良俊
藍博洲
魏以恩

王贊紘
呂興忠
林廷安
林宜瑩
侯坤宏
范曉嵐
張雅倫
莊永明
郭芝菁
陳彥竹
陳淇榜
陳獨蕾
葉丹青
廖明珊
廖繼斌
蒲浩志
劉立蕾
謝英從
韓良誠
魏以宣
藤井孝行

■ alphabetical

Mr. Wang Tien-Teng's Family
Mr. Hahn Shyr-Chyuan's Family

Academia Historica
ChangHua County Cultural Affairs Bureau
Chen Cheng Po Cultural Foundation
Chinese Taipei Film Archive
Chiang Wei-Shui's Cultural Foundation
Crony Information Technology CO., LTD
Formosa Vintage Museum Cafe
Green Film Production
Hahn Clinic (Internal Medicine & Pediatrics)
National Archives Administration
National Taiwan Library
National Taiwan Museum
Taipei City Archives
Thousand Bird Arts
Taiwan Provincial Consultative Council
Un Voeu d'Art Contemporain
Wu San-Lien Foundation for Taiwan Historical Materials

Chang Tsuan-Han
Chen Chien-Chuan
Chen Tsung-kuang
Chen Tsui-Lien
Cheng Nai-Wei
Fan Hsiao-Lan
Hahn Liang-Cheng
Ho Chia-Yu
Hsieh Ying-Tsung
Hung Wei-Chien
Gao Chin-Ching
Chi-Ching Lee
Liao Min-San
Lin Hsin-Chen
Lin Ting-An
Liu Li-Lei
Pu Hao-Chih
Pu Tzu-Chao
Wang Zan-Hong
Wei Yi-Hsuan
Chilling Yeh

Ellen Y. Chang
Chen Chi-Pang
Leiby Chen
Chen Yen-Chu
Chuang Yung-Ming
Takayuki Fujii
Hahn Liang-Jiunn
Hou Kun-Hung
Huang Tzu-Ching
Kao Huang-E
Lan Po-Chou
Liao Chie-Ping
Liao Te-Hsiung
Lin Pin-Pei
Lin Yi-Ying
Lu Hsing-chung
Pu Hao-Ming
Marika Sorimachi
Lan Wei
Yang Meng-Lun
Gisele Yeh

臺灣民主高峰會
二二八事件處理委員會紀念特展

發 行 人/ 倪重華
主　　編/ 何欣怡
編 著 者/ 純純文創
行政編輯/ 蕭明治　曾德宜
顧　　問/ 侯坤宏　陳翠蓮
撰　　稿/ 趙宏禧
視覺設計/ 洪于絜　何欣怡
文物攝影/ 張永晨
活動攝影/ 何廷華　金馥嫻
英文翻譯/ 那　凱　張雅倫 (p104-138)
日文翻譯/ 張滄漢
審　　稿/ 劉立蕾（英文）、韓良俊（日文）
出 版 者/ 臺北市政府文化局　　臺北市信義區市府路一號4樓東北區
　　　　　台北二二八紀念館　　臺北市中正區凱達格蘭大道3號
展覽策劃/ 純純文創
社長/ 黃嘉正　　行政總監/ 黃秀婉　　藝術總監/ 何欣怡　　行政助理/ 金馥嫻　金馥瑜　鍾蕙如
策 展 人/ 何欣怡
策展助理/ 張永晨
製版印刷/ 科億印刷股份有限公司
出版日期/ 西元2015年（民國104年）6月20日 初版

定　　價/ 新台幣400元
ISBN/ 978-986-04-5194-8
GPN/ 1010400948

Printed in Taiwan

Taiwan Summit for Democracy
──── The 228 Incident Settlement Committee

Issuer/ Ni Chung-Hwa
Editor-in-chief/ Ho Hsin-Yi
Acquisition Editor/ Sumiko Cultural & Creative Industries
Executive Editor/ Hsiao Ming-Chih, Paul T.Y. Tseng
Consultants/ Chen Tsui-Lien, Hou Kun-Hung
Author/ Chao Hung-Hsi
Graphic Designer/ Hung Yu-Chieh, Ho Hsin-Yi
Photographer/ Chang Yung-Cheng, Chin Fu-Hsien, Ho Ting-Hua
English Translation/ Nathaniel Carr, Ellen Y. Chang（p104-138）
Japanese Translation/ Tsuan-Han Chang
Publisher/ Taipei City Government, Department of Culture Affairs
       1, Shifu Rd., Taipei, 11008, Taiwan, R.O.C.
       Taipei 228 Memorial Museum
       3, Ketagalan Blvd., Taipei, Taiwan, R. O. C.
Exhibition Planning and Execution/ Sumiko Cultural & Creative Industries
President/ Huang Chia-Cheng   Executive Director/ Huang Hsiu-Wan
Artistic Director/ Ho Hsin-Yi   Executive Assistant/ Chin Fu-Hsien, Chin Fu-Yu, Chung Hui-Ju
Curator/ Ho Hsin-Yi
Assistant Curator/ Chang Yung-Cheng
Printing/ CRONY Information Technology CO., LTD.
Publication Date/ June 20, 2015
Edition/ First Edition

國家圖書館出版品預行編目 (CIP) 資料

臺灣民主高峰會- 二二八事件處理委員會紀念特展
純純文創編著
初版- 臺北市：北市文化局, 台北二二八紀念館
民104.06 面；公分
ISBN 978-986-04-5194-8（平裝）

1.二二八事件處理委員會　2.二二八事件　3.史料　4.文物展示

733.2913　　　　　　　　　　　104010505